THE FRONTIER CHALLENGE
responses to the trans-mississippi west

THE FRONTIER CHALLENGE

responses to the trans-mississippi west

edited by John G. Clark

The University Press of Kansas
Lawrence/Manhattan/Wichita

Essays in honor
of
George L. Anderson

PREFACE

In 1968, after nineteen years as Chairman of the Department of History at the University of Kansas, George L. Anderson resumed his place as a full-time teacher-scholar in the Department. As an appropriate means of recognizing and honoring Professor Anderson's years of distinguished service, the Department of History determined to host a conference focusing on the major area of Professor Anderson's research interests, the history of the Trans-Mississippi West. With the substantial support and encouragement of various officers of the University of Kansas, ten prominent scholars of Western America were invited to prepare papers for presentation at a Conference on the History of the Trans-Mississippi West that was held on October 16–17, 1969. The University Press of Kansas generously offered to publish the papers, both for their intrinsic value and as a permanent record of the honor accorded to Professor Anderson.

In addition to those presenting papers, numerous individuals contributed to the success of the Conference. The Conference Planning Committee of the Department of History, with the indispensable aid of their colleagues and University Extension, managed to get people where they were supposed to be—and on time. The Planning Committee wishes to thank William E. Unrau, Wichita State University, Stuart Levine, University of Kansas, and Donald F. Danker, Washburn University, for chairing sessions, and the discussants, Robert W. Richmond, Kansas State Historical Society, Homer E. Socolofsky, Kansas State University, Rosalie and Murray Wax, University of Kansas, and Lawrence H. Larsen, University of Missouri-Kansas City. Francis Heller, Dean of Faculties, and George R. Waggoner, Dean, College of Liberal Arts and Sciences, of the University of Kansas contributed pleasant glimpses into Professor Anderson's career, as did Nyle H. Miller, Kansas State Historical Society, John Unruh, Bluffton College, and Mark A. Plummer (in absentia), Illinois State University, Normal.

Conference Planning Committee

Donald R. McCoy, Chairman
John G. Clark
Grant K. Goodman
Lynn H. Nelson
W. Stitt Robinson
Ambrose Saricks

vii

CONTENTS

INTRODUCTION

John G. Clark
University of Kansas

In recent years, historians of the Trans-Mississippi West have increasingly focused their investigative and analytic energies upon the diversity of responses of people—individuals and groups—to a variety of unique geographical settings. Profiting from but pushing both empirically and methodologically beyond the land-oriented frames of reference employed by such significant innovators in the field as Walter P. Webb and James C. Malin, recent historians have demonstrated increasing awareness of the dangers in a reliance upon geographic (or any other) determinism as an explanation of the various paths of development manifest in the West.

Sufficient "chuck wagon" and "war bonnet" history has been written to furnish grist for a century's worth of Hollywood westerns and TV specials. It is no longer sufficient to chronicle the hardships encountered by travelers on the Mormon Trail, the inhabitants of sod houses in Kansas and Nebraska, or the cattle drovers along the Chisholm Trail. The problem now is to explain what happened to the people, including the Indians, who survived the great raid on Fort X; what did sod-house inhabitants do that enabled them to move into a balloon-frame house; what did migrants do when they reached the end of the Mormon Trail? In short, how did people develop and accommodate themselves to an environment which was itself constantly altered by the presence of a society in flux. Innumerable variables are encountered in explaining the process whereby American society penetrated and captured the West from its original human inhabitants and then domesticated the area by overcoming environmental obstacles of the gravest kind. In the unfolding of this process of Americanizing the West, tragedy and joy, victory and defeat, human fulfillment and human degradation are visible in roughly equal proportions. The historians whose papers follow are sensitive to the fact that the goals, both realistic and unrealistic, of one group, society, or culture are frequently pursued only at the expense of other groups.

A volume of this type, in which the contributors have pursued their own particular research interests, frequently results in an incoherent, mixed bag of themes. To be sure, a variety of topics and settings are encountered in the pages that follow. Nonetheless, two significant and related themes emerge—racism and a belief in material progress—both of which are indispensable to an understanding of the Trans-Mississippi West and both of which will continue to be of consequence as this vast region chases its future.

Skeletons abound in the closet of American history to a greater extent than a populace convinced of its own virtue has been willing to admit. Among the embarrassments of the American heritage is that of a conspicuous racism that has plagued the nation since its origins. White antipathy to non-whites, and other ethnocentric manifestations of intolerance, discrimination, and exploitation have corrupted and negated the promises of the American Dream and have caused blacks and Indians to speak of the American Nightmare.

Several papers deal with the alien or non-white populations on the different frontiers of the West. In each instance, the author speaks of the exploitive and destructive effects of Anglo-American society upon the alien groups or societies encountered as original inhabitants of the land or introduced for their labor. Paul W. Gates, William T. Hagan, and Rodman Paul narrate effectively the manner in which Anglo-American land laws and land usage were utilized by white majorities (and in some cases minorities) to despoil resident aliens of their property and livelihood. Chinese laborers, imported to work in the salmon canneries, were physically prevented from fishing on the Columbia River. In the gold fields, foreign miners were subjected to inequitable taxes, and white persecution drove most Hispano-Americans from the fields by 1850.

These papers demonstrate that the pressures generated against alien cultures were as much the product of attitudes toward economic development as of innate racism. The economic promises of the American West called forth formulas for economic growth that did not include ethical, moral, or legal protections designed to mitigate—let alone avoid—the suffering of the dispossessed or to accommodate the traditional life styles of minority peoples. The economic demands of the dominant race, as Francis Paul Prucha indicates, were transmuted into an intellectual rationale for the Americanization and Christianization of the Indians through their removal from ancestral lands. Thus, for many well-disposed and humane men, a shield was created, protecting their consciences from the knowledge that removal implied an unending trail of tears. The efforts of Prucha's reformers to isolate and educate their wards, undermined by white intruders and by the federal allotment and annuity policies described by Gates and Hagan, were shattered by the irrepressible expansionism of land-hungry whites. The American Mission of Stephen A. Douglas, as defined by Robert W. Johannsen, rooted in the same idealism and belief in progress that sustained the Indian Office during the 1840s, exploded all visions of Indian reform and made the reservation an inevitable experience for the American Indian.

Promises of progress and equality of opportunity, however irrelevant, if not actually destructive, to the life of many minority cultures in the United States, rang loud and clear with a precise meaning for the dominant elements in the nation. Stephen A. Douglas articulated a vision of the West as the adhesive of the Union, crisscrossed by railroads linking productive farms with ambitious towns and vigorous cities. A major responsibility of government at all levels throughout the West was the realization of the Little Giant's dream. State and territorial governments in the West, as those of Eastern states had before them, attempted to create an atmosphere conducive to economic growth. Federal policies sought similar ends both in the West and in the nation at large.

Variations in environmental circumstances conditioned responses within the different regions of the West. The frontier of the Far West, as delineated by Earl Pomeroy, was characterized by the development of cities—sometimes preceding almost all else—that served as advanced bases for the occupation of their hinterlands. A Western city such as San Francisco functioned as the Far West's major financial center, making major economic decisions for its backcountry. Kansas City, according to George L. Anderson, acquired similar capabilities within the Plains region. Access to urban populations and foreign markets, coupled with an apparently inexhaustible supply of salmon, led, as Carstensen describes it, to a canning industry characterized by relatively large-scale and technologically progressive organizations that called into being supportive industries in such growing communities as Portland and Seattle.

The federal government and state governments sponsored growth in a variety of ways. Oscar O. Winther emphasizes individual and corporate efforts to attract English capital and Englishmen to the "go-ahead" state of Kansas.* Alan G. Bogue offers an analysis of Kansas promotional, permissive, and regulatory legislation, each type shading into the next, designed to attract capital to the state through the medium of local bonding and land credit laws. At both the national and regional levels, Anderson traces the connection and interdependence between railroads, postal savings banks, postal money orders, and the Kansas City clearing house, all devices that worked to increase the amount of money circulating by speeding up remittances, enhancing the security and reducing the costs of transfers, and foreshadowing in some degree aspects of the Federal Reserve system. Bogue and Anderson, from different contexts, both offer suggestions relative to Populist motivation in the Plains region. Bogue points out a local institutional dimension of protest against local politicians who had allowed Kansas statutes to be drafted excessively in favor of non-state monied interests. Anderson questions Populist remedies for the so-called money problem as well as the actual shortage of a circulating medium, given the growing number and value of credit instruments in use.

The essays that follow, then, while adding up to less than a history of the Trans-Mississippi West, amount to considerably more than ten separate and unconnected views of isolated segments of that history. Each essay must obviously stand upon its own merits, but there are bonds uniting them, observational platforms shared, and common perspectives voiced which illuminate both the tragedy and the accomplishments of historical experience in the Trans-Mississippi West.

---

* Professor Winther's many friends were saddened by the news of his death in May, 1970.

1

The Urban Frontier
of the
Far West

Earl Pomeroy, University of Oregon

Five years ago, in August, 1964, the Bureau of the Census announced that as of July 1 the most populous state in the United States was California, succeeding New York. The announcement was no surprise to Californians who had been celebrating or deploring the fact before the census officially recognized it, and who had experienced it on the freeways entering San Francisco or a more hypothetical area, downtown Los Angeles. As an indicator of social condition it was both early and late. By virtue of being third largest of the states in area, following Alaska and Texas, California still was only thirteenth in density of population, well behind the states of the Atlantic seaboard, from Maryland to Connecticut. A more significant index to the quality of Western life will appear in the percentages of urban population, when they are ready. Sometime in the middle 1960s, probably 1965 or 1966, California became first in this category also, passing New Jersey. And probably in 1961 the Pacific states became the most urban in the country, passing the Middle Atlantic group. By the test of the census, they had been more urban than the nation as a whole since the 1860s.

As an index of urbanness, the census commonly has underdescribed the West. The nineteenth-century standard of eight thousand persons in incorporated places probably excluded most of the mining and cattle towns. Not until 1949–1950 did a definition include part of the unincorporated urban fringe.[1] Since then the new category of the standard metropolitan statistical area has shown the West leading in rate of urban growth.[2] In 1950 the limits of Los Angeles still enclosed more open fields than apartment buildings and skyscrapers, something like the plots laid out in the Florida real-estate boom of the 1920s; but they left out much more, both in the satellite towns that chose to maintain their separate governments and in unincorporated areas that were content to be simply parts of Los Angeles County. The awkward but indispensable category of rural nonfarm population appeared only in the census of 1920. It is particularly revealing for such nonagricultural states as Alaska, which in 1960 ranked third lowest in percentage of urban population, just above North Dakota and Mississippi, but highest in rate of urban growth and in percentage of nonfarm population. Los Angeles, which in the 1950s was the only one of the six largest American cities that gained population, grew only one-twelfth as fast as Anchorage. Persons living on farms in Alaska and other fast-growing Western states, moreover, often have been more interested in selling the land than in raising a crop on it. At the last census there were nearly thirty-five times as many farm workers in Los Angeles County, within and around the West's largest city, as in all the state of Alaska; and the two groups of farm workers were much alike, serving city people nearby, and emphasizing a factorylike kind of dairy-farming. It was not until 1950 that rural farm population specifically excluded persons in rural areas paying cash rents for house and yard only, and persons in institutions, summer camps, motels, and tourist camps, all of whom tended to occur more in the West than in other regions, and who were no more agricultural in occupations and concerns than Marie Antoinette at the Petit Trianon.

The Far West was urban, and urban in distinctive ways, long before the people of its cities spilled over into the countryside, before jet aircraft lifted modern industrial equipment and labor forces to a new mining frontier. (The public-address systems of Alaska Airlines ask passengers to put on their seatbelts in an ex-cruciating parody of Robert W. Service, but the red and gold flaps, fringes, and tassels on the planes and the stewardesses recall that the miners of '97, like those of '69, did not spend all their time in the wilderness.) Looking around the rim of the Pacific, one may be tempted to generalize that the newer the settlement, the greater its cities. Not only Los Angeles but also Sydney, Hongkong, and Jakarta, the children of other colonial powers, are larger than Rome, Madrid, Constantinople, and Vienna, the great European metropolises of the era of discovery; Mexico City is more than twice as large as any of them; and most of the growth of these new Romes has occurred within the last century.

Some of these Pacific cities may have developed at first chiefly because of their distance from the European heartland, as termini or way stations on world-wide systems of transportation so ex-tensive that they required secondary centers, as a long-distance telephonic cable requires amplifiers or repeaters. Anchorage, with its abundance of airplane service connecting three continents, re-calls Honolulu in the days when clipper ships out of New England stopped there on their way to Canton; or Singapore, which Sir Stamford Raffles founded as the most strategic stopping place midway between India and China, a then jungle-covered island that remains a great city now without either the Royal Navy or Malaya itself to support it. The thought cannot be altogether reassuring if it takes us to other way stations that have lost their traffic as trading routes have changed—to Gander, where we used to stop on the way to Europe; or Fort Benton, head of navigation on the Missouri River; or Greytown, which for a few years the Vanderbilts used as the eastern transfer point on the Nicaraguan route between the oceans and which might have been the Carib-bean terminus for a Nicaraguan canal; or Seville, European port for the Americas before the Guadalquivir River silted up; or countless heads of track on expanding railroad systems, each one declining as track moved beyond it.

Early Far Western cities were also advance bases for the occupation of their hinterlands. Instead of developing to handle the surpluses of farmers who raised more than they could eat, or, like some of the outposts of ancient Rome, to house the camp followers and sutlers and pensioners who gathered about frontier garrisons, Western cities sometimes preceded nearly all else. San Francisco was the staging area first for the American military occupation of northern California and then for the first great swarming into the Western mines, when the Golden Gate opened into the gold of the Mother Lode. The New York Volunteers came there in 1847, speculating in city lots even before the city was formally American. No one could know for several years where the chief city on the Bay would be, whether it would be instead at Benicia, or Alviso, or the half-forgotten site whose developers called it New York of the Pacific. Each of these and others had its boosters. But it was clear from the time the first Americans came that they would need a city. They learned that they could not move directly from the East to homesteads in this new West as pioneer settlers along the Ohio River and its tributaries sometimes had simply picked homes while drifting downstream on flatboats or rafts. The first important resident American merchant in California, Thomas Larkin, had settled first at Monterey, the Mexican capital and port for the cattle ranches of the Salinas Valley, and had later opened a branch office on the other bay, at San Francisco, as business developed there. And so Alaska has needed Anchorage, which has some of the qualities of San Francisco—and also some of Las Vegas, which began as a construction camp for the Salt Lake line and then for Hoover Dam—as Anchorage was construction camp for the Alaska Railroad and then for Elmendorf Air Force Base.

Most of the great treks of the emigrants overland to the Far West took place against backgrounds of wilderness, from the Platte to the Humboldt and the passes of the Sierra Nevada, or along the Snake and the Columbia. But they depended on settled places that became cities, beginning with those on or near the Missouri River, like Independence, where the companies assembled to gather supplies, make ready their wagons, choose their captains, plan the strategy of the journey, and await the day when the prairies were firm enough after the winter's snows to bear their teams and green enough to feed them. They headed, when they could, for a settled place on the way, above all others Salt Lake City, which lay off the direct route but was worth a detour to exchange worn animals for fresh and to prepare to cross the desert beyond.

The Mormons had planned Utah as a pastoral and agricultural colony, a modern Israel, but it became almost against their will one of the most urban of Western territories and states. (It was a Mormon with a taste for more urban opportunities than Brigham Young proposed to develop, Sam Brannan, who shouted the news of the first gold rush on the streets of San Francisco— "Gold, gold on the American River!"—after having first prudently invested in San Francisco real estate and cornered the market in mining tools.) Pushing on from the Mormon metropolis, most companies of emigrants dispersed only when they reached Fort Vancouver on the Columbia, where the Hudson's Bay Company opened its stores and offered refreshment, or Sutter's Fort on the Sacramento, or perhaps San Francisco itself.

The city remained important and necessary even when the discovery of gold made men who had come to seek their fortunes in San Francisco want to get away from it as fast as they could and to the mines. In fact, the gold rushes, which briefly emptied the city when the news first arrived, then filled it as never before and made it more necessary. The miners came there more than the farmers who had begun to make the journey in the early 1840s, both because there were more of them and because more of them, being Eastern men and in a hurry and well enough off to pay their passage, came by sea. Ships required a port, especially on a coast that has few natural harbors, and so did seafaring men and men who had begun their journeys at other ports and were accustomed to urban ways. They stopped for mail, for news of the new country, and for supplies they would need in it. Then if they found gold at the mines, they came to the city to spend it; or, if they did not, to work for men who had found it; or to invest in the new country; or to get out of it on their way back east. The city offered relief from the hardships of the mines, well-cooked food as a change from beans and salt pork, and other familiar creature comforts and entertainments. Along with store goods of all kinds, by the yard, pound, and bottle, the city imported the best and the worst of the theatre, and invented species of theatre peculiarly its own. The entertainers that play at the hotels of Las Vegas today descend from those that the saloonkeepers of San Francisco and Seattle and other Western cities hired to supplement and encourage the traffic at the bar: the miners who came there from the Mother Lode and later from the Yukon had much to make up for since they last saw city lights, and to save time they liked to look while they drank and drink while they looked. Eventually some acts moved from saloons to theatres as family entertainment, and miners' gold helped to finance vaudeville circuits that extended along the newly completed railroads from Puget Sound to San Francisco Bay, and to the north country as well.[3] Vaudeville became a significant item of export from West to East even before the Far Western states began to ship more fruit, vegetables, and lumber than gold, livestock, and wheat.

Much of the early Western city seemed temporary, expendable—composed of jerry-built houses that could not have lasted long even without the fires that from time to time swept over it. Where the climate permitted, and also where it did not, builders often used burlap and paper for partitions and substituted them for wooden siding. A decision to use masonry tended to represent a judgment that the city would last as much longer as the difference in time between laying brick and stretching cloth, as well as a judgment that the rates of return on trade had fallen to the point where a man might not easily recover costs between fires. Speculation in land under tidewater at San Francisco became profitable not because men joined in civic spirit to reclaim land but because they dispersed without it to seek gold: the Bay had seemed a forest of abandoned ships in 1849, as crews followed passengers to the mines. The rotting hulls compacted into the mud; speculators claimed their sites as city lots and built streets, houses, and conventional docking facilities over them; and the modern shoreline took shape.

Individual city dwellers sustained the transient dimension of the typical Western city well after it became clear that the city itself would last. Many of them were single males rather than heads of families, as the populations of some of the most Western of the Western states are still predominantly male today. We see this now most clearly in Alaska, newest of the Western states, where males exceed females by about one-third. But even California and Oregon, oldest of the Far Western states, are less female than the nation as a whole. When they married, the early city dwellers, like the Alaskans today, still lived more than other Americans in transient style, many of them in rented quarters, hotels and apartments, rather than in their own houses. The phenomenon of hotel-living in the early Far West was marked enough to inspire frequent attempts to explain it. Some traced it simply to the costs of rent, servants, and fuel. (Because they could not keep their homes warm, observed an agent of the Bureau of Labor Statistics, wives went out during the day and husbands after dinner, and so fell into temptation.[4]) An alternative was moving to a hotel, where the inconvenience of keeping children was such that most people had none or only one or two, and so could further postpone finding homes of their own. Mark Twain left a record of such domestic arrangements when he complained of trying to write to the accompaniment of childish voices at the Lick House in San Francisco, and of how he turned to devising lists of remedies to give to their mothers—for measles, tea with a tablespoonful of arsenic; for fits, soaking in a barrel of rain water overnight; for stammering, removing the underjaw; for brain fever, removing the brains.[5] Whether as cause or as effect, the low incidence of the traditional family household in Western cities made it appear that life there was unstable, poised for change.

The city was indeed a temporary abode for many who were there at any one time, tourists and fortune-seekers. But many remained, some predisposed by their backgrounds to favor urban residence and occupation. As a forty-niner observed, while the older Western states drew their inhabitants from the outer circumference of settlement, and therefore chiefly from the rural classes, California had drawn "a complete ready-made population of active and capable men of every trade and profession"—a cross section of the East.[6] Relatively few of the early inhabitants of the mining territories and states were prepared by experience or expectation for agriculture: either they came from commercial stock or at least they came hoping for the more rapid advancement of commerce and other urban occupations. For a long time the rich men of San Francisco and Portland and other cities, many of them originally merchants, felt that they could increase their riches more surely by reinvesting in merchandising than by venturing into the less familiar risks of agriculture or, for that matter, into mining and manufacturing.

The Americans' preference for city life left the Far Western countryside disproportionately to immigrants from Europe and Asia; to Englishmen who came to be sportsmen or ranchers rather than financiers or clubmen; to Italians, Yugoslavs, and Japanese who came to be freeholders (if possible, homesteaders) rather than tenants. A study of farmers in Oklahoma showed that those who personified the standard American rural virtues were not native Americans but Czechs: they raised the best crops, kept the neatest barns, bought the most machinery, earned the highest incomes, stayed the longest, went most often to church.[7] Yet immigrants also turned to the city, sometimes because alien land laws kept them from the agricultural life that they originally preferred, sometimes because, arriving without money to buy land, they had taken jobs digging ditches or carrying bricks, and then had found other opportunities. While the average early Far Western city offered little of the industrial employment that held so many newcomers in the East and Middle West in the late nineteenth and early twentieth centuries, wages in construction and at the docks were good. Irishmen moved from track-laying into the building trades. In many cities, particularly in the mining territories, German Jews dominated general merchandising. By the time some immigrants became rural proprietors, it was as financiers or as organizers of giant food-processing corporations that reached out to control their sources of supply in the classic style of the vertical trust, and with no more occasion to move to the land than J. P. Morgan had to live at a coal mine. Others, who had gone early to the land, in time became Americanized or Westernized enough to leave it. Even the Basques, who moved from the Pyrenees to take up their traditional occupation of sheepherder in Nevada and eastern Oregon, moved on to town predictably enough so that the stockmen insisted on special loopholes in the immigration laws, to permit others to replace them.

Meanwhile the rural Far West achieved much of the shape of the city, long before it became twentieth-century suburbs. Except in Utah, one of the geographically least promising parts of the West, agriculture was slower to develop than in the older states. Although some Western farmers made enormous profits in selling foodstuffs to miners, the high cost of transportation that justified local prices also discouraged raising crops for export, while the market at mining camps was too small and unstable to support substantial development. Insecure and experimental in the first stages of settlement, so that the rapid turnover of farm population that James C. Malin found in the first generation in Kansas[8] represented a fairly common pattern, Far Western agriculture tended to be highly capitalized when at last it came into substantial production. While practical farming experience was more useful than the promoters said, the dirt farmer often had to give way to the capitalist and executive, and with him disappeared many traditional rural ways. Profits in raising wheat in California in the 1870s, as the Grangers discovered, depended on access to capital for shipping as well as for machinery.[9] When the Southern Pacific sold land to family farmers, to foster more intensive agriculture, the irrigationists of the San Joaquin Valley ended by paying heavy tribute to the railroad and to Miller and Lux, who bought control of an undercapitalized irrigation system. By the time refrigerated cars were ready to carry Western fruits and vegetables to Eastern markets, in edible condition and at rates that the sellers could absorb, horticulture had changed along with transportation. The lemon and cantaloupe and lettuce crops of the Southwest required machinery and packing houses beyond the means of small owners. Some of the "associations" that distributed them were not true cooperatives but proprietors and processors on vast scales.[10] Advocates of irrigation agriculture liked to describe an urban way of life in the irrigated orchard lands of the Southwest, where a family might support itself on five or ten acres along an electric interurban railroad line that brought the city and its services to the doorstep. But irrigation might mean not urban neighborliness for small landowners but elaborate organization and heavy capitalization in units as large as the cattle ranches of Mexican times, and a society that was urban in the sense that its leaders were well-to-do businessmen and managers, who visited Los Angeles or San Francisco as often as the cattle barons of the high plains visited Cheyenne and Denver, if they did not live there.

New techniques of production and distribution meant that some of the mountain and desert states were able to shift from mining to agriculture as their gold and silver mines gave out or became less profitable in the 1880s and 1890s. For the most part, however, they did not become less urban in way of life even while vast new areas came under the plow or went into grazing. In the hard-rock mining country, prospectors gave way to hired laborers, most of them recent immigrants, though in the census records, since many Western mining towns were small, they often appeared as rural rather than urban population. The new miners were less conspicuous than the old—the press said little of their style of life, and politicians seldom catered to their interests—but the process of assimilation to the conditions of Eastern factory-town life that Rodman Paul has described in the gold mines of California[11] was more rapid and more complete in the technically more rural copper-mining states.

Consolidation and mechanization came later but more rapidly still in the Western lumber industry, which like mining developed along significantly urban lines despite its legendary picaresque heroes and its traditions of individualism. Frederick Weyerhaeuser, who bought 900,000 acres at six dollars an acre from the Northern Pacific in 1900, began manufacturing lumber on a large scale in 1915, in a new electrified mill at Everett.[12] The new organizations were slower to solve their human than their mechanical problems, and the lumber industry faced as radical and violent a species of unionism as the Western mining industry had faced a few years earlier. In 1917, the same year when the Russian Marxists established a Communist dictatorship in a country that according to Marxian dialectic was least ready for it among the major powers, strikes of loggers and millworkers in some of the newest Western American states threatened to stop production of airplanes and ships needed in war.

The desperate conditions and violent conduct of Western labor at Bisbee, Butte, Centralia, Everett, and other mining and lumber centers brought attention to conditions that represented concentration of control over natural resources in the West more than they represented either the nature of Western cities or the relation of Western society to them. Most Westerners have known as little of conditions in company towns as the members of the

Rockefeller family knew of conditions at their own mines at Ludlow, Colorado, in 1914. Dependent though they have been on outside capital, restless under the decisions that outsiders have made and the tolls that they have levied, Westerners have looked much to financial centers of their own. The more typical and vital instruments of Western economic development, at least since the era of the factories and forts that the great fur-trading companies, British, Russian, and American, built at York, Sitka, Astoria, and Vancouver, have not been the compounds of corporations but rather the Western cities themselves. Beginning often as facilities for outsiders and transients, whose purposes they serve much as the ports that an invading army builds handle military rather than civilian traffic, the principal cities have become in varying degrees autonomous forces. Even when they served to relay orders from higher authority, their distance from the East and from Europe permitted some of them to develop and exercise authority of their own. The agent received or took the means to become the independent capitalist. Sometimes cities have played mixed roles. Seattle was still waiting, hat in hand, on James J. Hill, whose pleasure gave it the terminus of his railroad, when it began setting conditions for life in Alaska. Especially on the coast, the regional metropolises have ruled much on their own behalf over wide though varying jurisdictions, rather than simply as agents of still greater masters to the East. Making some of the major economic decisions for their hinterlands, they have provided the financial and managerial services that complex economic systems require. San Francisco once was banker, broker, freight-forwarder, and commission merchant for the Western part of the continent from Alaska to much of Mexico. It is still the Far West's chief financial center, outreaching Los Angeles in bank clearances.

The authority of the Far Western city and the respect it commands rest on more than simple economic vassalage. For all the contrast in landscape between metropolis and interior, attitudes and ways of life differ less than between city and farm in the Middle West, the South, and the East. Westerners cherish animosities toward each other, but slurs against Seattle are not welcome in Seattle's territory as they are in Portland's, or against Los Angeles in Los Angeles's territory as in San Francisco's. The people of the Tanana Valley, the northern slope, and the southeastern panhandle may resent Anchorage as Anchorage resents Seattle, but they enjoy it and are proud of it, too. When Californians—at one time as far south as Los Angeles—and Nevadans spoke of San Francisco simply as "the city," they did so not in repugnance or enmity, as toward a Western Sodom or Nineveh (though they were not necessarily prejudiced against Sodom and Nineveh, either), but in familiar pride and affection. Mark Twain wrote to his mother that when he took leave from his job at Virginia City to visit San Francisco he felt as much at home on Montgomery Street as on Main Street back in Hannibal; he called the Occidental Hotel "Heaven on the half shell," since it would be sacrilege to say "Heaven on the entire shell."[13] Other Westerners rejoiced more soberly in Portland, more spiritually in Salt Lake City, more speculatively in Los Angeles, more alcoholically, if that were possible, in Seattle, but rejoiced nonetheless, in appropriate tones of hyperbole.

The Westerner's identification with his metropolis, his acceptance of its standards, appeared in what he did when he came into money. A few mining millionaires went to the East to live, or to Europe, like James G. Fair, or Darius Mills, or William Andrews Clark, whether because they were ashamed of the wives they had taken from behind the bar or before the washtub, or because their wives were ashamed of them and wanted more decorative husbands for their daughters. It was natural that some of them should look to urban centers and societies other than their own, especially since so many Westerners had thought of themselves as merely sojourners in a land too barbarous for permanent residence, while many of those who by chance became rich had been responsible enough for its reputation for barbarism so that they might prefer to live among those who had not known them when they were poor. Montana's graveyards were not big enough, the saying went, so that some of her rich men retired to Florida or to New York City, where William Andrews Clark spent seven million dollars building a chateau on Fifth Avenue that even in his time became a showpiece of bad taste, ridiculed in musical comedy. (Disappointed in his ambition to become ambassador to France, Clark spent his last years filling his mansion with paintings of which he boasted that they ceased to have monetary value from the moment that he acquired them. When he died in 1925, the Metropolitan Museum promptly agreed, in a sense he had not intended, by refusing to accept them as a gift.) But Clark and other copper millionaires may have had special reasons for leaving Montana, beyond millionaire-sized social ambition; few men formed strong sentimental attachments to Butte, a grim industrial slum dominated by its vast open mine and by smelters that poured out corrosive fumes on rich and poor alike. Other rich Montanans built their mansions instead on comfortable hillside sites in Helena and other towns where some of their families still live. The rich men of Colorado concentrated their pride and their ambitions on Capitol Hill; those of California first on Rincon Hill and then on Nob Hill in San Francisco, where the new cable-car system served the castles that the railroad tycoons built in the 1870s and 1880s. Rincon Hill, recalled a member of an old San Francisco family, was one of the few places "in those days where one could be born respectably."[14] For all the restless ambition with which Westerners moved about, like quicksilver, a contemporary said, staying nowhere longer than the gold attracted them, many sought respectability in such neighborhoods in the cities that ruled their parts of the West. What they did when they came into money tells something about their purposes and their values when they were still poor.

The members of the new Western plutocracy built their brownstone and marble monuments to themselves early enough to astound Eastern visitors by the speed with which they had transformed a wilderness. Tourists who made conducted tours to San Francisco in the 1880s saw town houses as Eastern or European as the Palace Hotel itself, finest of its kind anywhere when it opened in 1875. Yet the priorities that Western city-dwellers set for themselves appear more clearly in earlier scenes, within the first decade after the gold rush, as forty-niners began to have time to spend their money. Luxurious private residences usually came later than in Middle Western and Eastern cities of comparable wealth; most urban services came earlier. About all that tourists could desire were available when Richard Henry Dana, returning to San Francisco in 1859, found himself in a city of 100,000 inhabitants, his hotel on filled land in the sandy cove where he and his shipmates had beached boats from the ship *Alert* twenty-four years before. Dana marveled at newspapers, theatres, and cathedrals, as well as commerce surpassing that of Liverpool.[15] These represented some of the more portable of urban customs, already well established, as a bivouacking army establishes such services for its transient personnel alongside mess-hall and post exchange. If he had stayed longer, he would have noted also the unusual counts of restaurants and laundries, especially Chinese and French, at different price levels, and of commission merchants, lawyers, bankers, physicians, booksellers, photographers, and barbers. The service trades flourished, and especially those that served and exploited single men away from home. The distribution of occupations and facilities described a population younger and better educated than the national average, whose tastes and spending habits corresponded closely—with some allowance for youth and for distance from relatives and neighbors who might disapprove—to its urban Eastern background. Often its tastes outreached its condition; one had to take the measure of a Western city not merely by its size or even by the pace at which it lived within small space, but by its aspirations, which made it strive to make visitors recognize it as equal to the East, giving them Eastern entertainment within four walls instead of taking them into the wilderness. (It was only after Westerners were confident that they had destroyed their distinctive wildness that they joined the Sierra Club to celebrate it and to fight losing battles to preserve remnants of it.) The discrepancies between the raw Western setting of the nineteenth century and the ways of Eastern immigrants sometimes were as marked as those between the great cities of our time and the ways of refugees from rural poverty in Mississippi, Puerto Rico, or Mexico; and often imported ways were fully as persistent.[16]

Nearly four decades ago H. L. Mencken published in *The American Mercury* a long article, in three sections, entitled "The Worst American State." It consisted essentially of one hundred and six tables in which he listed the states in order of rank in different categories—literacy, income, rate of reproduction, alcoholism, reading habits, and so on—in most of which Mississippi stood at one end. For the purposes of this paper the more pertinent fact is that most of the Far Western states, and particularly those of the Pacific slope, clustered together at the other ends of most distributions along with the most urban states of the East.[17]

Similar resemblances between Far West and East have appeared in some other surveys, particularly those in which education is an essential factor.[18]

Mencken's data correspond both to considerable literary evidence of Far Western traits in earlier times and to studies of demography and of leadership. They do not, however, cover some interesting deviations from the Eastern urban model.

While in some respects San Francisco and the rest of the early Far West copied and imported Eastern cities in colors as bold and measure as generous as the originals, they also left some features behind. That the gold rushers and their successors from California to Alaska were an uncommonly literate breed was evident from their voluminous and inveterate diary-keeping and letter-writing, as well as from their appetites for newspapers, magazines, and books. Virtually all Western cities of any size had their printing and publishing businesses and their libraries, which sometimes were adjuncts to saloons, like early theatres, before they branched out on their own. As Mark Twain said, a flourishing literary paper was the surest sign, with a crowded police docket, that money was plentiful and business was good. Book peddlers and traveling librarians operated urban extension services far into the mining interior. But substantial colleges appeared much later than literary industries and college men.

The state of California established a university only in 1868, twenty years after the discovery of gold and eighteen years after statehood, when it had a population of about half a million. The delay is especially striking because California was both richer than other new states and more in need of the technical training, as in mining and hydraulic engineering, that Western universities have since emphasized. Oregon waited almost as long, thirteen years after statehood, to authorize a university, and then four years more after that, until 1876, before providing the money for buildings and a faculty. The states of the upper Mississippi Valley, which were roughly contemporary, established their universities either in the first legislature immediately following admission or even before admission, although in general their people were poorer than the Californians and Oregonians and less likely themselves to be college men. Thus Kansas—in this respect somewhat more Middle Western than Far Western—founded its state university in 1865, understandably waiting four years after statehood. Michigan had established its university in 1817, a full twenty years before statehood, authorizing the faculty "to establish colleges, academies, school libraries, museums, athenaeums, botanic gardens, [&] laboratories. . . ," when its population was less than eight thousand. But the territory's revenues and its intelligentsia were both so slight that it economized by dividing the thirteen professorships of the University between the president and the vice-president, who also served as Presbyterian and Roman Catholic clergy respectively. The president and holder of seven professorships received a salary of $25 a year, the vice-president and holder of six professorships $18.75.[19] Nor did the lag in publicly supported higher education in the Far West mean that instead private institutions had developed on the scale of the East Coast: the best-known private colleges appeared later still, Stanford and the California Institute of Technology both in 1891, Reed College in 1911, most of the Claremont group since the 1920s.

Eventually the Far Western states spent more on public colleges per student and per taxpayer than the rest of the country, which came to look to them for standards of support and service. When in 1947 a presidential commission published a statement of goals in higher education, it found that the states of the Pacific slope on the average had reached them and that California had exceeded them. From long before that, by the last decades of the nineteenth century, expenditures for subcollegiate education and public education as a whole had run high; and the earliest statistics available show that the Far West has been high in numbers of college graduates and years of school completed. Apparently the Pacific slope has lagged in building colleges while valuing education not less than other parts of the country value it but more. West Coast graduates of Eastern colleges, whose incidence from the earliest years of American settlement has been high (as in recent years the incidence of Western subscribers to the *New York Times*, the *Wall Street Journal*, and the *Christian Science Monitor* has been high on the coast), long have sent their sons and daughters to out-of-state schools. Living at Monterey in the 1840s, Consul Larkin sent his boys to a school that New England missionaries ran at Honolulu, and thence to Harvard—a fair distance away in the day of the clipper ship—thus exporting cattle hides and importing sheepskins. Down to the last years of the century most of the students at the Far Western state universities other than California's were in the preparatory departments, doing essentially secondary-school work; they were ahead of the clientele in Michigan Territory, where the University began by founding primary schools. If students went further, there was a good chance that it would be to a university out of state. The tradition of going away to college, and especially of going to colleges in older and more urban states, persists still in the newer states of the Far West, including the newest and most remote of them, Alaska and Hawaii.

To the extent that the argument of urbanhood depends on finding traits, values, and habits in the Far West associated with the urban Northeast, it may lose some of its force as the composition of the Western population changes. From the building of the first transcontinental railroads, and still more from the building of the first low-priced automobiles, migration to the Far West from rural Middle Western, Southern and South Central states has increased relative to migration from urban Eastern states. The growth of fundamentalist religious sects in the West, the recent national prominence of some practitioners of California's peculiar politics, and the failure of southern Californians to support effective public transportation and other urban services—or even to keep the system of public transportation that they once had—seem to reflect this shift in origins, first from New England and New York to Iowa and Missouri, then to Oklahoma and Texas.

Yet there are indications that there has not been an essential decline of urban traits, despite the changes in Far Western society that have come to focus recently, at the Cow Palace in San Francisco in 1964, at Watts in 1965, at the state capitol in Sacramento since 1967. Despite the visibility of emigrant sharecroppers from rural Arkansas and Oklahoma in the thirties and from rural Mississippi in the forties and fifties, the newcomers of the last half-century on the average have only confirmed the urban shape of the Far West; even at the height of migration from the dust bowl to California, they raised the educational level of California's cities.[20] Meanwhile, traditional patterns of behavior, including those of a more traditionally urban age, continue to prevail even in a region whose fluidity threatens to erode tradition: on close scrutiny, the new Western politics is not so new as it seems.[21] Further, much of the suburbanization and dispersion of Far Western urban life corresponds to what has been happening in other parts of the country, including the East. If New York City does not appear to be as fragmented a metropolis[22] as Los Angeles, it may be in part because more of it developed in the era of the horsecar, less in the eras of the electric streetcar and the automobile.[23] The opening of the Far West in the 1840s and 1850s had coincided not only with the acceleration of the American economy that W. W. Rostow and others have called take-off but also with still sharper shifts of population from countryside to city, which made it natural that the new states should share heavily in the new urban shape of the old. So the metropolitanization of the countryside in the Northeast that began about the time of the First World War inevitably had its counterpart in the rapidly growing Far West, which by the 1940s and 1950s was moving beyond the East in kind as well as in numbers.[24] This tendency of the more rapidly growing parts of the nation to partake of national trends in accentuated form is what a reporter for the *New York Times* referred to when, describing traffic in Los Angeles, he wrote, paraphrasing Lincoln Steffens, " 'I have seen the Future—and it doesn't work.' "[25]

Historians have been slow to recognize the urban dimension of the American West, even while in national historiography as a whole, as Roy Lubove has said recently, "the city threatens to subsitute for the frontier, or settlement of the West, as the key to . . . the evolution of American life."[26] Their slowness has been especially striking in the Far West, where the Middle Western frontier zone of two to six inhabitants per square mile meant as little in cattle-grazing and prospecting country as in its urban oases. Perhaps they could not easily believe in cities that not only preceded farms but also employed their populations in service trades rather than in either industry or agriculture, and whose immorality often was not that of the rough frontiersman that Bret Harte described for Eastern readers but rather that of the transient who refused to accept social responsibility, as Josiah Royce pointed out, or, as some might say today, refused to become involved, because he thought of himself as an outsider away from home.[27]

The urban Far West illustrates both the older and the newer interpretations of American life, not only in that it paradoxically has been and still is, more than other parts of the country, the site of opportunity on the land and in space, and at the same time has been and is urbanized, but also in that its people, who feel free from the land even while they find opportunity on it, have long resembled the immigrants of the urban East.[28] Well before Robert E. Park and other social scientists traced marginal man in East and West, one of the most eminent of applied sociologists, William Randolph Hearst, identified him by reaching clienteles on the two coasts that, despite their different schooling and social origins, turned together from their private concerns to listen to the message that Hearst shouted to them in large headlines.[29]

Building cities when Congress supposed that they wanted above all else farms, living in hotels rather than on homesteads, Far Westerners in our time have abandoned the city in its traditional form, sometimes, as at Los Angeles, before they had finished building it. By the time we recognized their urbanness, they were no longer interested in transplanting Manhattan but had turned more than other Americans to the intermetropolitan peripheries; the westward movement brought forth a continuing Western movement in a transurban civilization in which time replaced space.[30] At first Far Westerners were mobile essentially because most of them were male and, as economic men, so intent on their economic goals that they could not take time to build homes and raise families in the traditional settings of American family life; in time they were mobile because the pursuit of amenities loomed larger in their lives than the pursuit of gold and because in an affluent society where the family was no longer economically necessary, low birth rates continued even after the sexes were substantially equal.[31] Once they had aspired to build seaports and railroad termini where geography promised large commercial traffic; now they planned new towns for recreation and retirement, in areas whose main attraction was climate. Nineteenth-century visions of Far Western commerce, with that of the Orient surpassing that of North Atlantic and European ports, seem as remote as Macaulay's vision of the traveler from New Zealand at the ruins of London Bridge; but London Bridge itself is coming to a city that exists more in the minds of its promotors than on a new Thames in the desert. Wherever the West-to-come will build its principal metropolis, the prospect continues that by one definition or another the West will continue to be urban.

Notes

1. Leon E. Truesdell, "The Development of the Urban-Rural Classification in the United States: 1874–1949," *Current Population Reports,* Population Characteristics, Series P-23, No. 1 (Washington, D.C., 1949), 4, 6, 12.

2. Of twenty-seven SMSAs with increases of 20 percent or more, 1960–1966, twelve were in Pacific and mountain states. Of thirteen with increases of 200,000 or more, five were in California. *Estimates of the Population of Counties and Metropolitan Areas,* July 1, 1966, Population Estimates and Projections, Series P-25, No. 427 (Washington, D.C., 1969), 5.

3. Eugene C. Elliott, *A History of Variety-Vaudeville in Seattle from the Beginning to 1914* (Seattle, Wash., 1944).

4. Lee Meriwether, *The Tramp at Home* (New York, N.Y., 1889), 170; D. L. Phillips, *Letters from California* (Springfield, Ill., 1877), 84; John S. Hittell, *A History of the City of San Francisco* . . . (San Francisco, Calif., 1878), 443.

5. *Mark Twain's San Francisco,* ed. Bernard Taper (New York, N.Y., 1963), 31–33.

6. J. D. Borthwick, *3 years in California* (Oakland, Calif., 1948), 311.

7. Russell W. Lynch, *Czech Farmers in Oklahoma: A Comparative Study of the Stability of a Czech Farm Group in Lincoln County, Oklahoma* . . ., Oklahoma Agricultural and Mechanical College, *Bulletin,* XXXIX, No. 13 (Stillwater, Okla., 1942).

8. Malin, "The Turnover of Farm Population in Kansas," *Kansas Historical Quarterly,* IV (November, 1935), 339–72.

9. Rodman W. Paul, "The Great California Grain War: The Grangers Challenge the Wheat King," *Pacific Historical Review,* XXVII (November, 1958), 331–49.

10. As Gene M. Gressley has suggested in commenting on this paper, it would be interesting to investigate the failure of the orchardists of western Colorado and the pecan and cotton growers of New Mexico and Arizona to organize successful marketing cooperatives comparable to those of the coastal states. Have they lacked the commercial predispositions of the Californians as well as the stimulus of an active regional market such as San Francisco offered?

11. Paul, *California Gold: The Beginning of Mining in the Far West* (Cambridge, Mass., 1947), 332–33.

12. Ralph W. Hidy *et al., Timber and Men: the Weyerhaeuser Story* (New York, N.Y., 1963), 273–76.

13. *Mark Twain's San Francisco*, xi, 41.

14. Gunther Barth, "Metropolism and Urban Elites in the Far West," in *The Age of Industrialism in America* . . . , ed. Frederick C. Jaher (New York, N.Y., 1968), 162.

15. Dana, *Two Years before the Mast* . . . (Boston, Mass., 1911), 462–90.

16. There are opportunities for studies analogous to those of Peter Laslett, who has examined the low rates of illegitimacy in some industrial and industrializing cities of nineteenth-century Britain, especially in Liverpool, which he suggests may be attributed to recent immigrants bringing into the city habits formed in areas where bastardy was uncommon.

17. Charles Angoff and H. L. Mencken, "The Worst American State," *American Mercury*, XXIV (September-November, 1931), 1–16, 175–88, 355–71.

18. For example, Louis R. Wilson, *The Geography of Reading: A Study of the Distribution and Status of Libraries in the United States* (Chicago, Ill., 1938).

19. Burke A. Hinsdale, *History of the University of Michigan* . . . (Ann Arbor, Mich., 1906), 8–14.

20. Warren S. Thompson, *Growth and Change in California's Population* (Los Angeles, Calif., 1955), 175, 190, and cf. 237. Thompson points out that California's percentage of urban population declined, 1930–1950, but this was by the old definition, of persons living in incorporated places of 2,500 population and more. Metropolitan population merely increased at a lower rate than previously, and this may have been because it had already reached a point of saturation. *Ibid.*, 13–14.

21. Raymond E. Wolfinger and Fred I. Greenstein, "Comparing Political Regions: The Case of California," *American Political Science Review*, LXIII (March, 1969), 74–85, and "The Repeal of Fair Housing in California: An Analysis of Referendum Voting," *ibid.*, LXII (September, 1968), 753–69, test hypotheses pointing to new social factors in the politics of California, arising out of recent immigration, and conclude that tradition offers the most persuasive explanations.

22. Robert M. Fogelson, *The Fragmented Metropolis: Los Angeles, 1850–1930* (Cambridge, Mass., 1967).

23. George W. Hilton, "Transport Technology and the Urban Pattern," *Journal of Contemporary History*, IV (July, 1969), 123–35.

24. According to Eric Lampard, the rate of rural-urban shift in the East North Central Division in the nineteenth century exceeded any in Europe outside Britain. Lampard's figures for percentage of urban shift for the United States are 1800–1810, .9; 1810–1820, .0; 1820–1830, 1.8; 1830–1840, 1.8; 1840–1850, 4.0; 1850–1860, 3.6; 1860–1870, 4.8; 1870–1880, 1.8; 1880–1890, 6.3; 1890–1900, 3.9. Lampard, "Historical Contours of Contemporary Urban Society: A Comparative View," *Journal of Contemporary History*, IV (July, 1969), 3–25.

25. *New York Times*, March 3, 1959, 26.

26. Lubove, "The Urbanization Process: An Approach to Historical Research," American Institute of Planners, *Journal*, XXXIII (January, 1967), 33.

Richard C. Wade corrected the record for the Ohio Valley in *The Urban Frontier: The Rise of Western Cities, 1790–1830* (Cambridge, Mass., 1959), the pioneer and model study of Western cities; he calls attention to ambitions, roles, and processes similar to those of cities in the Far West. Yet he also indicates significant differences. "The towns," he says, "were the spearheads of the American frontier. *Planted as forts or trading posts* far in advance of the line of settlement, they held the West for the approaching population" (italics mine). "Urban Life in Western America, 1790–1830," *American Historical Review*, LXIV (October, 1958), 14. No major city of the Pacific and mountain states began as a fort or trading post in the sense of Pittsburgh or St. Louis; moreover, society in the Far West did not fall so neatly into rural and urban types (*ibid.*, 29–30) as in the Middle West. Adna F. Weber many years ago pointed out the indispensable role of cities in the growth of the United States: "A Mississippi Valley empire rising suddenly into being without its Chicago and its smaller centres of distribution is almost inconceivable to the nineteenth-century economist." He also noted the much higher percentage of town-dwellers in the Far West than in the Middle West, suggesting that it might follow on the importance of commerce and the nature of Far Western agriculture, which did not call for a dense population. *The Growth of Cities in the Nineteenth Century: A Study in Statistics*, Columbia University Studies in History, Economics and Public Law, XI (New York, N.Y., 1899), 20, 30–31.

27. Royce, "Some Characteristic Tendencies of American Civilization," Royce papers, vol. 92, p. 47 (Harvard University Archives); Royce, *California, from the Conquest in 1846 to the Second Vigilance Committee in San Francisco: A Study of American Character* (New York, N.Y., 1948), 393–94 and passim.

28. Everett S. Lee, "The Turner Thesis Reexamined," *American Quarterly*, XIII (Spring, 1961), 77–83.

29. Delos F. Wilcox, "The American Newspaper: A Study in Social Psychology," *Annals of the American Academy of Political and Social Science*, XVI (July, 1900), 70–71, 79–80; Carey McWilliams, *Ambrose Bierce; A Biography* (New York, N.Y., 1929), 175; and cf. George P. West, "Hearst: A Psychological Note," *American Mercury*, XXI (November, 1930), 301.

30. John Friedmann, "The Role of Cities in National Development," *American Behavioral Scientist*, XII (May-June, 1969), 18; Friedmann and John Miller, "The Urban Field," American Institute of Planners, *Journal*, XXXI (November, 1965), 315–16. As Melvin M. Webber points out, use of the automobile has facilitated departure from the old pattern of the central business district in some Middle Western and Eastern cities as well as in Western cities—in Detroit and Washington as well as in Los Angeles. The more distinctive pattern of settlement in Far Western cities may concern the rapid expansion of industries far from both raw materials and consumers,

attracted by climate and other amenities, and dependent on long-distance transportation and communication. Lowdon Wingo, ed., *Cities and Space: The Future Use of Urban Land; Essays from the Fourth RFF Forum* (Baltimore, Md., 1963), 35, 45. Promoters had predicted a dispersed, suburban pattern of settlement in southern California even before the boom of the 1880s, but based on agriculture rather than on industry. Charles H. Shinn, "Southern California," *The Californian*, III (May, 1881), 448.

31. Robert A. Nisbet, *The Quest for Community: A Study in the Ethics of Order and Freedom* (New York, N.Y., 1953), 68–69.

Commenting on this paper, Professor Lawrence H. Larsen observed that as late as 1880 the only Far Western cities (west of the Rockies) with populations greater than 10,000 were San Francisco, Oakland, Sacramento, San Jose, Stockton (all five of these within a radius of less than seventy miles in northern California), Salt Lake City, Portland, and Los Angeles; and that whereas some of these became national metropolises, others did not; and that San Diego, Seattle, and Vancouver, unlike smaller cities in other regions apart from the Great Plains and Florida, grew to urban greatness after the initial urban mosaic had taken shape and despite extended opposition from the older cities.

As Professor Larsen suggests, entrepreneurial leadership was important in overcoming the natural advantages of the first wave of Western cities. This has been especially evident in Los Angeles, which lacked a natural harbor, and in Seattle and San Diego, which lacked extensive natural hinterlands and which were late in getting satisfactory direct overland railroad and highway connections; their promoters were unusually resourceful and aggressive. Yet it would be easy to overemphasize the effectiveness of Western entrepreneurs relative to those in older regions whose agriculture, port facilities, and financial institutions were well developed before their first trunk railroads. Some of the earliest Far Western metropolises, moreover, also faced unpromising geographical settings: San Francisco attained reasonably satisfactory approaches across the Bay by automobile ferry and bridges only in the period 1921 to 1937; Salt Lake City got direct transcontinental railroad service only in the period 1908 to 1910 and highway connections across the Utah desert still later; Denver got the direct railroad route westward, to which William Gilpin and other early prophets looked, only in 1934, when railroads were already giving way to automobiles and airplanes. Critics of labor unions in San Francisco complained of burdens that unions imposed; some of these were related to San Francisco's location and the extra handling of cargoes that followed it. The peculiar geography and chronology of the Far West should not obscure developments that it shared with other sections. The historian of the West has no obligation to demonstrate the uniqueness of his region.

2

The Spanish-Americans
in the Southwest,
1848-1900

Rodman W. Paul, California Institute of Technology

One of the mysteries of the current demand that more attention be paid to the history of ethnic minorities has been the surprisingly slow development of an agitation to give the Mexican-Americans a more prominent place in our histories. Probably one reason for the moderate nature of the protest has been uncertainty as to how to classify the Mexican-Americans. Are they really a racial minority, when they range through every degree of admixture of Indian and white blood? Or are they more properly a cultural minority, rather like the Mormons, a cultural minority whose special status is the result of a complex blend of ancestral origins, language, religion, habits and attitudes, level of vocational skills and education, and geographical influences?

As a minority the Mexican-Americans have lacked cohesiveness. Groups in one of the Southwestern states have not been in close touch with comparable groups in other Southwestern states, and thus there has been little foundation for a regional, much less for a national, movement of protest. Unity of effort has been particularly elusive because the flow of immigration has continued for so long that at any given historical moment there have been among the Mexican-American population many quite different degrees of cultural adaptation to the peculiar mores of the United States.

Today all but a small proportion of the four million people of Mexican or Spanish antecedents[1] are either recent arrivals or are the children or grandchildren of immigrants who have come to this country since 1900, and more probably since 1910 or even 1920. In the main these Spanish-speaking Americans have come here to work as seasonal or unskilled laborers, and in most Southwestern communities they have been relegated to minority status, which means that they have been excluded from full participation in the life of the predominant society.

But in a historical sense there stand behind these twentieth-century Mexican-Americans several small but exceedingly interesting groups of nineteenth-century predecessors. To call them ancestors would be an exaggeration. Some were in the Southwest when the Anglo-Americans arrived, and had been there for periods varying from several decades to several generations; others infiltrated from northern Mexico during the half-century after 1848; still others were the offspring of these pioneers, and being born under the American flag, were American citizens from the beginning, however Hispanic their daily life.

Roughly speaking, and with some allowance for the later addition of the Gadsden Purchase territory, there seem to have been a little less than 75,000 Spanish-speaking people, other than Indians, in the Southwest at the time of the Treaty of Guadalupe Hidalgo in 1848. To this original 75,000 should be added a second 75,000 who were recorded by the census of 1890 as constituting the Southwest's Mexican-born *immigrant* population in that particular census year.[2] Neither of these two ascertainable figures gives any clue to two large unknowns: how many children were born to Spanish-speaking United States citizens during the second half of the nineteenth century and were raised in what the social scientists term a "culturally Spanish" environment; and how many Spanish-speaking immigrants other than the 75,000 Mexicans recorded in 1890 had come and gone since 1848, after having been for a few years or a few months a part of the life of the Southwest.

Both of these unknown elements must have been of significant size. One would expect a high birthrate among a rural Catholic population that traditionally has loved children and emphasized the family. As for temporary immigrants, we are told that during the Gold Rush years a folk migration of several thousand Mexicans came north each year and returned home at the end of the mining season, while Chileans and Peruvians, in smaller numbers, likewise formed a part of the Gold Rush population.[3] After the migrations of the Gold Rush, there was the unascertainable factor of Mexicans from the northern provinces of Sonora, Chihuahua, and Coahuila who crossed and recrossed the long and largely unguarded border between Brownsville and Baja California during the course of fifty years. Lacking a reliable basis, any estimate of the size of the "culturally Spanish" population of the late nineteenth century becomes guesswork. It is hard to see how the total can have been less than several hundred thousand by the end of the century.

Generalization about these nineteenth-century stocks is difficult. Carey McWilliams has remarked that "there is no more heterogeneous ethnic group in the United States than the Spanish-speaking."[4] Looking back upon the Spanish-speaking pioneers who made the first settlements in the Southwest, a modern Hispano-American scholar has declared:

> The colonial Hispanos were not culturally homogeneous. The Nuevo Mexicanos, settled in the region as early as 1598, were different from their cousins, the Californios and the Texanos, who arrived much later. The date of migration and settlement, the attendant cultural concomitants, geographic isolation, natural resources, the number and kind of Indians among whom they settled, and many other factors resulted in not one Spanish-speaking people but several, each with distinctive cultures. The outlook on life and the values, the allegiances, the biology, the very speech of these colonial

settlers varied greatly; and though all were Spanish-speaking, they can be thought of as different peoples.[5]

If they differed in their colonial origins, so did these older stocks continue to display a high degree of diversity in their later history. Everything made for dispersion. Their principal centers, such as San Antonio, Santa Fe, Tucson, San Diego, and Monterey, were separated from each other by extraordinarily great distances and geographical obstacles, not to mention hostile Indians in the earlier years and Americans in the later ones. In the pastoral, agricultural, and semiliterate societies in which most Hispano-Americans lived, there were neither economic, social, nor intellectual incentives to frequent contact and communication between widely separated points. A few engaged in long-distance freighting, packing, or driving in order to haul in American-made goods and export hides, wool, livestock, and other simple products, but most of them rarely ventured beyond visits to kinfolk, fellow villagers, or not-too-distant rancher-friends.

Localism was pronounced, and nowhere was localism more evident than in the richly varied pattern of assimilation to Anglo-American culture. The adjustment made in California was quite different from that of Texas; Arizona's was unlike that of its neighbor New Mexico. Within the single territory of New Mexico there were upper-class families that became so thoroughly Americanized as to be able to slip into Anglo-American society at will, while the mass of the rural population remained "culturally Spanish" and spoke English with difficulty or not at all, even after their families for several generations had passed their entire lives under the jurisdiction of the United States. With medieval agricultural practices and rudimentary economic arrangements, these New Mexican farm villages survived into modern times as retarded alien enclaves of American citizens on American soil, precisely as if they were candidates for economic aid to an underdeveloped foreign country.

To a surprising degree the older stocks of Hispano-Americans held themselves apart from the several populations that in successive periods surrounded them. In the very beginning of the colonial era, the small number of Spanish men of course bred with Indian women—as the early settlers in Old Mexico had, because there was no alternative—so that the Spanish-speaking people of the Southwest became of predominantly mixed descent (mestizo); but once a supply of eligible young women of mixed blood had been established, intermarriage became infrequent. Something similar happened when the first Anglo-Americans arrived. As with all frontier populations, women were scarce among the new arrivals. Therefore some took brides from among the Hispano-American women, and today many a Southwestern family that boasts of its pioneer lineage claims an ancestress with a Spanish name. At the annual fiestas much is made of these ties with a romanticized "Spanish" past. But the scant evidence as to matrimonial arrangements after, say, 1880 suggests that as a large "Anglo" population developed, intermarriage became much more rare. Nor have the older Hispanic stocks been eager to associate with the twentieth-century Mexican immigrants. Looking down upon the latter as social inferiors, in most communities the older stocks have shunned intermarriage, just as they have sought to keep their residential districts separate.

At the opening of the American era, New Mexico had by far the largest Spanish-speaking population, perhaps as much as four-fifths of the total in the Southwest. Most of the New Mexicans were illiterate peasants who led an unprogressive, poverty-stricken life in small villages or as hands on great ranches. They were very much subject to the authority of the small class of rich land-owners (*ricos*) or the much larger number of those who served as *patrón* or headman in each village. Only the priest approached the power of the patrón and rico over the lives of the common people. Between them, rico, patrón, and padre ruled a thoroughly paternalistic society that was medieval in the serflike dependency of the many upon the few.

Some of the peasants of the mid-nineteenth century were held in debt-peonage that constituted virtually permanent bondage— and through the ignorance and helplessness of its victims this practice continued for many years, despite the Thirteenth Amendment to the United States Constitution and despite a specific prohibitory federal statute of 1867. A federal territorial official asserted in 1856 that, on the whole, Southern Negro slaves were better off than New Mexican peons.[6]

For most peasants life centered in the village and the extended family (the *familia*). Both were organized as authoritarian structures. The patrón was the father figure of his village. He controlled what little credit was available, owned the store if there was one, and performed the limited middleman functions that connected the isolated peasants with the outer world. Politically he controlled "his" peasants, and when the Americans introduced notions of elective government, the patrón was quick to discover the profit involved in delivering whatever popular vote had been contracted for by higher authority. Within each family the senior married man was not only a husband and biological father, but was also the dominant, decision-making figure whose presence gave definiteness and unity to the extended family group.

This authoritarian pattern of village and family, when taken in conjunction with an unchanging, labor-consuming type of crop-raising and livestock-herding that was medieval if not biblical in inspiration, made the life of the peasant seem to the contemporary "Anglo" observer to be utterly devoid of incentive or opportunity for progress, while at the same time the frequency of crop failures and stock losses in that high, dry, and sometimes Indian-infested land seemed a guarantee of perpetual debt or at least poverty. More discriminating observers, especially after the social sciences began to suggest whole new frames of reference for judging alien societies, have pointed to the psychological values inherent in this unquestionably unprogressive rural society. Life in both the family and the village were familiar, predictable, and congenial, however pinched in terms of income and food supply. They were based upon a highly developed pattern of community cooperation, best illustrated by the decisively communal nature of New Mexico's local irrigation systems. Together the family and the village offered a certainty in relationships and values and a sociability unknown to the Anglo-American who, as an individual, was aggressively trying to thrust his way into the life of the Southwest.[7]

The weakness of this psychologically tranquil, resigned existence was that it prepared the villager and his children for nothing but a continuation of the same. Physically there was a margin neither for safety against bad years nor for growth and change; intellectually there was no basis for experimentation and innovation. (The federal census of 1870 reported that more than half the population over ten years of age could neither read nor write.) Natural increase of population would have put an unbearable pressure upon the scant supply of irrigable and pasture land even if no other factors had changed. But in fact the amount of land available to the villagers decreased greatly because acquisitive Anglos found ways to displace ignorant peasants by substituting new written land titles for the familiar unwritten customary use of the soil. By the end of the nineteenth century the need for additional income was so pressing that the men of the villages were absenting themselves for months at a time in order to work as transient laborers in other parts of the West. For a unit as cohesive as the *familia*, this meant a severe social strain, mitigated only by the role of the women, who by Hispanic tradition were supposed to remain at home, and thus were available as a force to hold the family together during the absence of the male head of the household. The practice common among Negro families of sending the wife and mother out to work as a domestic was not popular among Spanish-speaking people.

By the opening of the twentieth century the high, dry lands of rural New Mexico began to stand forth as a cultural island of poverty, illiteracy, and premodern customs—however picturesque and quaint to the eyes of Eastern visitors. While this was the fate of probably a majority of New Mexicans during their first half-century under the American flag, there were some notable exceptions that showed how alert men with the right "connections" could actually profit from the stratified and unprogressive nature of New Mexican society. The *rico* class of landed proprietors—masters of great estates *(haciendas)* whose varied economies produced most of the articles that they consumed and still had an exportable surplus—had a remarkably strong position in New Mexican life. Linked together by extensive intermarriage and united in a typically Latin American acceptance of nepotism and "influence," they were the obvious ruling class with whom the incoming Anglo-Americans must deal.

Even in the 1840s some of the great families, such as the Otero and Chavez clans, had in fact anticipated the new era by sending their sons across the plains to the Missouri frontier to be forwarded to American schools and colleges located all the way from St. Louis to New York. Other young New Mexicans, whose families wished them to have practical training, were placed in the dispatching-point headquarters of the mercantile and freighting firms that sent American-made goods to New Mexico and handled in return New Mexico's few productions, such as wool and hides. A class of English-speaking aristocrats was thus developed who soon moved still further into Anglo-American life by intermarrying and forming business partnerships with "Anglos."[8]

The simplicity of New Mexican economic life prior to the railroads, with a stress on freighting across the plains and handling government supplies on contract, permitted a type of business in which merchandising, transportation, and finance were essentially one operation and had distinct political overtones. The abler of the American-trained Hispano aristocrats fitted easily into this undifferentiated politico-economic activity.

A similar development characterized the field of land titles. Shrewd, opportunistic Anglo lawyer-politicians found their chance in the fact that, unlike the expedient adopted for California, no special agency to handle the tangled land titles was created by Congress until 1891. For more than forty years land titles were determined by special acts of Congress and by surveys, investigations, and decisions made by appointive officials in Santa Fe and Washington. This was just the type of opening that determined lawyer-politicians wanted, and in exploiting it they formed what came to be known as the "Santa Fe Ring," an informally constituted, frequently changing group dedicated to fattening their own pocketbooks through speculation in land and land titles.[9]

Just as Anglo businessmen and English-speaking Hispanos found it both advantageous and pleasant to form matrimonial and business alliances, so the Ring impartially drew into its transactions anyone whose influence could further the group's profits. Since Hispanos occupied most of the seats in the territorial legislature, dominated elections in the local constituencies, held some of the territorial offices, and in the beginning controlled the big landholdings, quite a few of them were able to share in the plunder.

Whether Hispanos really were the big gainers from the operations of either the Ring or the early business houses may be doubted. One suspects that their Anglo associates were too resourceful for that. And in any event, while some of the Hispano upper class were prospering, many of their cousins, through inexperience with American ways, including the intricacies of acquiring legal titles to real estate, and through a proneness to borrow and spend too freely, were losing ownership of the land that had been the traditional basis of their power. So at best only a portion of even the favored class were better off at the end of the century than they had been in 1848. Still, for them the opportunity had been there, and the prominence of a few of them, symbolized by the appointment of Miguel Antonio Otero as governor of New Mexico under McKinley and Theodore Roosevelt, suggests that so long as New Mexico remained a predominantly Hispanic, tradition-bound society, its accustomed Spanish-speaking leaders, quite unlike their peon dependents, might expect to play a role of considerable importance.

Immediately adjacent to New Mexico, and at one time legally a part of it, was the territory of Arizona. The key to understanding early Arizona is to appreciate that even at the peak of Spanish pioneering, Arizona had never had but a very small population, and when Mexico succeeded Spain, devastating Apache raids very nearly brought Hispanic settlement to an end. By the close of the 1840s Spanish-speaking civilization had shrunk back to the single frontier garrison town of Tucson. Through the Gadsden Purchase of 1853 Tucson and Arizona south of the Gila River were transferred to the United States. This was the only part of Arizona that had been touched significantly by Spanish and Mexican efforts to establish missions, ranches, farms, or mines.

During the later 1850s Tucson became a crossroads and supply center for California-bound traffic, and a few mines, ranches, and farms were reopened. In the almost abandoned and hitherto dispirited region, a bicultural society began to emerge, with Tucson as its focal point. In addition to the little group of Spanish-speaking settlers that had never left Tucson (probably less than one thousand in total),[10] a few English-speaking men, not always of the most desirable sort, drifted in from both California and the Missouri frontier, while a much larger number of Mexicans from Sonora and Chihuahua came in to form the biggest single element in the new society. The latter came chiefly as laborers and brought with them some of their womenfolk and some unattached girls. Raids by Confederates, Sonoran bandits, and Indians during the American Civil War temporarily cleaned out the territory once more, but with the arrival of volunteer federal troops from California, the bicultural society resumed its slow growth, and this time with the additional asset that some distinctive personalities from the California military contingent decided to remain in Arizona when they were mustered out of the volunteer force.

In several senses Arizona was more Hispanic than American between 1853 and the later 1870s. Tucson, the largest and most important community and the headquarters for the major business of supplying the Army and the Indian reservations, was decisively "Spanish" in appearance, language, and customs.[11] Throughout the territory as a whole, the census of 1870 showed that of the nearly ten thousand total population, somewhat more had been born in Mexico than in the United States.[12] On the other hand, in the 1860s and 1870s most Arizonans with Spanish names were employed in simple jobs, especially in the catchall category of "laborer." They served also as miners, teamsters, farmers, and ranchers, with only a few functioning as craftsmen, small tradesmen, saloon keepers, liquor dealers, butchers, or merchants.[13]

A disproportionately large amount of leadership in business and local government was supplied by Americans and by immigrants from the United Kingdom and Germany—in other words, by what was the minority element in the population. Poor education, lack of capital, unfamiliarity with American economics and politics, and perhaps a differing set of values that made for different incentives, all of these factors worked to discourage the Spanish-speaking settlers and Mexican immigrants from seizing the opportunities that the numerically fewer Anglo-Americans and European immigrants found in this reconstituted society. It is significant that the leading Spanish-speaking merchant and political figure, Estévan Ochoa, was a Chihuahua-born person who, like the New Mexico aristocrats, had as a boy gone to Independence, Missouri, to learn English and business methods.[14]

Some members of the so-called old Spanish families of Tucson were always to be found in lesser political offices, including one or two in each session of the territorial legislature. More significantly, until the 1880s some of the larger business firms in

Tucson included partners from both the "Spanish" and "Anglo" elements. If few Hispano-Americans save Ochoa rose to the levels achieved by the rico class in New Mexico, that was partly because the opportunities were so much more limited in Arizona.

But the fact that the Spanish-speaking population tended to take a secondary place in business and political life does not indicate the totality of their influence. Those early English-speaking settlers of the 1850s and 1860s rarely brought their womenfolk with them. Instead, as they began to establish themselves as merchants, they married the daughters of Tucson's "old Spanish" families. Lesser Americans and European immigrants married, or in many cases simply bred, with the graceful, black-eyed girls who accompanied the supply trains and crews of laborers that came up from Mexico. Not infrequently the resourceful Mexican girls entered a household by taking employment as cook and housekeeper, graduated to the status of mistress, and won promotion to the rank of de facto wife by the simple expedient of producing several children. Any estimate of the significance of the Spanish-speaking people in early Arizona must allow for influence exercised via the bedroom, nursery, and kitchen.

What happened in the thinly settled, initially almost empty territory of Arizona was thus quite unlike developments in the stratified, more populous territory of New Mexico. California's experience revealed still a third variant. Here the controlling force was the unbelievable number of people from all over the world who started coming to California during the gold rush and kept on coming throughout the nineteenth century. Beginning with an 1848 population of perhaps 14,000, other than Indians, California boomed to about 100,000 by 1850 and nearly 1.5 million by 1900. Of that original 14,000, only about 7,500 were of Spanish or mestizo stock.

Sudden engulfment by so immense an alien society was more than any small provincial group could have endured without suffering virtually total eclipse. Perhaps, instead of asking, Whatever happened to the original Hispano-Californian element? one should ask, How did they manage to preserve their identity at all? As a distinctive group, they were ill-prepared to cope with the Americans and European immigrants who so soon became their competitors. Quite aside from an imperfect command of

English, few Hispano-Californians of any class had had experience with American legal, financial, or business practices, least of all with sharp practices. The harsh realities of taxes, loans, and mortgages, and the use of politics by pressure groups, all had to be learned abruptly. Often they were either not learned, or were learned reluctantly and imperfectly, because of the difference between the values and incentives of the newcomers and those familiar to the established Hispano-Californians.

The latter's had been a slow-moving pastoral and agricultural rather than a rapidly changing commercial and money economy and society. The level of education, even among the upper class, had not been high. Fewer modern ideas and less familiarity with English than might have been expected were introduced by the assimilation into Hispano-Californian society during the 1830s and 1840s of several hundred Americans and Britons, who learned Spanish, married daughters of the local families, acquired land, and entered into a variety of business relationships characteristic of the undifferentiated Californian economy of that day. It is worth noting that some of these Hispanicized Anglo-Americans were not much more successful than their in-laws in adjusting to the revolutionary changes that swept California after the gold discovery of 1848.

That sudden event, with its vast unforeseen results, took place in the northern half of the province, which was precisely the part of California in which Hispano-Californian influence had been challenged even before Marshall made his great discovery. Most of a large new influx of Americans just before and during the Mexican War had settled in areas tributary to the province's one great interior waterway, the chain of bays and rivers that led from San Francisco past fertile valleys to the lower reaches of the Sacramento and San Joaquin. It could be argued that the effect of the gold rush in northern California was simply to accelerate immensely a transfer to Anglo-American dominance that was already foreshadowed by the geographical pattern of settlement of the middle and late 1840s.

In the coastal cow country from Monterey down through Santa Barbara and Los Angeles to San Diego, on the other hand, the older Hispano-Californian way of life was unchallenged in 1848, having successfully absorbed most of the few Anglo-Americans that had appeared, and was to yield only slowly during the 1850s and early 1860s. What makes generalization so difficult in the case of California is that both before and after 1848 Hispano-Californian influence shaded off from south to north, and was able to last especially long in some rural areas and back country.

Finding themselves in a hopelessly small minority within the northern half of California, the upper-class Hispano-Californians struggled ineffectively against the unfamiliar language, legal system, tactics, and, above all, the values of a formerly alien minority that overnight had become their masters. To survive at all they needed, and to some degree received, extensive help from American lawyers in coping with the confusing, expensive, and delaying procedure set up in 1851 for confirming title to Spanish and Mexican land grants. They needed equally, and by nature of the problem could rarely receive, help in dealing with an Anglo-American population that pushed them aside, outsmarted them at law and politics, threatened them with physical violence, and led them into such booby traps as mortgages and loans at high interest. In a masterly understatement a historian recently summed up the fate of the ranch lands that had been the traditional source of the Hispano-Californians' wealth, prestige, and power: "In the north of California, then, the basis of landownership had changed drastically by 1856. Through armed struggle, legislation, litigation, financial manipulation, outright purchase, and innumerable other tactics, Yankees had obtained a good deal of interest in the land."[15]

South of Monterey, and more particularly south of Santa Barbara, the Hispano-Californian upper class fared better. Their land-title cases seem to have been settled with less contention in court and much less squatter violence outside of court, presumably because land in southern California did not yet have a high value and was not yet subject to population pressure. Economically the great cattle ranches not only continued but indeed flourished with a temporary and quite misleading prosperity, caused by the high price of meat required for the greatly enlarged northern consumer population.

Through bad judgment on their part, instead of using their unexpected income to clear debts and develop their ranches for the future, the southern "Californios" tended to spend for current desires, including the luxuries and elaborate parties that have been described so often, and when even their inflated income proved insufficient, they borrowed. Horace Bell, whose life in southern California from 1852 onward brought him into contact with everyone, claimed that most of his friends lost their money and land not through gambling, idleness, and profligate living, as critical "Anglos" customarily alleged, but through the fact that they "knew not the value of money or the crushing power of compound interest" on debts.[16]

A later observer, whose years as a Los Angeles lawyer handling land cases gave him an especial insight, pointed to the effect upon Hispano-Californians of another unfamiliar device—real estate taxes. Frequently lands were lost for a "meager tax" due. Again, to pay off one lien, a mortgage would be taken out on an undivided interest in lands. Such a step could lead to long, expensive, and disastrous litigation if the rights to the undivided interest fell into the hands of a new owner who insisted on bringing action to divide the property.[17]

And yet, despite a continuing loss of land to Anglo-Americans, the southern Californios as a whole retained enough of their estates to live in style and remain "the dominant influence" until they were struck by blows inflicted not by man but by nature. California rather favors extremes: either too much or not enough. Heavy floods in the winter of 1861–1862 gave way before an unprecedented drought, which began in 1862 and did not really yield until the fall of 1865. Long before it was over, ranch managers were reporting that "there is absolutely no grass," and were forcing their emaciated cattle upon the market regardless of price. Soon thereafter cattle were sold for the hides alone, and later still were left upon the range to die beside the dried-up water holes and vanished creeks. Coming on top of the Hispano-Californians' earlier troubles over land titles, debts, taxes, and extravagances, this natural disaster meant the loss of most of the ranches and the end of the dominance of the ranchero class.[18]

It is well to speak first of the ranchero class, because the members of that privileged order were once the controlling force. They were the California equivalent of the ricos of New Mexico. Like the ricos, each lived in patriarchal style on his big, undeveloped estate or in his sprawling town house. At either place children, relatives, and retainers swarmed about the large adobe building to create a typically Hispano-American sense of living in the midst of an extended family. The authority of the ranchero over the considerable assemblage that ate at his board was unquestioned. These places were unlike the haciendas of New Mexico, in that Indians, under the supervision of major-domos who were usually mestizos, did most of the manual labor, domestic service, and handling of animals that in New Mexico was performed by peons. Horace Bell scornfully described such ranch Indians as being the "vassals" of their lordly employers.[19]

Neither at the ranches nor in the relatively few towns did a class of debt-bonded peons develop; nor were there peasant villages, each ruled by its patrón, on the New Mexico model. The nearest approximation was a practice sanctioned by the city fathers of Los Angeles during the American era of selling the services of Indian jail inmates in lieu of fines or punishment.

But there was a population of working-class mestizos. Some were to be found serving as vaqueros and major-domos on the ranches; others, who dwelt in the towns, earned their living as small farmers, craftsmen, tradesmen, teamsters, and the like. Often a miserable colony of former mission Indians lived a bare existence on the edge of the town, apparently content with what little work they could get. Typical of a Spanish-American community, the sum total of all available talents still left wide openings in the trades, crafts, businesses, and professions. It was these opportunities that attracted a steadily growing number of Americans and European immigrants.[20]

A most intriguing question is, What happened to the mestizos as the ranchero class lost control of its lands and the towns began to fall under the economic control of "Anglos"? An answer is difficult to give, because so many were largely illiterate people who left no personal records, and because such evidence as we do have is confused by a circumstance that stemmed directly from the gold rush. In the early phase of the gold rush literally thousands of Spanish-speaking people of both sexes were to be found in the mines, engaged sometimes in mining or running pack trains, sometimes in operating restaurants, saloons, gambling houses, and brothels. Many a fight in the mining towns started in rivalry for possession of a "Spanish" woman.

A grossly unfair tax on foreign miners and a virulent persecution of the Spanish-speaking people drove most of the Hispanic element out of the mining regions in 1850. In bitterness some packed up and returned to their native countries; others fled to the seacoast to take refuge in the towns where the humbler Hispano-Californians had long been established. In Los Angeles so many Mexicans came in from the mines that the "quarter" they occupied came to be called "Sonora-town" and so continued until at least as late as 1888, at which time a guidebook reported that "this Spanish population is rapidly disappearing. Death and emigration are removing them from the land."[21] In its early years Sonora-town's fame rested more on its "hells," lawlessness, and squalor than on the picturesqueness that attracted tourists in the 1880s. After 1850, therefore, the population of Los Angeles and other towns included a mixture of the original Hispano-Californians, numerically chiefly mestizos, and these later additions of other Spanish-speaking people, chiefly from northern Mexico, together with a remnant of bedraggled Indians.

If the census reports are to be trusted, there must have been little continuing immigration from Mexico or other Spanish-speaking countries after the early 1850s, for the figures for California residents born in those countries show a stationary or slightly declining total for the censuses of 1860 through 1890. A severe epidemic of smallpox in southern California in 1862–1863 was particularly hard on Indians and other poor Spanish-speaking people in the congested districts, where no medical help was available and the disease spread fast. Deaths were so numerous as to retard considerably any expansion of the working-class part of the Spanish-speaking community.[22]

As the years passed and their familiar jobs disappeared, some of the mestizo ranch hands drifted into the growing cities and towns to join the colonies of their own cultural group and, too often, there to deteriorate in unaccustomed idleness. Others sought continued employment at the tasks they knew best. Throughout the remainder of the century, scattered reports of "Californian cowboys" indicate the continuing presence of these expert riders and livestock handlers out on the remote, by now American-owned ranches to which the cattle industry had retreated after the disasters of the 1860s. Still others withdrew into the mountains and deserts, to places so isolated or arid that no one would bother them. There, in lonely dignity, they and their families ran small "ranches" that were little more than hardscrabble homesteads.

In what has been said so far, emphasis has been on the attempts of the several kinds of Spanish-speaking Californians to continue their familiar ways despite an increasingly unfamiliar surrounding society and economy. The most striking venture into entirely new ways was the readiness of upper-class Hispano-Californian girls to marry "Anglos" and the willingness of their parents to sanction such unions. Marriage and the establishment of family lines that thereafter bore Anglo-American surnames may well have been one of the most enduring contributions of Hispano-Californians to the new mixed society.

In business and politics the position of the Hispano-Californians was inherently weaker than that of their compeers in New Mexico, where the continuance of a Spanish-speaking majority throughout the rest of the century ensured respectful attention from alert Anglo-Americans. Parallels with the Spanish-speaking community in southern Arizona are dubious, because basic conditions were so very different. Although there were "Spanish" partners in some "Anglo" business and law firms in Los Angeles for many years after 1848,[23] it is difficult to point to Hispano-Californians who achieved a prominence in economic life comparable to that of the Otero clan in New Mexico or Ochoa in Arizona, and even such eminence as they did achieve passed as the city's population shifted away from a Spanish-speaking majority. Of the two earliest known directories of Los Angeles, the one for 1875 shows that all but a very few of those with Spanish surnames were in simple, often humble occupations. Most were "laborers," others were grocers and fruit dealers, clerks, saddle and harness makers, shoemakers, farmers, saloon and billiard-hall proprietors, barbers, waiters, dressmakers, hostlers, and so forth. Only three, all well-known figures, were listed under such substantial-sounding categories as "capitalist."[24]

This paucity of Spanish names among the higher-income businesses and professions at as late a date as 1875 is the more interesting because by then there had been ample time for a new generation to come to maturity. Contemporaries remarked that whenever a young Hispano-Californian sought a good education and made an effort, he did as well as anyone else, but that too many seemed unwilling to compete on Anglo-American terms.[25]

That same Los Angeles directory for 1875 reveals something else about Hispano-Californian participation in American life. Some locally famous names appear in the pages devoted to public officials. One of the Sepúlveda family was district judge, a Carrillo was city marshal, three members of the common council of the city bore Spanish names, and on the county's board of supervisors at least two members plus the interpreter had names of Spanish origin. So did two policemen, a deputy sheriff, and all of the officers of a forty-member militia company.

Since the average proportion of people with Spanish surnames in Los Angeles County was down to one-fourth or less by 1880,[26] this list correctly suggests that the Hispano-Californians did well in "cow county" local politics—that is, at town, city, and county level in southern California—prior to the 1880s. In addition to the fairly solid support that they were able to count upon from the large Spanish-speaking bloc, the patriarchal nature of Hispano-Californian society and the network of marriage relationships and blood ties gave them an initial advantage in soliciting votes locally. When they moved outside southern California local politics, the Hispano-Californians became relatively ineffective. They did elect two of their members to the office of state treasurer, several to the state legislature, and for a few months had the psychological satisfaction of seeing Romualdo Pacheco, who had been elected lieutenant governor, serve out the remainder of the former governor's term.

To complete this study, something should be said about Colorado and Texas. Colorado had no Spanish-American communities in 1848. When a few courageous Spanish-speaking pioneers came into the San Luis Valley from New Mexico in 1851, they sought to duplicate in southernmost Colorado the rural life they had known in the province to their south. The isolated villages that they built were planned as compact, enclosed units, with an eye partly to protection from the dangerous surrounding Indians, and partly to preserving the social values so fundamental to New Mexican rural society. In the late nineteenth century these villages, while no more progressive than those in New Mexico, showed a remarkable stability and continuity. As in New Mexico, a well-established pattern of community cooperation, especially in regard to water supply, was of key importance.[27]

Texas involves a more complex story. There is no intent here to talk of the Texan Revolution and the Texan Republic, nor indeed of relations between cultural groups in eastern Texas after 1848, for the dominance of Anglo-Americans in the more-developed part of the state was well established by that date. Bancroft guessed that in Texas as a whole "the Mexican element," as he termed it, "at this time numbered about 4,000 souls." This was in contrast to a total population that different censuses from 1847 to 1850 listed as ranging from 136,000 to 213,000.[28] All that will be attempted here is to say something concerning life in the western-most part of Texas, where the Spanish-speaking element continued to be important. Roughly, this is the area from the coast at Corpus Christi, up through San Antonio, and across the Edwards Plateau and Staked Plains (Llano Estacado) to Amarillo.

Even within this western strip the influence of the Spanish-speaking people was subject to challenge from an early date. When Frederick Law Olmsted, the noted traveler, visited San Antonio in 1857, he found that that town was already a "jumble of races, costumes, languages and buildings." On the streets Olmsted noticed "sauntering Mexicans . . . bearded Germans and sallow Yankees," just as he observed buildings that clearly reflected the work of those three distinct nationalities. As he reflected on the probable future of relations between the English-speaking and the Spanish-speaking, Olmsted coined some unforgettable phrases: "The mingled Puritanism and brigandism, which distinguishes the vulgar mind of the South, peculiarly unfits it to harmoniously associate with the bigoted, childish, and passionate Mexicans. They are considered to be heathen; not acknowledged as 'white folks.' Inevitably they are dealt with insolently and unjustly. They fear and hate the ascendant race, and involuntarily associate and sympathize with the negroes."[29]

Whatever possibility there may have been of developing better relations was made vastly more difficult by the lawless nature of society throughout broad strips on both sides of the Rio Grande international border. On the Mexican side, in addition to persistent problems of poverty, political instability, and erratic law enforcement, there was a hatred for Anglo-Texans that dated back to the Texas Revolution but was refreshed in each few years by some new act of arrogance or cruelty alleged against the Texans. On the Texan side there was the controlling circumstance that the area between the Nueces River which had its mouth at Corpus Christi, and the Rio Grande was a no-man's-land for many years, starting with the Texas Revolution. So great was the confusion and danger that the Spanish-speaking ranchers who had pioneered the region had to abandon it, and down into modern times a tradition has persisted that when reoccupation became possible, the original Spanish-speaking grantees transferred their lands to Anglo-Texans under conditions suggestive of forced sales.[30] To this the reply has been that only the courage and ability of Anglo-Texans made it possible to resume life at all in that region.

It was a situation in which misunderstanding and bitterness came easily. Wild Indians, bandits, smugglers, and cattle thieves plundered on both sides of the Rio Grande and took refuge on whichever side temporarily offered the better haven. Runaway American slaves and Mexican peons fled past each other in opposite directions. Vigilantes, filibusters, and revolutionaries gathered on both sides of the line and were not particular about whom they killed or robbed.

In this turbulent setting, relations between English-speaking and Spanish-speaking groups deteriorated rather than improved as the years passed. Speaking of the period prior to the American Civil War, a well-known historian has remarked of the two linguistic stocks: "The former were sometimes selfish, aggressive and overbearing; the latter were suspicious, underhanded, often proud and sensitive."[31]

Nor was there improvement after the Civil War. The principal student of this problem has asserted:

> From the close of the War between the States to 1880, friction along the Texas border was intense, and almost continuous. The lawlessness of a frontier cattle range was aggravated by international complications and inter-racial hostility involving Mexicans, Indians, and Americans. There were thieving, murder, arson, armed expeditions of outlaws or irregular bands of both Mexicans and Americans, and clashes

of troops of two nations and of the State of Texas. It is not strange that there was also intensification of animosities already well developed by the experiences of many years.[32]

Despite these towering international and intercultural difficulties, the land south of the Nueces began to enjoy successive booms in the last third of the nineteenth century. First it was cattle, then sheep, then cotton and vegetables. Anglo-Texans were the dominant force and the principal landowners, although they were always a numerical minority of the total population of the area. Spanish-speaking workers came into the region in relatively small numbers in the days when cowboys, sheepherders, or sheep shearers were all that was needed; their numbers increased sharply after irrigated agriculture began. Some of the workers came from Texas itself, many from Coahuila Province, Mexico, and others from more distant Mexican provinces. As in Arizona at an earlier date, the Spanish-speaking population thus became in the late nineteenth century a mixture of American-born and immigrant stocks.

Most were of too simple origins to play much of a role beyond that of low-paid wage earner. Their slowness to learn English proved a severe handicap. In sharp contrast, the survivors of the older "Spanish" upper-class families remained near San Antonio, just as they did near Santa Fe, Santa Barbara, or Tucson. They intermarried with the "Anglos" and received a comparable education. Like the daughters of the California aristocracy, their womenfolk were said to be "quite as white as the Americans, . . . a fine-looking and elevated race . . . of wonderful beauty."[33] They contributed to the founding of many a family that today bears an Anglo-American surname.

Politically the importance of the Spanish-Americans of Texas varied greatly. In the rural areas their influence was never great, even if they were in a majority. In some towns and cities they were courted briefly at each election, occasionally paid so much per head for their vote, and then dismissed until needed next time. Where they lived in towns that were overwhelmingly Hispanic, they sometimes had real power. In Laredo in the 1880s the leading Mexican-American families were supplying the chiefs for both local parties, even though the merchants and professional men included people of many national origins.[34]

To conclude this study it would be well to look back across the whole spectrum of events in the era, so as to examine the several conclusions that stand out. First, in their initial half-century under the American flag the historical experiences of Spanish-speaking populations in the several Southwestern states were strikingly varied. In considerable part this was the result of their respective histories prior to 1848. New Mexico, by far the oldest, had built up a sufficiently substantial population base and a sufficiently cohesive society so that throughout the rest of the century the Spanish-speaking remained in the majority and rural New Mexican culture remained largely unchanged, save for the very serious loss of needed farm and pasture lands. Arizona had been so thoroughly cleaned out by Indian troubles that when revival came under American auspices, a new mixed society emerged on a basis that for two decades at least offered to all hands an equal chance to profit from the new opportunities, even though in practice it was Americans and European immigrants who took advantage of the possibilities. In California the gold rush so accelerated the process of Americanization that had already begun that thereafter the performance of the relatively small population of Hispano-Californians constituted a kind of prolonged retreat from one area to another, as the Americans and European immigrants increased in numbers and gradually took possession of the land, business, and politics. In westernmost Texas, recent history had already established an unhappy pattern of mutual antagonism, lawlessness, and violence. Retention there of a Spanish-speaking majority was not sufficient to prevent a takeover by Anglo-Americans under turbulent, angry conditions that left a heritage of bitterness.

Secondly, it is hard to see that in any of the Southwestern states Spanish-speaking cultures proved resilient or resourceful in meeting the challenge of the aggressive, acquisitive Anglo-American intruding groups. To no small degree the encounter between the two stocks was a collision between old-fashioned pastoral and agricultural societies, characterized by practices that dated back to the Renaissance if not to the Middle Ages, and an advancing society that had already experienced to the full the commercial revolution and was now well into the industrial revolution and a comparably great change in transportation and finance. A poor level of education throughout the Hispanic lands and a limited knowledge of the modern world made the contest an unequal one, but so did the one group's instinctive wish to have life continue without basic alteration, while the other was opportunistically ready either to promote change or to exploit the status quo, whichever seemed more profitable.

In New Mexico more than in any other state some members of the well-to-do upper class did show a high degree of agility in taking advantage of the economic and political opportunities brought by the invasion of Anglo-Americans. The initial status of upper-class New Mexicans was one of unusual strength, and their position was preserved by the very slowness of their state to develop or grow. To a lesser degree, upper-class Californians were able to exploit their land ownerships and otherwise favored situation so as to profit at least temporarily, although many proved unable to keep wealth once they had it, or to find for themselves a permanent place of distinction in the new society that they found arising around them.

Thirdly, the great majority of the Spanish-speaking people who were in the Southwest in 1848, or came as immigrants thereafter, were simple people who stood far down on the social and economic ladders of their own societies. Of mixed blood and often much darker-skinned than the aristocracy, they were the ones most likely to encounter racial prejudice when they came into contact with Anglo-Americans. Being illiterate or semiliterate, without capital, and possessed of only modest skills vocationally, they had little more chance of advancing in the unfamiliar, pushing world of the Anglo-Americans than they had had in their own. As manual laborers, miners, cowboys, mule packers, sheepherders, sheep shearers, and agricultural workers, they made a contribution to the labor force of a region that was perennially short of manpower.

Unwittingly, by so doing they prepared the way for a veritable flood of new immigration from Mexico that began at about the turn of the century, when many new job openings were created in railroad construction and repair, in the new intensive agriculture, in mining, and in some types of industry. Coming in numbers many times greater than any previous influx of Spanish-speaking people, the newcomers drowned from sight the struggling older groups, except in slow-moving rural New Mexico. In the twentieth century the "Spanish-American problem" thus became a question of how to help recently arrived immigrants who were only just beginning acculturation. The public tended to forget that hidden somewhere were older groups, composed partly of much earlier immigrants who had been long in the United States, but partly of people who should not be called immigrants at all, since they were the descendants of pioneers who were second in time only to the Indians in their occupancy of the Southwest. Perhaps the most important service this paper can contribute is to recall to our momentary attention this often-forgotten aspect of Western history.

Notes

1. The estimate of George I. Sánchez, "History, Culture, and Education," in Julian Samora, ed., *La Raza: Forgotten Americans* (South Bend, Ind., 1966), 1.

2. See Seventh Census, 1850, pp. 972, 993, 996, 505; Hubert H. Bancroft, *Works* (39 vols., San Francisco, Calif., 1882–1890) XVI, 346, 390, XXI, 649, XXII, 643; Walter P. Webb *et al.*, eds. *Handbook of Texas* (2 vols., Austin, Texas, 1952), I, 321; Eleventh Census, 1890, *Population*, 606.

3. Doris M. Wright, "The Making of Cosmopolitan California: An Analysis of Immigration, 1848–1870," *California Historical Society Quarterly*, XIX (December, 1940), 324–26.

4. Carey McWilliams, *North from Mexico: The Spanish-Speaking People of the United States* (Philadelphia, Pa., and New York, N.Y., 1949), 7.

5. Sánchez, "History, Culture, and Education," *La Raza*, 5.

6. William W. H. Davis, *El Gringo: or, New Mexico and Her People* (New York, N.Y., 1857), 232.

7. For an admirable modern analysis, see Margaret Mead, ed., *Cultural Patterns and Technical Change* (paperback edition, New York, N.Y., n.d.), 151–77. A UNESCO study originally published 1955.

8. Cf. Miguel Antonio Otero, *My Life on the Frontier, 1864–1882. Incidents and Characters of the Period when Kansas, Colorado, and New Mexico Were Passing through the Last of Their Wild and Romantic Years* (New York, N.Y., 1935), passim.

9. Howard R. Lamar, *The Far Southwest, 1846–1912: a Territorial History* (New Haven, Conn., 1966), 136–70.

10. Bancroft, *Works*, XVII, 475, cites a Mexican census of September,

1848, that reported 760 people in Tucson and 249 in Tubac. Later in that year Tubac was abandoned.

11. Cameron Greenleaf and Andrew Wallace, "Tucson: Pueblo, Presidio, and American City: A Synopsis of its History," *Arizoniana*, III (summer, 1962), 24–25.

12. Ninth Census, 1870, *Population*, 3–4, 299, 341–42.

13. Compare Historical Records Survey, WPA, *The 1864 Census of the Territory of Arizona* (mimeographed, Phoenix, Ariz., 1938) with W. C. Disturnell, comp., *Arizona Business Directory and Gazetteer: Containing the Names of* . . . (San Francisco, Calif., 1881).

14. Elizabeth Albrecht, "Estévan Ochoa: Mexican-American Businessman," *Arizoniana*, IV (summer, 1963), 35–40.

15. Leonard Pitt, *The Decline of the Californios: A Social History of the Spanish-Speaking Californians, 1864–1890* (Berkeley and Los Angeles, Calif., 1966), 103.

16. Horace Bell, *Reminiscences of a Ranger or, Early Times in Southern California* (Los Angeles, Calif., 1881), 449.

17. Jackson A. Graves, *My Seventy Years in California, 1857–1927* (Los Angeles, Calif., 1927), 135–36.

18. Robert G. Cleland, *The Cattle on a Thousand Hills: Southern California, 1850–1880* (2nd ed., San Marino, Calif., 1951), 126–37.

19. Bell, *Reminiscences*, 288.

20. Cf. Harris Newmark, *Sixty Years in Southern California, 1853–1913*. Maurice H. and Marco R. Newmark, eds. (3rd ed., Boston, Mass., 1930), passim, but especially 60–111.

21. Walter Lindley and J. P. Widney, *California of the South . . . Being a Complete Guide-Book to Southern California* (New York, N.Y., 1888), 85.

22. Cleland, *Cattle on a Thousand Hills*, 132.

23. Pitt, *Decline of the Californios*, 123–24.

24. *Directory of Los Angeles for 1875* (Los Angeles, Calif., 1875).

25. Bell, *Reminiscences*, 455; Graves, *My Seventy Years*, 137.

26. Pitt, *Decline of the Californios*, 262–63, 271.

27. Cf. Olibama Lopez, "Pioneer Life in the San Luis Valley," *Colorado Magazine*, XIX (September, 1942), 161–67; and Emilia Gallegos Smith, "Reminiscences of Early San Luis," *ibid.*, XXIV (January, 1947), 24–25.

28. Cf. Bancroft, *Works*, XVI, 390, with Webb, *Handbook of Texas*, I, 321.

29. Frederick Law Olmsted, *A Journey through Texas: or, A Saddle-Trip on the Southwestern Frontier* (New York, N.Y., 1857), 456.

30. Paul S. Taylor, *An American-Mexican Frontier: Nueces County, Texas* (Chapel Hill, N.C., 1934), 184–88.

31. J. Fred Rippy, "Border Troubles along the Rio Grande, 1848–1860," *Southwestern Historical Quarterly*, XXIII (October, 1919), 93.

32. Taylor, *An American-Mexican Frontier*, 49.

33. Nathaniel A. Taylor, *The Coming Empire: or Two Thousand Miles*

in *Texas on Horseback* (rev. ed., Natalie Taylor Carlisle, ed., Houston, Texas, 1936), 107. Original edition 1877.

34. Seb. S. Wilcox, "The Laredo City Election and Riot of April, 1886," *Southwestern Historical Quarterly*, XLV (July, 1941), 1–23.

3

The Fisherman's Frontier
on the Pacific Coast:
The Rise of the
Salmon-Canning Industry

Vernon Carstensen, University of Washington

The rise of the salmon-canning industry on the Pacific Coast represents a minor theme in the long story of the ardent exploitation of the "inexhaustible" resources of North America. In a way, it also represents a minor failure of the exploiters and destroyers. Like the sky-darkening flocks of passenger pigeons of the Midwest and the enormous herds of buffalo of the Western plains, the great salmon runs invited the attention of market hunters and sportsmen, but the West Coast salmon, although hard pressed, were not pushed to extinction, as were the passenger pigeons, or nearly to extinction, as were the buffalo. They have survived in sufficient numbers to serve both commercial and sports fishermen.[1]

In 1874 the Portland *Oregonian* claimed that the salmon industry of the Columbia River was surpassed in value only by the wheat crop, and for many years the claim would be made by the fishing interests that the canned-salmon industry, not gold, provided the true economic base for Alaska.[2] Whatever the relative importance of the industry, there can be no doubt that the salmon fisheries and the salmon-canning industry were very important for varying periods of time in the developing economies of Oregon, Washington, British Columbia, and Alaska. Yet the fisheries, like the lumber industry, have attracted the interest of relatively few historians. The interest of American historians in the North American fisheries could almost be said to have begun and ended with the great cod fisheries of the Atlantic. The history of the freshwater fisheries, like that of the West Coast, has been largely ignored except when someone has said something about Ramsey Crooks' attempt to shore up the declining fur business by developing a trade in whitefish or has wanted to explain the presence of Icelandic people in the area of the Great Lakes. West Coast salmon have been much written and talked about by icthyologists, newspaper reporters, editorial writers, and politicians, but not by historians. Yet the salmon had been in view and of great importance to the people of the Pacific Coast long before the first whites visited the area.

Salmon were found in large numbers in the Pacific from Monterey north to the Arctic. They seemed designed to serve the needs of man, since the mature fish returned from the sea to spawn in the fresh-water streams that fall into the Pacific.[3] Just as the great herds of buffalo played a large part in sustaining the Plains Indians, so the great salmon runs of the West Coast served the Indian tribes of the area. The runs became a vital part of their economy and of their religion. No doubt some of the late-eighteenth-century traders considered trying to make something out of the great quantity of salmon, but they left no record. When Lewis and Clark reached The Dalles on the Columbia in October, 1805, they saw the Indians catching and packing fish. The dried, pulverized salmon was packed into woven basketlike containers lined with dried salmon skins. Each container, they estimated, held from ninety to one hundred pounds of salmon pemmican. "Great quantities," they recorded, "are sold to white people who visit the mouth of this river as well as to the natives below."[4]

Whatever business in salmon pemmican the Indians had developed with the occasional maritime fur traders was not to be theirs for very long. Shortly, Astor's men built a post at the mouth of the Columbia, and in a few years they gave way to the Northwest Company. Then, in the early 1820s after the union of the Hudson's Bay Company (HBC) and the Northwest Company, the HBC organized the Columbia District and installed John McLoughlin as chief factor. His primary business was to collect furs, but almost immediately he sent barreled salmon to England to see whether a market could be found. In July, 1824, the governor and committee of HBC wrote saying that the fish could not be used. A year later a second shipment arrived in London, and although it was found to be in better condition than the first, the company officers declared that they were "of the opinion that from the difficulty of curing the fish properly, and the length of time it must unavoidably continue in pickle, that it will not answer as an article of commerce."[5]

Although discouraged from packing salmon for the London market, the HBC men in the Columbia District during the next decades barreled salmon and sought and found markets for it in San Francisco, South America, and Hawaii.[6] But much as Governor Simpson and McLoughlin would have liked to maintain a monopoly of the salmon fisheries, they did not succeed. In April, 1831, Josiah Marshall's brig *Owhyhee* returned to Boston after three years of trading in the North Pacific. Besides fur and some sperm-whale oil, she brought fifty-three barrels of pickled salmon which, it was reported, had been "taken by the Indians, sold green to the master of the ship and cured by him." The collector of customs at Boston accordingly ruled that they were "foreign caught fish" and imposed a duty of two dollars a barrel. The fifty-three barrels were sold to a Boston buyer at fourteen dollars a barrel, but one observer wrote disparagingly that the Pacific Northwest salmon was a "large white and coarse fish" more like the hake than the Atlantic salmon. He added with malicious pleasure that the buyer of the cargo had not yet been able to sell any of the fish. Nevertheless a ship leaving Boston that fall carried salt and staves and hoops for a thousand barrels—it was assumed that it would seek Pacific Coast salmon.[7]

Apparently the Boston fish market, like that of London, saw

little more of West Coast salmon during the next decades, but Boston investors must have heard a great deal. In the early 1830s Nathaniel Wyeth launched substantial ventures to exploit the Columbia River salmon fisheries, but he failed, and, in the next years, in the correspondence of McLoughlin, we have glimpses of other New Englanders who entered the river with the intention of taking fish. Few returned for another try, and this pleased McLoughlin.[8] Presumably for every New Englander who actually ventured to take fish in the Columbia or elsewhere on the Pacific Coast, there were many others who dreamed of developing the salmon fisheries. Indeed, in 1871 J. L. McDonald wrote a book under the title *Hidden Treasures or Fisheries around the Northwest Coast,* which was intended to publicize the great promise of the western fisheries. Appropriately enough the book was published in Gloucester, Massachusetts, and it exhibited a proper attitude toward fishing and fishermen. Not only did McDonald describe in glowing terms the abundance of desirable fish in the North Pacific, but he showed that he was aware of what went into the settlers' and immigrants' guidebooks that sought to encourage the migration of farmers into the new areas of the West. In many of the immigrant guides—and of course in many other places—the argument was advanced that farm settlers deserved special treatment and privileges because they were, after all, carriers of civilization. McDonald suggested that fishermen who ventured into new waters were also carriers of civilization.[9]

But whether the fisherman was the carrier of civilization or not, it seems reasonably clear that neither the HBC nor those it regarded as interlopers enjoyed a substantial success in exploiting salmon in the years between 1823 and 1864. The fish-taking gear employed by the whites was somewhat more efficient than that of the Indians, but no new methods of preserving fish were introduced. Fish were dried or they were pickled in brine. A few attempts were made to develop a market for dried salmon bellies —probably because the Indians had used this part of the fish as a kind of primitive K ration—but salmon bellies had little appeal in the marketplace.[10] San Francisco newspapers in 1864 reported a small but widespread international trade in barreled salmon. Shipments of barreled salmon were reported as having gone to New York and Boston, Mexico, the Hawaiian Islands, Australia,

China, Japan, and "other countries."[11] In 1864, however, a salmon cannery was established on the Sacramento River, and the day of rapid expansion of the salmon fisheries was at hand.

The art of preserving food in hermetically sealed containers was discovered in France early in the nineteenth century. Shortly thereafter an Englishman contributed the idea of using tin-plated iron to make the container, so that before the end of the second decade of the century the principal ingredients for this new method in the art of preserving food were brought together. Not until the 1890s would the art move toward becoming a science, when H. L. Russell of the College of Agriculture, University of Wisconsin, and other bacteriologists began to bring the relatively new discipline of bacteriology to the service of the food-canning industry, and by that time canning had become a big business. In the intervening years canners of fish, meat, fruit, and vegetables had measured their success by such crude devices as the number of filled cans that exploded in their warehouses or elsewhere, the amount of other spoilage, and the extent to which their customers complained of food poisoning or succumbed to botulism.[12]

The French and English were relatively quick to adopt the new art of canning, and some Americans, by the 1830s, sought to preserve fruits and vegetables by this method. By the 1840s some seafood was canned with success along the East Coast, and it is reported that in 1843 lobsters and salmon were canned at East-port, Maine. Canned sardines were known, if not widely used, for a decade before the California gold rush. In fact, it might be said that "modern food technology" touched the Late Stone Age when Sir William Drummond Stewart carried canned sardines into the Rocky Mountains in the 1830s.[13] San Francisco newspapers of the early 1860s show a regular importation of canned goods such as lobsters, scallops, and sardines and suggest that canned salmon was fairly widely known. In May of 1865 the San Francisco *Daily Evening Bulletin* reported that canned salmon was quoted in Australia at sixteen shillings per dozen one-pound tins. In the middle 1860s a fruit and vegetable cannery was established near Sacramento and attracted some newspaper attention. Perhaps the remarkable thing is that no one tried to can salmon on the West Coast until 1864.

Three men from Maine, William and George W. Hume and

Andrew Hapgood, launched their business across the river from
Sacramento in the spring of 1864. William, the oldest of the
Hume brothers, had come to California in 1852, and after a try at
gold mining, had turned to earning his living as a fisherman and
hunter for the San Francisco market. His father had worked as a
salmon fisherman in Maine, and William apparently knew something about the business. In 1856 he had been joined by two of
his brothers, John and George, and the three continued as fishermen and market hunters. In 1863 George, on a visit to Maine,
encountered a boyhood friend, Andrew Hapgood, a tinsmith, who
had done some canning on the Maine coast and had even canned
a few salmon on the Bay of Chaleur. Fisherman and canner
worked out an arrangement to pool their skills, and Andrew Hapgood came to California in March, 1864, with the tools and equipment to launch a cannery.

Later reminiscences have it that the partners obtained tin-
plate on credit from a San Francisco dealer, borrowed a boiler
from a neighboring farmer, and purchased a scow on which they
built their cannery. They anchored it across the river from Sacramento and enlarged their cabin to serve as a tinshop. No news-
paperman visited this pioneer cannery, and no contemporary accounts of the operation have come to light. In 1904, however,
R. D. Hume, youngest of the Hume brothers, furnished for the
Pacific Fisherman a detailed and probably fairly accurate description of the laborious and awkward work of making cans, the
process of butchering, cleaning, and cutting up the fish and filling
the cans. The lid was then soldered on and the filled can pushed
into the cooking department, which was called the bathroom.
Here Andrew Hapgood presided over what was supposed to be
the secret process. The cans of fish were cooked for a period of
time, the cans were then vented, resoldered, and cooked some
more. They were then cooled, cleaned, and painted red—the
color which for several years was to mark canned salmon. The
amount of the first pack is usually given as 2,000 cases, forty-eight
one-pound cans to a case, and is probably approximately correct.
It was also recalled that only about half of the pack exploded, and
what was left found a slow sale in San Francsico, at about five
dollars a case. The first season was not a brilliant success, but
neither was it a failure. Indeed, in view of the inexperience of the

canners, and the crudeness of the machinery and the procedures, perhaps the remarkable thing is that the whole pack didn't explode.

The partners continued on the Sacramento River for two more seasons, but in 1866 they moved to the Columbia River. Several reasons were given for this move. Salmon were decreasing in the Sacramento in consequence of pollution of the stream and the destruction of spawning grounds by the gold dredges. Perhaps more important was the far greater supply of salmon reported on the Columbia. The Humes were apparently satisfied that they had mastered the canning process and that they could find a market for a greater amount of fish than they could produce on the Sacramento. They sought to keep the process a secret for the next few years, but in view of the amount of work that had to be done in the "bathroom" this was impossible.[14]

The Humes and Hapgood enjoyed wonderful early success on the Columbia. In 1867, 18,000 cases of salmon were packed; the next year, 28,000; and in 1869, a total of 100,000 cases.[15] Markets apparently developed to absorb all they could produce. In March, 1868, the *Oregonian* carried a story on the salmon fisheries on the Columbia and reported that Hapgood and the Humes expected to pack 300,000 pounds of salmon that season by employing a new process that involved putting the fish in tin cans which, the reporter declared, "keep fresh for years." Hume and Hapgood, the report said, already had a good reputation. Most of the canned salmon would be sent to Australia.[16] Scattered details on the search for markets are found in a small miscellaneous collection of letters and accounts of the Hapgood and Hume cannery at Oak Point for the years 1869 to 1872. Apparently the commission merchants Platt and Newton of San Francisco and New York managed the sale of the Hapgood and Hume canned salmon. Incomplete accounts for 1870 show sales in Hong Kong, Valparaiso, Singapore, and Melbourne. There are later references to additional sales in Wellington, Callao, New York, and London. Entry into the English market was vigorously pushed. In early 1872 George Brett, the London agent of Platt and Newton, reported that he had been unable to sell Columbia canned salmon to Crosse and Blackwell. He found that some English purchasers complained "of the red color of American salmon and thought it to be artificial." Nevertheless Brett was elated that he had an order for 5,500 cases of salmon from J. T. Morton of Leadenhall Street, the largest handler of canned salmon in London. He also reported to his employers a conversation during which Morton remarked that in view of the quantity of salmon in the North Pacific, the canners in that area could capture the London market. Brett responded, "I said that was *exactly* what I had come to do." But he warned the Columbia canners to maintain the high quality of their goods and to conform to English taste. He sent out several cans of Scotch and Irish salmon to show the men on the Columbia what their competitors were doing, and he bought and shipped some red paint of the color preferred by the English. Parenthetically, the same year that Brett reported his large sale in England, Platt and Newton reported to Hapgood and Hume that they had sold first 100 and then 500 cases of canned salmon to the commissary department of the U.S. Army.[17] This may not have been the first sale, but it shows the very early use of canned salmon by the army —a use that would continue, although canned salmon was challenged on the army menu during the Second World War by Spam.[18]

The sales in England grew rapidly in the early 1870s. In 1877 it was reported that well over half the entire pack on the Columbia was shipped directly to England. Very little found a market inside the United States. A decade later this situation had changed substantially.[19]

Accounts of the great riches made in salmon-canning on the Columbia brought a number of other canners to the Columbia, which was the principal salmon-canning stream until the middle 1870s. In 1873 there were fourteen canneries on the river, more than half of which were either wholly or partly owned by the Humes, and competition for the fish was beginning to be very keen. After the middle 1870s the canners established themselves on the coastal rivers of Oregon and California, in the Puget Sound area, in British Columbia, and in Alaska. Before 1900 an American-built cannery was established on the Kamchatka River, and it was only a few more years before canneries would be tried on the rivers flowing into the Siberian Arctic.[20]

In 1878 R. D. Hume took the first steps toward obtaining virtually complete control of the Rogue River in Oregon. He purchased the fishery already in operation there and set about to obtain possession of all land on both sides of the Rogue from the ocean to the mountains, and an appropriate amount of ocean frontage. He built a cannery, a fish hatchery, a company town— he even established his own newspaper and race track, and once brought his steam-powered automobile there for the summer— and he sought to enjoy complete possession of his own river. Until his death in 1908 he claimed his prescriptive right to all salmon in the river. He also claimed, and perhaps deserved, the title of King of the Rogue, although he did have unruly subjects, some of whom he dealt with directly, others he faced in courts of law.[21]

The rapid expansion of the business is reflected in the production figures. In 1882 the North Pacific canneries reported over one million cases of salmon packed, more than half of which came from the Columbia; in 1895 the total pack exceeded two million cases; in 1900, three million; and in 1901, five million. The spread of the productive fisheries to the new districts is reflected in the annual statistics of the industry compiled by John N. Cobb. Salmon-canning was resumed on the Sacramento in 1875 and built up to 200,000 cases in 1882, before it declined again and virtually disappeared. In 1876 there were reports of the first canned salmon from British Columbia, where the business grew slowly but steadily. In 1893 the pack there exceeded a half-million cases for the first time, and four years later, in 1897, it exceeded a million cases but promptly dropped again. There was a modest return from Alaska in 1878; in 1889 production passed the half-million mark; and ten years later more than a million cases were packed. From that time on, Alaska would be the largest producer of canned salmon. Around five thousand cases were produced in the Puget Sound area in 1877, but the business increased relatively slowly. In 1895 the canneries of the Puget Sound area produced more than a hundred thousand cases, in 1897 almost half a million, and in 1901 a million. These rapid increases in production did cause some marketing problems in the late 1880s. In 1891 the Alaska canners formed a marketing pool that led to the formation of the Alaska Packers Association, which sought to control both production and marketing. This was shortly followed by similar associations in the Puget Sound area and in British Columbia, but not until the end of the 1890s did something approaching an association find acceptance on the Columbia River.[22] By this time the old Hapgood and Hume cannery at Oak Point was in the hands of two men whose conservatism was reflected in their annual boast that they still packed salmon in the old-fashioned way and still painted their cans red. They had few customers. Meanwhile the supply and marketing center was in process of moving northward from San Francisco.[23]

The spectacular increase in the productivity of the canneries reflected rapid technological advances in almost every part of the business from taking the fish to can-making, butchering, packing, processing, and packaging, and in the related businesses. The Indians and the first white fishermen had used dip nets, spears, and small seines. The first drift or gill nets were apparently used in the Columbia in 1851. In 1877 the *Daily Astorian* printed a letter from an old fisherman who claimed that when he began fishing in the lower Columbia in 1847, he could catch more salmon than he could manage in a thirty-fathom seine—now such a seine would not bring in a single fish. R. D. Hume stated that in 1871 a cannery on the Columbia had been able to pack 25,000 cases of salmon in a ninety-day season and employed only four fishing boats, each supplied with a drift net 125 fathoms in length and twenty-five to thirty meshes deep. Nets were initially hand woven, but in 1877 a Portland mechanic devised a machine to weave nets at half the cost of handweaving. By this time nets had lengthened to 200 fathoms and shortly would reach 300.[24] So efficient and abundant did the fishing gear become, that by 1883, sixteen years after the business was launched, the Columbia River registered the largest production of Chinook salmon in the history of the river. In 1888 the Corps of Engineers made an inventory of the fishing gear in use on the Columbia. There were 1,600 drift nets in use, averaging 300 fathoms, or 1800 feet; this amounted to about 2,888,000 feet or 545 miles of net. There were also 136 fish traps installed on the lower Columbia. In addition there were an unknown number of seines—some worked by boats, some by horses—and seven fish wheels located at the Cascades and The Dalles. The first fish wheel was put in operation at The Dalles in 1878 and attracted much attention. Upriver canners declared it to be a marvelous fish-catching machine which took fifty thousand pounds of fish a day. Downriver gill netters denounced it as a murderous device that took all fish regardless of size or species. They called it the fish pump.[25] The remarkable thing is that any fish at all reached the spawning grounds. The Engineers thought that all this fishing gear actually slowed down the flow of water in the Columbia.

The large amount of fishing gear in the river reduced the number of fish a single fisherman could catch and forced up the price. When the business started in 1867, fishermen were paid twenty cents a fish. It was expected that three fish would produce forty-eight pounds of canned salmon. Hence fish weighing less than twenty pounds often were not paid for. As the gear improved, the number of fishermen increased, and the catch per boat diminished. Fishermen asked for more money and occasionally struck to enforce their demands. The price per fish went to twenty-five cents in 1873, to fifty cents in 1879, and to seventy-five cents in 1882. After the price reached one dollar in 1890, the canneries began to pay fishermen by the pound.[26]

The gill netters on the Columbia were mostly transients, drawn from San Francisco for the fishing season. An observer in the early 1880s characterized them as mostly Italians, although they included some Slavs, Greeks, Portuguese, and Spaniards. More than two-thirds were unmarried, and most were illiterate. Astoria served as their headquarters during their stay on the Columbia, and the *Oregonian* viewed that city as "the most wicked place on earth for its population." It once declared, however, that some respectable men also fished on the lower Columbia. The *Post-Intelligencer,* no doubt in a mood of exasperation, described the fishermen of the lower Columbia as a rough, tough, lawless group of Greeks, Austrians, Russians, and Finns, and later as a bunch of "piratical dagoes" who were trying to terrorize the peaceful upriver American fishermen. The Americans, according to the *Post-Intelligencer,* consisted of "Scandinavians and others."[27]

The life of gill netters on the lower Columbia was rough and dangerous. In George Brown Goode's great compendium on fisheries and fishing, twenty-two pages are given to the dangers of fishing. Three short paragraphs dispose of the Columbia. Some skillful sober fishermen and others who were drunk or asleep, drifted too close to the bar and were lost. The statement continues "in stormy weather some men are drowned every night," and unless their bodies were caught in drift nets, they were carried out to sea and never found. In 1879 forty fishermen were drowned and "more than that number" in 1880. Neither the canners nor the local newspapers seemed much interested in making public announcements of the loss of itinerant and nameless gill netters. In a great storm on the Columbia on May 3 and 4, 1880, somewhere between sixty and three hundred and fifty gill netters lost their lives on the Columbia bar, but newspaper interest in the disaster subsided within four days.[28]

George Hume began using Chinese laborers inside his cannery in 1872, and thereafter the Chinese furnished most of the cannery labor throughout the industry, although no Chinese were permitted to fish on the Columbia.[29]

The fishing season was relatively short and the catches often very large, so successful canners were forced to take whatever steps they could to speed the work and to mechanize all processes that would yield to mechanization. Work was carefully scheduled and often highly specialized. For example, when tin cans first were used for canning, it was claimed that a good tinsmith could make only sixty cans a day when he performed all steps in the process by hand. Can-making had improved somewhat by the time Hapgood and the Humes opened their first cannery, but even so, a large part of the winter and early spring was spent in making cans. But very quickly machines were devised to cut out the ends and body pieces, and crews of can makers were carefully organized. A visitor to a cannery in 1877 reported that can-making had been broken down into fourteen necessary steps and that a gang of twenty-two men produced 15,000 cans a day. The next year the *Daily Astorian* announced with great pleasure that a local mechanic had a soldering machine, run by a two-horsepower steam engine, that could solder twenty-five to thirty thousand cans a day.[30] It appears that almost every canner contributed something to the mechanization of can-making. Gordon Dodds, in his biography of R. D. Hume, credits Hume with twenty-four patents on can-making machinery, including one machine that shaped and soldered the body and then attached and soldered the bottom of the can.[31] The most impressive innovations were made in the

1890s and later by Axel Johnson, a Swedish immigrant, who came to the industry by way of Chicago machine shops.[32]

Much of the apparently inescapable handwork of the cannery came in cleaning and cutting the fish for packing. Gang-knives for cutting the cleaned fish appeared early, but a mechanical fish-cleaner and -slimer was slower in coming, although by the 1890s there were reports that such a machine would soon be invented—and it was. Edmond Augustine Smith, the inventor of the first successful fish-cleaning machine, was as alien to the salmon-canning business as Axel Johnson. Born in London, Ontario, his farmer-parents brought him to Victoria, British Columbia, as a youngster. He worked at various jobs and then came to Seattle as a brickmaker and terra cotta presser. A natural tinkerer, he got interested in the problem of making a mechanical fish-cleaner around 1901, and in 1903 he had a machine ready. It was tried at Bellingham in 1903 and cleaned 22,000 fish during the first eight-hour run. Improvements were added, and within a few years it was claimed that one machine could do the work of a crew of fifty Chinese butchers. Smith was described as a fat and happy man. A Seattle newspaper once stated that he weighed under five hundred pounds, but not much.[33]

There were innumerable less dramatic improvements. For example, it was thought that the English customer would buy canned salmon only if the cans were painted red; and besides the can needed some protection against rust. When only a few thousand cases of salmon were produced during the season, this was not an impossible arrangement; but paint dried too slowly to serve well when production increased. The canners sought a fast-drying paint and failed to find one. They tried varnish and found it unsatisfactory. They then experimented with shellac and found that it served admirably. The shellac bath became a part of the canning process. Similarly, once the salmon pack passed fifty thousand cases a year, the canners faced a minor problem of obtaining the wooden boxes in which to store and ship their goods. Manufacturers in Portland organized box-making factories, and in 1877 John Harlow's factory employed a crew of forty-five men and produced 2,500 boxes a day using a box-nailing machine.[34]

The salmon-canning business hardly fits the pattern most historians like to employ in describing economic development in the Western United States—although in some respects it resembles the fur trade. Almost from the beginning it was characterized by relatively large-scale organization and absentee ownership; it was seasonal, it depended on transient labor, and it sought a world market. Moreover, although the salmon canners were beneficiaries of whatever technology they could borrow from Europe and the Eastern United States, they also made numerous important contributions to canning technology themselves. Perhaps they shouldn't have done this in an economically underdeveloped area, but they did.

The canners conducted their business in isolated places, unsupervised except by the market. They were either responsible or lucky in that they were not touched by anything resembling the "embalmed-beef scandal" of the Spanish-American War, and only a little harassed by Upton Sinclair's disclosures of conditions in the stockyards of Chicago; but analysis of their product by the North Dakota state chemist did embarrass them. It was more in amusement than in anger that the *Pacific Fisherman* reported in 1912 that an English newspaper had charged that American salmon was nothing more than cod dyed pink by the Yankees, and that another, no doubt influenced by Upton Sinclair, charged that American salmon were usually packed in brothels and often were unintentionally adulterated with the human hands, feet, and other parts lopped off during the canning operation.[35] In 1918 the whole Alaska salmon pack was purchased by the U.S. government and subjected to a cursory inspection. The stuff stood up fairly well. Most of what was found in the cans was reported to be salmon, but it had not been carefully packed. Of 817,000 cases inspected in Seattle, 108,000 were rejected.[36] This experience led the leading salmon canners to propose industry-wide inspection at the canneries.[37] The proposal itself probably indicates that the old order had vanished beyond recall.

Notes

1. A. W. Schorger, in *The Passenger Pigeon: Its Natural History and Extinction* (Madison, Wisc., 1955), 199 ff., recounts in full detail the melancholy story of the destruction of the passenger pigeon, a species which once had an annual population estimated at various numbers over a billion. There

are a number of accounts of the destruction of the vast buffalo herds. E. D. Branch, *The Hunting of the Buffalo* (New York, N.Y., 1929), is as useful as any in showing how the indestructible buffalo herds melted in the face of avarice, technology, and an insatiable market. It is true that the salmon runs into the New England rivers were virtually destroyed by mid nineteenth century and so, too, were the runs in some of the California rivers. However, by the mid 1870s, less than a decade after the salmon canners reached the Columbia, steps were being taken to try both to protect the salmon and to provide for artificial propagation, see Gordon Dodds, *The Salmon King of Oregon: R. D. Hume and the Pacific Fisheries* (Chapel Hill, N.C., 1959).

2. *Morning Oregonian* (Portland), July 16, 1874. This story was reported from Astoria. On March 3, 1875, the *Oregonian* modified the claim to say that the salmon canneries were next after wheat and wool in commercial importance.

3. There is an enormous amount of scholarly and popular literature based on observation and imagination that deals with the life cycle of the salmon. A. D. Hasler, *Underwater Guide Posts: Homing of Salmon* (Madison, Wisc., 1964), offers a hypothesis to explain the homing mechanism of salmon and provides a useful bibliography. R. L. Haig-Brown, *Return to the River* (Vancouver, B.C., 1946), presents a fictional account of the life cycle of the chinook. The special work done by Professor Lauren R. Donaldson and his associates in the College of Fisheries, University of Washington, in getting salmon to return to the college hatcheries has occasionally been reported in national magazines since the return of the first "class" in 1951: see *Time*, November 12, 1951, p. 70, October 20, 1961, pp. 61–62; Murray Morgan, *Harpers*, 231 (July, 1965), 47–51; *Readers Digest*, 87 (October, 1965), 193–98.

4. October 21–22, 1805, *Original Journals of the Lewis and Clark Expedition, 1804–5*, R. G. Thwaites, ed. (8 vols., New York, N.Y., 1904–5), III, 146–48.

5. *Fur Trade and Empire: George Simpson's Journal, 1824–25*, Frederick Merk, ed. (rev. ed., Cambridge, Mass., 1968), 240, 252.

6. The work of HBC in catching, packing, and peddling barreled salmon can be followed in the correspondence of John McLoughlin. See *Letters of John McLoughlin from Fort Vancouver to the Governor and Committee*, E. E. Rich, ed. (3 vols., Toronto, Ont., 1941, 1944, 1945); *Letters of Doctor John McLoughlin, 1829–32*, Burt Brown Barker, ed. (Portland, Ore., 1948). The persistent hope of HBC officers of developing a profitable salmon trade is reflected in a letter of Simpson, written to the governor and committee from Honolulu on March 1, 1842. He reported the abundance of superior salmon in the North Pacific, for which he was sure U.S. and Chinese markets would grow. The fish commanded from ten to twelve dollars for a 180-pound barrel in the Sandwich Islands. "I think," he concluded, "the fisheries of this coast are highly deserving of attention as a growing and almost inexhaustible source of trade." "Letters of George Simpson, 1841–42," Joseph Shafer, ed., *American Historical Review*, XIV (October, 1908), 83–84.

72 / *Vernon Carstensen*

7. S. E. Morison, "New England and the Opening of the Columbia River Salmon Trade, 1830," *Oregon Historical Quarterly*, 28 (June, 1927), 111–32.

8. In a letter to the governor and committee, October 29, 1832, McLoughlin reported the arrival of Wyeth with eleven Americans and said they proposed to investigate the possibility of going into the salmon-curing business as well as the fur trade. *McLoughlin Letters from Vancouver*, I, 108–9. Wyeth recorded his salmon-fishing experience in his *Journals*, F. G. Young, ed. (Eugene, Ore., 1899), and in a letter of February 4, 1839, printed in *Report from Mr. [Caleb] Cushing from the Committee on Foreign Affairs. Territory of Oregon, Supplemental Report, Feb. 16, 1839. House of Representatives Document* No. 101, pt. 2, 25 Cong. 3 Sess., serial 351, pp. 12–14. Scattered through the McLoughlin letters are angry and denunciatory references to American sea captains who entered the Columbia to take salmon.

Although HBC never managed to get barreled salmon to England in good shape, efforts continued and are reflected in the letters. The business never attained the prosperity in the Pacific that officers of the company apparently hoped for; so long as HBC remained at Vancouver, however, the company continued to take and pack salmon. An 1846 drawing of Fort Vancouver shows the salmon store and wharf prominently among the buildings of the establishment. *McLoughlin Letters from Vancouver*, III, 48.

9. Apparently spokesmen for the fishermen had over the years sought to reap such benefits as might accrue from identifying themselves as "carriers of civilization." Eighty years before McDonald published his book, Talleyrand, having engaged in land speculation in New York and New England, declared that lumbermen and fishermen were among the less valuable members of society. "Fishing," he said. "closely resembles idleness"; and of fishermen, "There is no place they love, they know the land only by the poor house in which they live. . . . When some political writers have said that fishing was a sort of agriculture they have said something which seems brilliant but which has no truth. All the qualities, all the virtues which are attached to agriculture are lacking to the man who engages in fishing." *Talleyrand in America As a Financial Promoter, 1794–96: Unpublished Letters and Memoirs*, H. Huth and Wilma J. Pugh, trans. and eds. (*Annual Report of the American Historical Association, 1941*, 3 vols., Washington, D.C., 1941), II, 81.

10. There are scattered references to the salmon trade on the Columbia in the 1850s in H. H. Bancroft, *History of Oregon* (2 vols., San Francisco, Calif., 1888), II, and *History of Washington, Idaho, and Montana 1845–1889* (San Francisco, Calif., 1890). James G. Swan, *The Northwest Coast, or Three Years Residence in Washington Territory* (New York, N.Y., 1857), 107 and passim, provides a description of the nets and seines used in salmon-fishing in the 1850s and a brief comment on the decaying Indian ceremonies that attended capture of the first salmon in the spring.

11. *San Francisco Daily Evening Bulletin*, October 19, 1864, January 14, 1865. I am indebted to Peter C. Carstensen, now an attorney in the

Department of Justice, for searching the files of California newspapers for trade and other data relating to the salmon fisheries.

12. General histories of the canning industry are both rare and inadequate. James H. Collins, *The Story of Canned Foods* (New York, N.Y., 1924) has some useful information but is seldom reliable on details; Earl Chapin May, *The Canning Clan: A Pageant of Pioneering Americans* (New York, N.Y., 1937), 31–38, also untrustworthy on details, devotes a chapter to Russell's work, with wild disregard for accuracy of detail. He provides, pp. 433–41, a list of somewhat capriciously selected "important dates" in the history of canning. Most useful is A. W. Bitting, *Appertizing: or, The Art of Canning: Its History and Development* (San Francisco, Calif., 1937), who has looked at many of the important documents and who, on pages 47–49, reprints H. L. Russell's report on gaseous fermentation in the canning industry from the *12th Annual Report of The Wisconsin Agricultural Experiment Station, 1895*, 227–31. See also E. H. Beardsley, *Harry L. Russell and Agricultural Science in Wisconsin* (Madison, Wisc., 1969), 19–21; and Paul F. Clark, *Pioneer Microbiologists of America* (Madison, Wisc., 1961), 266.

13. Historians of canning, like most other historians, supply dates and places to identify beginnings and "firsts," but they seldom agree. Bitting, *The Art of Canning*, 796, 805, 812, states that lobsters were "first" canned at Eastport, Maine, in 1842; salmon at Aberdeen, Scotland, 1824; and sardines at Nantes, France, 1834. May, *The Canning Clan*, 435, states with a (?) that Crosse and Blackwell established "the world's first salmon canning factory" at Cork, Ireland, in 1849. The authors of a recent biography of William Drummond Stewart mention that among the supplies Stewart took to the mountains on his trips into Western America during the early and middle 1830s were canned sardines which he doled out on rare occasions to mountain men and presumably Indians. See Mae Reed Porter and Odessa Davenport, *Scotsman in Buckskin: Sir William Drummond Stewart and the Rocky Mountain Fur Trade* (New York, N.Y., 1963), 132, 146.

14. Few contemporary records give so much as a glimpse of this enterprise on the Sacramento. Robert E. Draper, *Sacramento Directory for 1866*, lists neither the Humes nor Hapgood. *The Sacramento Union* says nothing from June to October about the salmon canners working across the river from the city. A year after the Humes established their cannery on the Columbia the *Oregonian*, March 10, 1868, carried a brief account of their cannery. Thereafter newspaper and other accounts appear. The story of the establishment and management of the Sacramento cannery rests almost entirely on the recollections of R. D. Hume, the youngest of the seven Hume brothers, four of whom played a part in the salmon-canning industry. R. D. arrived in California in the spring of 1864 in time to help with the first salmon pack. Details of his account changed from time to time, but the story remains much the same. See R. D. Hume, *Salmon of the Pacific Coast* (n.p., 1893); "The First Cannery," *Pacific Fisherman*, January, 1905, pp. 19–20 (printed with the article was a sketch picturing the first cannery made under "direct supervision" of R. D. Hume), and *ibid.*, January, 1908, pp. 25–26; obituaries of

R. D. Hume and George W. Hume appear in *ibid.*, February, 1909, p. 21, and March, 1912, p. 17 respectively. A biography of William, who died in 1902, by R. C. Clark is in the *Dictionary of American Biography*. The *Daily Astorian*, January 6, 1883, carried an article on George W. Hume. R. D. Hume wrote an autobiography of sorts and published it serially in his newspaper, the *Radium* (Wedderburn, Oregon), 1904–6. This has been reprinted, with Gordon B. Dodds as editor, under Hume's title, *A Pygmy Monopolist: The Life and Doings of R. D. Hume Written by Himself and Dedicated to his Neighbors* (Madison, Wisc., 1961).

There is some confusion about the date of the first pack of salmon on the Columbia. Most writers give 1866 as the year during which the Humes and Hapgood began canning salmon on the river. However, the best evidence—the recollections of George W. and R. D. Hume and the report in the *Oregonian* in 1868—clearly indicates that the 1867 season marked the beginning of salmon-canning on the Columbia. For many details on the Columbia River fisheries see also T. E. Craig and R. L. Hacker, *History and Development of the Fisheries of the Columbia,* Bull. 32, Bureau of Fisheries, 1940.

15. John N. Cobb assembled the data on the salmon fisheries for the U.S. Bureau of Fisheries. His first bulletin was published under the title of *The Salmon Fisheries of the Pacific Coast* in 1911, and thereafter the bulletin appeared in enlarged editions in 1917, 1921, and 1930 under the title of *Pacific Salmon Fisheries.*

16. The *Daily Oregonian* (Portland), March 10, 1868.

17. Hume and Hapgood Business Records, University of Oregon, include the George Brett letters, January 10, 1872, to the New York and San Francisco offices of Platt & Newton. The Army sales were reported to Hume and Hapgood on May 4, 1872, and in June, 1872.

18. The long relation of the Army with canned salmon is underscored by three pages or so devoted to salmon and salmon-canning in the *Handbook of Subsistence Stores,* published by authority of the Secretary of War, for use in the Army of the United States, *War Department Document* No. 19 (Washington, D.C., 1896), 146–49.

19. *A Review of the Commercial, Financial and Industrial Interest of the State of Oregon for the Year 1877* (Portland, Ore., 1878), 11–12; Cobb, *Pacific Salmon Fisheries* (1917), 162. The *Review* reports a total of 274,360 cases of salmon sent to England in 1877 out of a pack of 380,000. *Oregonian,* September 8, 1881, reported that 1881 was the first year of substantial canned-salmon trade with the United States. It was anticipated that 150,000 cases would be sent to New York by sea and that soon it would be possible to ship by railroad. *Oregonian,* January 1, 1890, reported that in 1883–1884 the pack was almost equally divided between domestic and foreign sales; in 1884–1885 domestic sales exceeded foreign substantially.

20. Cobb, *Pacific Salmon Fisheries* (1917), provides the principal statistical and other data showing the spread of the canneries. The *Pacific Fisherman Yearbook, 1915,* 66–67, offers a short account of salmon-canning

in Siberia. It reports that the first plant was bought in San Francisco by the Kamchatka Trading Company and put in operation in 1898, and lists other canneries established after that.

21. See Gordon B. Dodds, ed., *A Pygmy Monopolist,* and *The Salmon King of Oregon: R. D. Hume and the Pacific Fisheries* (Chapel Hill, N.C., 1959), for full accounts of R. D. Hume.

22. Statistical data is all drawn from Cobb, *Pacific Salmon Fisheries* (1917). Two volumes prepared by Jefferson F. Moser, both bearing the title *The Salmon and Salmon Fisheries of Alaska* and reporting the operations of the United States Fish Commission Steamer *Albatross,* the first for the year ending June 30, 1898, the second for the year ending June 30, 1901 (Washington, D.C., 1899, 1902), provide a full account of the Alaska fisheries at the end of the century and offer some descriptive data on the Alaska Packers Association, although one must look elsewhere for a characterization of the often coercive tactics employed by the APA. The association grew out of a pooling arrangement made in 1890 by several Alaska salmon packers. The next year, in the expectation of a substantial glut of the market, a larger number of packers combined to dispose of some 360,000 cases of salmon. In 1892, according to Moser, thirty-one canners formed an association under which a committee was created to direct all operations of the members. Under this arrangement only nine canneries were operated that season and profits were prorated among all members whether their canneries worked or not. In 1893 steps were taken to provide formal organization and incorporation under the name Alaska Packers Association. The association sought to control both production and marketing of Alaska canned salmon. Although the APA reduced substantially the number of canneries operating in Alaska, this reduction had slight effect on total quantity of canned salmon produced in Alaska. Production increased throughout the decade. The competition for markets was, however, much reduced. Moser estimates that the APA controlled 74 percent of the production in 1897. In 1901 the amount was down to 50 per cent. For an account of the tactics employed by APA against one competitor, see Dodds, *The Salmon King of Oregon,* 70–78. The full history of the APA, and indeed the history of the West Coast fisheries, richly deserves to be written.

23. In 1915 the *Pacific Fisherman* reported that only the Alaska Packers Association still used San Francisco as a base. Other salmon business tended to center in Portland, Astoria, and Seattle, with Seattle as the dominant supply, storage, and marketing point. The move to Seattle had probably been heralded in 1912 when the *Fisherman* reported that through the efforts of the Seattle Chamber of Commerce, the Astoria Iron Works was in process of arranging to transfer its plant to Seattle. Land had been leased on the Duwamish from the county commissioners, "and after the bodies of the Potter's Field, for which the ground is now being used, have been disinterred and incinerated, work will start on the construction of the large buildings which the Astoria Iron Works will occupy." The company was a large manufacturer of canning machinery, marine gasoline engines, etc.

24. F. F. Victor, *All over Oregon and Washington* (San Francisco, Calif., 1872), 61; *Daily Astorian*, October 24, 1877; *Radium* (Wedderburn), November 7, 1907; *The West Shore*, June, 1877, p. 159; Cobb, in an article in the *Pacific Fisherman Yearbook, 1916,* provides a detailed description of virtually all types of fishing gear used to catch salmon. Much of this material is found in the various editions of his *Pacific Salmon Fisheries.*

25. *Letter from the Secretary of War transmitting, in response to Senate Resolution of Jan. 27, 1887, report of the salmon fisheries of the Columbia River,* Senate Executive Document No. 123, 50 Cong., 1 Sess., serial 2510, provides a full and somewhat melancholy picture of the fisheries on the Columbia of that year and indicates the enormous speed with which fish-taking gear had developed. The number of fishing boats had increased from 15 reported in 1867 to 1,500 by 1882. See also *Daily Astorian*, October 22, 1882, for an early comment on the fish wheel. The gill netters disliked the fish-trap men as intensely as they did the fish-wheel operators, and this conflict led to a number of "salmon wars" and many casualties. Violence followed the fishermen to other fishing places and is appropriately celebrated by Rex Beach, *The Silver Hoard* (New York, N.Y., 1909). The *Pacific Fisherman* approved of Beach as the truthful chronicler of the fisherman's epic.

Improvement of gear was of course coupled with a relative decline in the efficiency of the gill netters and others. The *Oregonian* reported in 1887 that in 1876 the average catch had been 3,850 fish per boat for the season. In 1887, with nets twice as long, it was 600 per boat, *Oregonian*, August 11, 1887.

26. The price data is provided in the letter from the Secretary of War cited above, 59–60. The *North Pacific Coast* (Portland), August, 1881, p. 51, reported that on the Columbia it was still expected that three salmon would provide seventy-two pounds of raw fish, enough to make a forty-eight-pound case of canned salmon.

27. George Brown Goode and Associates, *The Fisheries and Fishing Industries of the United States,* prepared through the cooperation of the Commissioner of Fisheries and the superintendent of the tenth census. *Senate Miscellaneous Documents* No. 124, 47 Cong., 1 Sess., serials 1998–2003. Section 2, 608, and Section 4, "The Fishermen of the United States," 29–43. The data was collected in the early 1880s but was not published until several years later. *Oregonian*, September 8, 1881; *Post-Intelligencer* (Seattle), April 30, 1890.

28. Goode, *The Fisheries and Fishing Industries of the United States,* pt. IV, 104–26.

Newspaper reporting of the great disaster of May, 1880, was tentative and capricious. During most of April the fishermen at Astoria were on strike, and the events surrounding the strike were followed regularly by the Portland *Oregonian* (April 22, 23, 24) and the *Daily Astorian* (April 24), and there was much approval when the strike was settled on April 24. Fishermen apparently tried to make up for lost earnings by taking risks they might otherwise have avoided. Almost the whole fishing fleet went out on May 3 (fishermen went out in the evening and fished at night) and were caught in a great gale followed by sudden squalls. In a report dated May 4, the reporter for the *Oregonian* said there were rumors that many fishermen had been lost in the storm, that some boats had been towed in without crews. The reporter further declared that such accidents wouldn't happen if fishermen would not drift close to the bar and would also avoid drinking whiskey after spreading their nets. (*Oregonian,* May 6, 1880.) The *Daily Astorian* reported on May 5 that there were rumors that many fishermen had lost their lives in the great storm, but the editor was reassuring. He was sure the reports had been "exaggerated." On May 7 the *Oregonian* carried another story on the disaster in which it was estimated that at least twenty-five men and ten to fifteen boats were lost. The next day the *Astorian* told its readers that there had been a great loss of life in the storm and that the reporter of the *Oregonian* had apologized for charging fishermen with drunkenness. With this account the interest of the newspaper waned. On August 1 the *Daily Astorian* announced the end of a very successful salmon-canning season but also remarked that "Not less than from seventy-five to a hundred men have been lost." The editor promised his readers that he would get more details on this loss and present them in a later article, but seems not to have gotten around to it. Early in September, however, many of the fishermen having returned to San Francisco, the San Francisco *Chronicle* carried a somewhat garbled account of losses on the Columbia and quoted fishermen whose estimates of loss of life ranged from 200 to 350. Cannery owners, it was reported, admitted that sixty men were lost. One of the fishermen said that cannery men never reported half their losses. The *Daily Astorian* reprinted the piece from the *Chronicle* on September 10, 1880, but the editor expressed his doubts about the truth of the reports. A year later the *Oregonian,* in a review of the industry and the fishing season, acknowledged that sixty men had been lost in the storm the year before (*Oregonian,* September 7, 1881). This figure was subsequently adopted officially. (*Fifth and Sixth Annual Reports, Fish and Game Protector* and *Report of the State Fish Commissioner of Oregon,* 1898.) But even that number shrank through time. In December, 1950, an Astoria newspaper, the *Columbia Press,* declared that "more than a dozen" gill netters were lost in the great storm of May 3–4. However, J. A. Gibbs, *Pacific Graveyard: A Narrative of Shipwrecks Where the Columbia River Meets the Pacific Ocean* (2nd ed., Portland, Ore., 1964), 238, says two hundred fishermen were drowned in the storm.

29. The Chinese were restricted to work in the canneries. It was reported that if they tried to enter fishing, they disappeared at night. *Daily Astorian* (quoting San Francisco *Chronicle*), September 10, 1890. However, on the Columbia and elsewhere from 1872 until well into the twentieth century, they performed most of the work in the canneries. Proportions of Chinese to other laborers in the canneries were often given at four Chinese to one white (*North Pacific Coast,* August, 1881). The *Oregonian,* September

8, 1881, reported some 7,500 persons engaged in the business on the Columbia, 4,000 of them Chinese. Chinese labor was supplied to the canneries by Chinese labor contractors, some of whom appear as shadowy figures in the pages of the *Pacific Fisherman,* see January, 1903, p. 13; April, 1903, p. 2; February, 1903, p. 4; April, 1906, pp. 7–8.

30. *The West Shore,* June, 1877, p. 160; *Daily Astorian,* May 24, 1878.

31. Dodds, *The Salmon King of Oregon,* 195.

32. *The Pacific Fisherman, Yearbook, 1916,* pp. 58 ff., paid tribute to Johnson with a full page picture accompanying the article.

33. The *Pacific Fisherman* carried stories early in 1903 about the Smith fish-cleaning machines and about several other mechanical fish cleaners that were in process of being built. In September, 1903, p. 12, the *Fisherman* printed an article reporting the successful use of the Smith machine, soon to be called the Iron Chink, by the United Fish Packing Plant at Fairhaven, Washington. The editors declared that the manager of this plant was the only one in the whole industry who had been freed from the necessity of hiring Chinese labor. Despite the enthusiasm of the editor, canners were wary. Smith continued to improve the machine in the next years, and in 1907 he announced there were no further improvements he could make, *ibid.,* September, 1907, p. 26. Meanwhile, in 1904, he had announced the machines would be leased, not sold, to canneries for a royalty of three cents a case on all salmon packed, *Fisherman,* December, 1904, p. 16. This permitted him to improve all machines already in operation or substitute improved models. By 1906 the *Fisherman Yearbook* assumed that the Iron Chink had captured the market and that the Chinese butcher gangs would soon disappear. The Iron Chink, it was reported, could handle three thousand fish an hour, two of the machines could supply enough cleaned fish to keep seven lines of packing machinery busy, the machine wasted less than hand-butchering, and one machine could do the work of fifty Chinese (*Fisherman Yearbook, 1906,* pp. 19–30, 45–47). The *Fisherman* returned to the story with more superlatives in the *Yearbook, 1907,* pp. 53–54; in February, 1909, the *Fisherman* announced that the Smith Iron Works had been moved to a new building. In June the *Fisherman* announced the death, following an automobile accident, of Edmond Augustine Smith. Smith's short obituary appeared in June, 1909, pp. 19–21.

34. From time to time the *Pacific Fisherman* presented accounts of the supporting industries of the canning industry. An article on salmon labels with many color reproductions appeared in *The Yearbook, 1905,* pp. 24, 27–31; lacquer is discussed in the *Yearbook, 1916,* pp. 85–86 and in *The West Shore,* June, 1877, p. 160. Misbranding and fraudulent labels were matters of dispute from time to time throughout the early years of the industry.

35. *Pacific Fisherman,* August, 1903, p. 5; September, 1912, p. 26.

36. *Hearings before Subcommittee No. 3 (Quartermaster Corps) of the Select Committee on Expenditures in the War Department,* 66 Cong., 1 & 2 Sess., 1919–1920, pts. 17–20 of serial 5, are devoted to purchase and return of canned salmon. Part 19, 919–26, contains data on the inspection of Alaska

canned salmon at Seattle. A sketch of the dimensions, organization, and operation of the business as of 1918 appears in a publication of the Federal Trade Commission as a part of a general investigation of canned foods, *Report of the Federal Trade Commission on Canned Foods: Canned Salmon,* December, 1918 (Washington, D.C., 1919).

37. John N. Cobb gives a laconic account of the development in *Pacific Salmon Fisheries* (1930), 529–31. He says that the widespread suspicion that the 1918 pack was below standard caused the canners a substantial monetary loss and led to the approval by the salmon canners in February, 1919, of an arrangement for inspection of their plants under the direction of the National Canners Association. This in itself did not prove effective, but it was accompanied by the establishment of a branch laboratory in Seattle in 1919 with scientists to assist canners in dealing with their problems. "The quality of the annual pack," he wrote, "has been wonderfully enhanced."

American Indian Policy
in the 1840s:
Visions of Reform

Francis Paul Prucha, Marquette University

The decade of the 1840s was an interlude of relative quiet in American Indian relations, and it gave the federal government the opportunity to promote with sincerity and enthusiasm a program for the civilization and advancement of the Indian nations with whom it had long been in contact. By 1840 the removal of these Eastern Indians to new homes west of the Mississippi had largely been accomplished, bringing to a culmination the removal policy that had been the answer to the "Indian problem" of the generation of James Monroe, John Quincy Adams, and Andrew Jackson. Now there stretched ahead an indefinite future in which the officials of the Indian Office envisaged the flowering of earlier attempts to ameliorate the condition of the Indians. In their visions these men shared in the vital optimism of their age. Betterment of all mankind seemed within easy reach, and concern for society's unfortunates (the delinquent, the insane, the indigent poor, the deaf, and the blind) appeared everywhere. Crusades for peace, for women's rights, for temperance, for education, and for abolition of slavery marched with reforming zeal and a strange naïveté through the land. Words like "benevolence," "philanthropy," and "perfectability" slipped easily from men's tongues. The plans for civilizing and Christianizing the Indians who had been removed from the main arena of American life partook of this evangelizing spirit. The Indian policy of the 1840s, indeed, must be considered in the light of what Arthur M. Schlesinger has called "the first great upsurge of social reform in United States history."[1]

Such a reform movement, of course, was not new, for there had always been voices raised on behalf of the Indians. Removal itself, its advocates within the federal government thought, was a humanitarian measure. They did not think that they were acting as harshly toward the Indians as their critics at the time and as later historians have claimed. Rejecting infeasible alternatives to solving the Indian problem, they sought to remove the red men from contact with white society and beyond the reach of jurisdictional disputes between the states and the federal government. The War Department put together what it considered a liberal offer to the Indians. In return for the agreement on the part of the Indians to give up their lands east of the Mississippi for comparable lands west of Missouri and Arkansas, the federal government offered to assume the costs of removal, to subsist the Indians for a year in the new land, and to provide substantial annuity payments. Beyond this simple exchange the United States committed itself to provide more general aid and protection. Altogether, the stipulations and pledges were thought to be so beneficial to the tribes that the Indian leaders could not refuse to accept removal.

President Monroe, in a special message to Congress on Indian removal delivered on January 27, 1825, set the general tone and pattern. He urged for the Indians "a well-digested plan for their government and civilization, which should be agreeable to themselves, would not only shield them from impending ruin, but promote their welfare and happiness." He recommended some sort of internal government for the tribes in the West, with sufficient power to hold the tribes together in amity and to preserve order, to prevent intrusion on the Indian lands, and to teach the Indians by regular instruction the arts of civilized life. "It is not doubted," he concluded, "that this arrangement will present considerations of sufficient force to surmount all their prejudices in favor of the soil of their nativity, however strong they may be."[2]

Andrew Jackson, in his first annual message on December 8, 1829, spoke in the same way. In the West, he asserted, the Indians "may be secured in the enjoyment of governments of their own choice, subject to no other control from the United States than such as may be necessary to preserve peace on the frontier and between the several tribes. There the benevolent may endeavor to teach them the arts of civilization, and, by promoting union and harmony among them, to raise up an interesting commonwealth, destined to perpetuate the race and to attest the humanity and justice of this Government."[3] Similarly, Lewis Cass, in his first annual report as Secretary of War, spoke of removal as presenting "the only hope of permanent establishment and improvement." He recommended instruction in the "truths of religion, together with a knowledge of the simpler mechanic arts and the rudiments of science," and he listed seven fundamental principles, which he asserted would constitute the best foundation both for American efforts and for Indian hopes. In addition to a solemn pledge that the land assigned to the Indians would be a permanent home and that an adequate force would be provided to suppress intertribal hostilities, he encouraged severalty of property, assistance in opening farms, and employment of persons to instruct the Indians. He spoke also of leaving the Indians free to enjoy their own institutions insofar as they were "compatible with their own safety and ours, and with the great objects of their prosperity and improvement."[4] The government clearly intended, therefore, to promote the civilization of the Indians in their new homes.

The 1840s were years for fulfillment of the promises. The men in charge of Indian affairs in that decade were convinced of the wisdom of the removal policy and eager to make it work for the Indians. "It will be the end of all," T. Hartley Crawford, the Commissioner of Indian Affairs appointed by President Van Buren, wrote after his first year in office, "unless the experiment of the Government in the Indian territory shall be blessed with success." He admitted that the outcome was uncertain, but he was not disheartened and he urged perseverance.[5]

As Crawford warmed to his job, he became bolder in his praise of removal as essential for Indian betterment. He considered other alternatives that might have been pursued—assimilation of Indians into the mass of white society and life as farmers on their lands in the East—and rejected them as infeasible. Removal to the West, he judged, was "the only expedient—the wisest, the best, the most practicable and practical of all." His view of the advantages to the Indians was idyllic, his goals utopian. The Indians, he prophesied, would find "a home and a country free from the apprehension of disturbance and annoyance, from the means of indulging a most degrading appetite, and far removed from the temptations of bad and sordid men; a region hemmed in by the laws of the United States, and guarded by virtuous agents, where abstinence from vice, and the practice of good morals, should find fit abodes in comfortable dwellings and cleared farms, and be nourished and fostered by all the associations of the hearthstone. In no other than this settled condition can schools flourish, which are the keys that open the gate to heaven and God." He foresaw for the Indians in their new Western homes a great flowering of the solid Puritan virtues—"temperance and industry, and education and religion." Imbued with this attitude, he could not but urge the speedy removal of those Indians who had not yet migrated.[6]

These sentiments Crawford repeated year after year while he was Commissioner of Indian Affairs. A treaty with Wyandots in Ohio was looked upon as a means to promote their comfort and, as a consequence, their advance in morals, civilization, and Christianity, although the Commissioner was not so obtuse that he did not appreciate the advantages to the whites in obtaining the Wyandots' Ohio acres. Like so many others, from Thomas Jefferson on, he rejoiced that the duty of Americans toward the Indians coincided with their own interests. Removal from the lands that the whites wanted would bring to the Indians seclusion and protection from the contaminating influences of white civilization.[7]

Crawford's vision was reflected in the statements of the Secretaries of War. Joel R. Poinsett in 1840 spoke of removal as the only way, not only to civilize the red man, but to perpetuate his existence. John C. Spencer remarked two years later that the end of the removal process was in sight. "It is to be hoped that the red man will then be suffered to rest in peace," he concluded, "and that our undivided efforts will be bestowed in discharging the fearful responsibilities we have incurred to improve his intellectual and moral condition as the only means of rendering him happy here or hereafter."[8]

For the whites, the removal of the Indians from the East was an end in itself, since the lands they coveted could then be acquired and developed. For the Indians, on the other hand, removal was only a means to an end. Relocation was to make possible their civilization. The instrument that would bring all this about, the panacea for all the ills besetting the Indians, was education.

That the Indians were educable was a basic tenet of the reformers. It was admitted, of course, that the present state of the Indians was one of semibarbarism. The aborigines were indolent, a condition aggravated by the lack of individual property, which alone would give incentive to work. They were erratic, wandering from place to place without permanency of residence. They were warlike, for their culture elevated war into an advantage and violence into a virtue. Contrasted with the Americans, who extolled thrift, perseverance, enterprise, domestic peace, and Christian morality, the Indians were an inferior people, standing in the way of progress. But the unfortunate condition of the red men was not irremediable. The government officials did not believe in a racial inferiority that was not amenable to betterment. "It is proved, I think, conclusively," Crawford remarked of the Indian race, "that it is in no respect inferior to our own race, except in being less fortunately circumstanced. As great an aptitude for learning the letters, the pursuits, and arts of civilized life, is evident; if their progress is slow, so has it been with us and with masses of men in all nations and ages."[9] Circumstances and education alone made the difference between them and the whites; and Indian agents, missionaries, and traders contributed evidence that the red men were suspectible of improvement. There would be no racial obstacle to the eventual assimilation of the Indians into the political life of the nation.[10]

So, schools for Indians were advocated with great enthusiasm, befitting an age in which education was considered the "universal utopia."[11] The promotion of schools as the agency to swing the Indians from a state considered to be barbarous, immoral, and pagan to one that was civilized, moral, and Christian took on new exuberance when the Indians were safely ensconced in the West, where the "experiment" could be carried out unhindered. Indian schools, Commissioner Crawford asserted in 1839, formed "one of the most important objects, if it be not the greatest, connected with our Indian relations. Upon it depends more or less even partial success in all endeavors to make the Indian better than he is." The Commissioner hammered tirelessly at this same theme. "The greatest good we can bestow upon them," he said in 1842, "is education in its broadest sense—education in letters, education in labor and the mechanic arts, education in morals, and education in Christianity."[12]

The initial problem was how to intrigue the Indians, both the youths to be educated and their parents, into accepting the schooling. It was all too evident that simply duplicating white schools in the Indian country or sending Indian children to the East for formal education was not the whole answer. Learning in letters alone was not appreciated by the Indians and did not give any practical advancement to the young Indians, who became misfits within their own community. The answer, rather, lay in manual-labor schools, whose full importance was made explicit by Crawford:

> The education of the Indian is a great work. It includes more than the term imports in its application to civilized communities. Letters and personal accomplishments are what we generally intend to speak of by using the word; though sometimes, even with us, it has a more comprehensive meaning. Applied to wild men, its scope should take in much more extensive range, or you give them the shadow for the substance. They must at the least be taught to read and write, and have some acquaintance with figures; but if they do not learn to build and live in houses, to sleep on beds; to eat at regular intervals; to plough, and sow, and reap; to rear and use domestic animals; to understand and practise the me-

chanic arts; and to enjoy, to their gratification and improvement, all the means of profit and rational pleasure that are so profusely spread around civilized life, their mere knowledge of what is learned in the school room proper will be comparatively valueless. At a future day, more or less remote, when those who are now savage shall have happily become civilized, this important branch of Indian interest may be modified according to circumstances; but at present, when every thing is to be learned at the school, and nothing, as with us, by the child as it grows up, unconsciously and without knowing how or when, the manual labor school system is not only deserving of favor, but it seems to me indispensable to the civilization of the Indians; and their civilization, with a rare exception here and there, is as indispensable to real and true Christianity in them.[13]

This apotheosis of white cultural traits and insistence upon them, willy-nilly, for the Indians is an overpowering indication of the ethnocentric viewpoint of the white reformers. Once the way of life was accepted, then more formal education in arts and letters would be seen to be advantageous, and the desire to attain it would motivate the Indians to attend and promote traditional schools. As civilization advanced, Christianity could be promoted, and moral improvement would follow. The desire for material well-being would stimulate industry, which would in turn accelerate the whole process. It was a wonderful white man's carrousel.

The practical model for the Indian Office planners was the Methodist mission school established in 1839 for the Shawnees at the Fort Leavenworth Agency, which seemed to embody all the characteristics demanded to accomplish the goal. In 1840 it had some fifty students, in about equal proportions of boys and girls, running in age from six to eighteen years. "They can nearly all read, many can compose and write sentences, and a number are acquainted with the rule of three," Crawford reported. "They are taught out of school to split wood, plough, mow, &c.; and when all the appliances are ready for use, will learn the mechanic arts. The girls have made the same average progress in letters, and are taught the various branches of housewifery." Two three-story brick buildings had been erected and a third was under way.

There were houses for the principal and for the blacksmith, and a shop, a barn, and stables. Between five hundred and six hundred acres of land were fenced and in cultivation. "The spirit manifested in thus reclaiming the wild woods," the Commissioner noted, "has been extended to the much more important work of mental culture." Plans called for accommodations ultimately for two hundred students, at a yearly expense of not more than seventy dollars each. Crawford considered the school as "the strongest evidence I have yet seen of the probability of success, after all our failures, in the efforts made by benevolent and religious societies, and by the Government, to work a change in Indian habits and modes of life; while it is conclusive proof that these sons of the forest are our equals in capacity."[14] For its good work, and even more as a harbinger of greater things to come within the Indian territory, the school won praise from the highest sources. Manual-labor schools for all the Indians became the goal of the War Department and the Indian Office.[15]

Two other principles, in connection with manual-labor education, were adopted by the Indian Office. One of these, as was appropriate in a period that saw the first organized crusade for women's rights, was that Indian schools should teach girls as well as boys, if civilization was to be forwarded. When Crawford, early in his term of office, noted that more boys than girls were being educated, he asked, "Upon what principle of human action is this inequality founded?" And he set forth his argument in strong terms:

> Unless the Indian female character is raised, and her relative position changed, such an education as you can give the males will be a rope of sand, which, separating at every turn, will bind them to no amelioration. Necessity may force the culture of a little ground, or the keeping of a few cattle, but the savage nature will break out at every temptation. If the women are made good and industrious housewives, and taught what befits their condition, their husbands and sons will find comfortable homes and social enjoyments, which, in any state of society, are essential to morality and thrift. I would therefore advise that the larger proportion of pupils should be female.[16]

"The conviction is settled," he reiterated in 1841, "that the civilization of these unfortunate wards of the Government will be effected through the instrumentality of their educated women, much more than by their taught men."[17] Although the Commissioner's goals were never met, promotion of female education continued.

A second principle, gradually developed during the decade, was that Indian youths should be taught in the Indian country where they lived and not sent off to Eastern schools. There had been a tradition of sending select Indian boys to white schools in the East, where it was supposed they could more quickly absorb the white man's civilization. The Cherokee leaders John Ridge and Elias Boudinot, for example, had been educated at Cornwall, Connecticut. The Choctaws had made arrangements with Richard M. Johnson of Kentucky, by which he established an academy for boys at Blue Springs, Kentucky, in 1825. The school was directed by the Baptists and supported enthusiastically for many years by the Choctaws. Twenty-five boys entered this Choctaw Academy in 1825, and the enrollment in some years ran to more than one hundred and fifty students. Other tribes, too, sent their boys to the school.[18] But complaints arose about the school, and by 1841 the Choctaws had decided to educate their sons within the nation. Such a move was in accord with the Indian Department's views.

Crawford advised from the first against sending Indians away from home to distant schools, and in 1844 Secretary of War William Wilkins argued that education should be diffused as equally as possible through the whole tribe by establishing common schools within the Indian country. The education of a few individuals in a college or school away from their tribe did not promote the designs of the government, Wilkins argued, for he was afraid that men more highly educated than the mass of the tribe might employ their talents for selfish acquisition and oppression of their uneducated brothers.[19] By 1846 the Indian Department had clearly decided to adhere to the new policy.[20] "The practice so long pursued of selecting a few boys from the different tribes, and placing them at our colleges and high schools," Commissioner William Medill repeated in 1847, "has failed to produce the beneficial results anticipated; while the great mass of the tribe at home were suffered to remain in ignorance." The plan would be completely discontinued as soon as existing arrangements could be changed, and the resources of the Indian Office would be applied solely to the schools within the Indian country, where education could be extended to both sexes and generally spread throughout the tribe.[21]

To carry out the educational reform considerable money was expended in the Indian country. The civilization fund of $10,000 a year, which Congress had authorized in 1819, was apportioned among the various missionary societies in small amounts of a few hundred dollars each.[22] The effect of these small allowances in stimulating contributions by missionary groups is hard to evaluate, for other federal funds also were poured into the mission schools. Chief among these were the funds specified for education in treaties made with the Indians or designated from annuity moneys by the tribes themselves for educational purposes. Thus the Choctaw treaty of 1830 stipulated that the government was to pay $2,000 annually for twenty years for the support of three schoolteachers, and the tribe itself in 1842 voted to apply $18,000 a year from its annuities to education.[23] A treaty with the Ottawas and Chippewas in 1836 specified that in addition to an annuity in specie of $30,000 for twenty years, $5,000 each year would be given for teachers, schoolhouses, and books in their own language, and $3,000 more for missions. These payments were to run for twenty years and as long thereafter as Congress would continue the appropriation.[24] In the year 1845, $68,195 was provided by treaties for Indian education, to which was added $12,367.50 from the civilization fund.[25] Subsequent treaties added to the school funds available. A treaty with the Kansas Indians in 1846, for example, provided for the investment of the sum paid for the cession of lands, and $1,000 a year from the interest was directed to schools within the Indian country. The treaty of 1846 with the Winnebagos provided that $10,000 of the cession payment was to be applied to the creation and maintenance of one or more manual-labor schools.[26] To these government funds were added those supplied by the missionary societies themselves. The government also built schools and churches and supplied agricultural implements and domestic equipment, which could be used in the manual-labor sort of education that the men of the 1840s advocated.

Although the number of students in the Indian schools was small, the optimism of the Indian Office and the missionaries was not without foundation. The Choctaws, although more interested in education than many of the tribes, offered an example of what was possible. They began to build schools as soon as they arrived in the West. The missionaries of the American Board reported eleven schools with 228 Choctaw students in 1836, and in addition there were five schools supported by the Choctaw Nation and the three district schools provided by the 1830 treaty. In 1842 a comprehensive system of schools was begun. Spencer Academy and Fort Coffee Academy were opened in 1844; Armstrong and New Hope academies two years later. The national council also supplied support to four schools established earlier by the American Board. By 1848 the Choctaws had nine boarding schools supported by tribal funds, and neighborhood schools had been opened in many communities.[27] The Commissioner in that year reported exceptional progress as well among the Osages, Chickasaws, Quapaws, and Miamis.[28] The Cherokees also made remarkable progress, until they had a better common-school system than either Arkansas or Missouri.[29]

Comparative numbers give some indication of the progress, although reports were often incomplete. In 1842 forty-five schools (out of a total of fifty-two) reported 2,132 students enrolled. In 1848 there were sixteen manual-labor schools with 809 students and eighty-seven boarding and other schools with 2,873 students; in 1849, although some reports were missing, a further increase in students was noted.[30]

These schools would have been impossible without the devoted work of Christian missionaries, and Indian education was a beneficiary of the missionary impulse of the Protestant churches that was an important element in the reform ferment of the age.[31] The Indian Office felt this influence strongly, for its goals and those of the missionary societies in the 1840s were identical: practical, moral, and religious education of the Indians, which would bring both Christianity and civilization to the aborigines.[32] Since the civilization fund that the federal government had at its disposal was small, the money had been used from the beginning as a stimulus to missionary societies to enter the work of Indian education. The government thus consciously and eagerly consummated a partnership with the churches by which federal funds and church funds were united to support the Christian missionaries— a union of church and state in which the participants seemed unaware of any Jeffersonian wall of separation.[33]

Reliance on the missionaries, indeed, was uppermost in the minds of the federal officials. Commissioner Crawford noted in his report of 1839: "No direction of these institutions [Indian schools] appears to me so judicious as that of religious and benevolent societies, and it is gratifying to observe the zeal with which all the leading sects lend themselves to this good work; discouragements do not seem to cool their ardor, nor small success to dissuade them from persevering efforts."[34] So successful was the Methodist school for the Shawnees that the War Department was eager to support similar establishments directed by other religious groups, "equally zealous, no doubt, in spreading the light of the Gospel among the Indians, and equally disposed to advance their moral culture."[35] The report of the Commissioner of Indian Affairs in 1847 indicates how enamored the Indian Office had become of its missionary auxiliaries:

> In every system which has been adopted for promoting the cause of education among the Indians, the Department has found its most efficient and faithful auxiliaries and laborers in the societies of the several Christian denominations, which have sent out missionaries, established schools, and maintained local teachers among the different tribes. Deriving their impulse from principles of philanthropy and religion, and devoting a large amount of their own means to the education, moral elevation and improvement of the tribes, the Department has not hesitated to make them the instruments, to a considerable extent, of applying the funds appropriated by the government for like purposes. Their exertions have thus been encouraged, and a greater degree of economy at the same time secured in the expenditure of the public money.[36]

Agents in the field who were close to the missionaries and their work were strong in praise of the efforts of the churches. Thus Thomas H. Harvey, Superintendent of Indian Affairs at St. Louis, argued that the schools for the Indians should always be entrusted to missionaries. "I conceive that the missionary, or teacher of the Christian religion, is an indispensable agent in the civilization of the Indians," he said. "No one who is not steeled in prejudice can travel through the Indian country where they have missionaries without observing their beneficial influence." Harvey saw the schools of the missionaries as the centers of ever-widening influence, for the educated Indians would soon give tone to the larger society.[37]

Much of the optimism of the officials in Washington regarding Indian improvement rested upon the reports of the missionaries. It was common for the church groups to describe the results of their efforts in highly favorable terms, and the Indian Office seemed ready to accept the reports uncritically. But this acceptance, unwarranted as it might have been at times, emphasizes the utopian, reform-minded views of the age.[38]

The visions of reform that the Indian Office and the missionaries had for the Indians, however, met serious obstacles. Removal of the Indians to lands west of the Mississippi had not in fact sequestered them from all contact with evil men. Traders under license were permitted in the Indian country according to the laws governing trade and intercourse with the Indians, and whereas traders had traditionally been drawn to the Indians in search of furs, they now came to the emigrant Indians principally to provide goods in return for annuity money. Concern for the Indians in the 1840s included a critical attack upon the system of annuity payments as it then existed and strenuous efforts to have the system changed.

Commissioner Crawford in his annual report of 1841 devoted a long section to the problems connected with annuity payments. The annuities did the Indians for whom they were intended little good, for the money was almost completely absorbed by traders, to whom the Indians had become indebted and who sat at the annuity-payment grounds ready to pounce upon the funds. "The recipients of money," Crawford complained, "are rarely more than conduit pipes to convey it into the pockets of their traders." He objected, too, to provisions in treaties for payment of debts owed to the traders by the Indians.[39] The annuities aggravated the very conditions that the Indian Office was trying to correct. As long as the Indians were assured of receiving their annual stipend, they did not exert themselves to earn a living, thus defeating the efforts of the reformers to turn them into hard-working farmers. Much of the annuity money was spent for worthless goods or trivial objects, so that the bounty of the government was misappropriated.[40] The annuity problem, furthermore, was closely tied to the problem of intemperance among the Indians, for the money was easily drained off into the pockets of the whiskey venders.[41]

The attack on the problem was made on several fronts, all aimed at directing the annuities toward the benefit of the Indians. A change was demanded, first, in the method of paying the annuities. The act of 1834 that reorganized the Indian Department provided for payment to the chiefs of the tribes.[42] The funds often did not reach the commonalty but were siphoned off by the chiefs and their special friends for purposes which might not benefit the tribe as a whole. To correct this deficiency, Congress on March 3, 1847, granted discretion to the President or the Secretary of War to direct that the annuities, instead of being paid to the chiefs, be divided and paid to the heads of families and other individuals entitled to participate or, with consent of the tribe, that they be applied to other means of promoting the happiness and prosperity of the Indians. The new law, in addition, struck boldly at the liquor problem. No annuities could be paid to the Indians while they were under the influence of intoxicating liquor nor while there was reason for the paying officers to believe that liquor was within convenient reach. The chiefs, too, were to pledge themselves to use all their influence to prevent the introduction and sale of liquor in their country. Finally, to protect the Indians from signing away their annuities ahead of time, the law provided that contracts made by Indians for the payment of money or goods were null and void.[43]

The War Department immediately took advantage of the discretionary authority provided by the act, and instructions were sent to the superintendents and agents to pay the annuities in all cases to the heads of families and other individuals entitled to them. The law, Commissioner Medill said in sending out instructions, "is probably one of the most salutary laws affecting our Indian relations that has ever been passed."[44] Although there were complaints from parties adversely affected by the new policy, the Indian Department was well pleased. Medill reported in 1848 that the per capita mode of paying annuities had been attended with "the happiest effects." It prevented extortion of the Indians through the means of national credits, and it gave to everyone a knowledge of his just rights. "In the whole course of our Indian policy," he said, "there has never been a measure productive of better moral effects."[45]

The profligacy of the Indians who squandered their annuities in quick order and then were destitute for the rest of the year was attacked by Medill at the same time. The annuities of many tribes were much larger than their wants required at the time of payment. In consequence, when immediate necessities had been provided for, the excess in funds enabled the Indians "to indulge in idleness and profligacy" or to buy items of no real value to them. Then when spring came they would be in a state of destitution and would resort to hunting for subsistence instead of turning their attention to farming. The Commissioner's solution was to divide the annuities when they were sufficiently large and to pay them semiannually. Benefits were sure to follow. "The spring payment will so far supply their necessities as to enable them to put in their crops, and, to some extent at least, await their maturing," he wrote; "where not sufficient for the latter purpose, a portion can resort to hunting, and the others remain to attend to the cultivation of the crops; and they will be encouraged to pursue this course. In this way much more attention may be paid to the peaceful and more profitable pursuits of agriculture, which will tend greatly to their advancement in civilization, and to increase the resources and comforts of civilized life among them."[46] The results of this policy, too, seemed satisfactory, and Medill, noting that opposition had been less than anticipated, recommended that the policy be continued.[47]

The stipulations of past treaties about payment and use of annuities were rigorously adhered to, but it was the sentiment of the Indian Office that efforts should be made to encourage the Indians to make use of their funds for worthwhile purposes that would lead toward the ultimate goal of civilization. Medill noted in 1848 the pernicious effects of large money annuities upon the welfare and prosperity of a tribe, and in all future negotiations with the Indians he wanted the government to have as much of the purchase money as possible set aside for purposes that would elevate and improve the condition of the tribes. He wanted, further, to induce tribes to whom large sums were already due to consent to the application of the funds to such purposes. The goal was always the same: "The less an Indian's expectations and resources from the chase, and from the government in the shape of money annuities," he said, "the more readily can he be induced to give up his idle, dissolute, and savage habits, and to resort to labor for a maintenance; and thus commence the transition from a state of barbarism and moral depression, to one of civilization and moral elevation."[48]

Another attempt to meliorate the condition of the Indians was a renewed attack upon the private traders. Secretary of War John C. Spencer declared in 1842 that the system in operation did not lead to the "improvement of the moral and intellectual condition of the Indians." Although Spencer acknowledged the presence of many honest and faithful traders, he noted the recklessness of the Indians, who purchased worthless goods or quantities of supplies far beyond their needs. These they wasted or bartered for liquor and soon were as destitute as before. He noted, too, the undue influence that the traders acquired over the Indians, which was greater than that of the government agents and sometimes used in opposition to government policy.[49]

The Secretary of War supported the plan put forth by Indian Commissioner Crawford for a new government "factory system," which Crawford first broached in his annual report of 1840. While emphatically asserting that he did not propose a return to the old factory system, which had been "rightly abolished," Crawford deemed its principle to be valuable. Because of the increased annual disbursements to the Indian tribes, the improved facilities for transportation, the greater need the Indians had for protection as they became surrounded by white population, and the growing dependency of the Indians upon their annuity payments, he urged an alternative to the existing system that would be more beneficial to the Indians. He outlined his plan in some detail:

> I would make a small establishment of goods, suitable to Indian wants, according to their location, at each agency. I would not allow these goods to be sold to any one except Indians entitled to a participation in the cash annuities, and

I would limit the purchases to their proportion of the annuity; so that the Government would, instead of paying money to be laid out in whiskey and beads, or applied to the payment of goods at two prices bought from others, meet the Indians to settle their accounts, and satisfy them that they had received, in articles of comfort or necessity, the annuity due them for the year, at *cost*, including transportation. The Indians would be immensely benefited; and the expense would not be greater than that of the money-payments now almost uselessly made them.[50]

Under such a system Crawford believed that the government Indian agents would gain the position of weight with the Indians that they ought to have. The Indians would look to the government as its best friend, for from it would come the goods they needed. He was sure that the secret of the great attachment of the Indians in Canada to the British government was that the Indians received everything from the officers of the government. In contrast, the United States government paid the Indians what it owed them but then left them a prey to the traders, who absorbed all that the Indians had received. There was no intention, however, for the agents to enter into the fur trade as the old factors had done. Such business would be left to traders under license; but with competition from the government agents, the traders would be forced to furnish quality goods at fair prices or get out of the business.[51]

In subsequent years Crawford repeated and strengthened his original recommendations.[52] The House Committee on Indian Affairs took up the proposal in 1844 and reported a bill to authorize the furnishing of goods and provisions by the War Department, but the action died in the House.[53] Crawford did not give up. His plan, he asserted, would increase the comfort of the Indians; the comfort in turn would be a "leading string . . . to conduct them into the walks of civilization," and general improvement of the Indians would soon be seen everywhere.[54] But Crawford left office, and his scheme died. It was too much to ask in an age of private enterprise that the government go back into the Indian trade. Control of the evils of the Indian trade reverted to the old attempt to enforce the licensing system that was part of the traditional setup.

A strong movement in that direction came in 1847, under the direction of William Medill, Commissioner of Indian Affairs, and W. L. Marcy, Secretary of War. Although previous laws and regulations called for a careful surveillance of the traders and the elimination of those deemed unfit for dealing with the Indians, Medill found that lax enforcement had allowed licenses to be given to many persons who should never have been permitted to go into the Indian country. He insisted that licenses should be granted to "none but persons of proper character, who will deal fairly, and cooperate with the government in its measure for meliorating the condition of the Indians." He drew up new and tighter regulations, therefore, which were promulgated by the War Department.[55] The Secretary of War reported in 1848 that the new regulations and the rigid supervision over the conduct of the traders had put an end to many evils and abuses. How much real success this new drive had, nevertheless, is hard to judge, for at the end of the decade Orlando Brown, the new Commissioner of Indian Affairs, again urged circumventing the traders by paying the annuities in goods rather than in money.[56]

All problems or obstacles in improving the Indians' condition seemed to stem from or to be aggravated by intemperance. The cupidity of white men, who were eager to sell vile concoctions to Indians at exorbitant prices, could not be struck at directly, and restrictions on the sale of liquor to Indians were impossible to enforce. A primary justification for removing the Indians to the West had been to place them in a home free from temptations. In an age of reform, when many considered excessive drinking to be an important factor in the problems of delinquency and dependency among the general public, temperance was to be one of the agencies opening up "the fountains of hope" for the red man in the new lands.[57]

But removal alone did not prevent intemperance among the Indians. The whiskey venders were if anything more virulent on the Western frontier than in the settled regions of the East, and the means of stopping their nefarious commerce were less effective. Crawford began the decade almost with a cry of desperation:

. . . [any] improvement, or attempt at benefiting the Indians, will meet the great obstruction to every effort of meliorating their condition—the inordinate use of ardent spirits. If you could civilize and christianize them, you might possibly correct the evil; but the misfortune is, that it must be eradicated before you can effect the former. To reason with them, experience has shown to be vain; to rely upon their own reflection and resolution for doing the good work, would be infatuation; . . . The remedy lies in keeping the poison beyond their reach.[58]

The Commissioner did not quite believe in the vicious circle he described, and as a man of his times, he pinned much of his hope for eradicating the vice upon education. "Whatever we can do to save them from self-immolation we are bound to do," he declared in 1841, "but, after all, the great security against this, as against every other vice, is education and civilization—for men have in all ages cast off the grosser vices, particularly, in the proportion in which they have advanced as social and intellectual beings." He believed that if the Indians themselves turned their attention earnestly to the subject, they could accomplish more than the United States and the states or territories combined.[59] In 1843 he reported that the exertions of the Indian Department had been strenuous and unremitting to prevent the use of ardent spirits by the Indians, and he described attempts on the part of the Territories of Iowa and Wisconsin to prevent the trade. But his outlook was pessimistic that any final solution would come from legal enactments. His hope lay with the efforts of the tribes themselves, and he noted with pleasure that temperance societies had been organized in several of the tribes and that some tribes had passed laws to put down the sale and use of whiskey.[60]

Crawford professed to see signs of success. "The increase of temperance, and a contempt for the degradation of drunkenness, which has been most strikingly manifested in the Southwest," he wrote, "has been accompanied by a strong disposition to extend the means of Indian education." There were other indications, too, that there was some lessening in the evil. The Superintendent of Indian Affairs at St. Louis reported "a wonderful decrease in the quantity of spirituous liquors carried into the Indian country," which he attributed mainly to the increased vigilance of the officers of the Indian Department.[61]

While Crawford and others worked diligently to promote temperance through education, they did not neglect the frontal attack on the liquor trade in the Indian country that had long been a staple of American Indian policy. Laws in 1802, 1832, and 1834 had prohibited the introduction of whiskey into the Indian lands and had provided for fines for violations.[62] But the legislation had not been completely successful, and liquor continued to flow. Secretary of War James M. Porter in 1843 called for further legislation to prevent persons from introducing ardent spirits among the Indians, and his successor, W. L. Marcy, in 1845 called for a revision in the system of trade with the Indians by imposing more restrictions and severer penalties upon those who brought in liquor.[63]

Finally, on March 3, 1847, Congress acted. In addition to the fines provided by the act of 1834, the new law provided imprisonment up to two years for anyone who sold or disposed of liquor to an Indian in the Indian country and imprisonment up to one year for anyone who introduced liquor, excepting only such supplies as might be required for the officers and troops of the army. In all cases arising under the law, Indians were to be competent witnesses.[64] The Commissioner of Indian Affairs and the Secretary of War, however, were not satisfied to let the law serve by itself. New regulations, dated April 13, 1847, were promulgated by the War Department, which called attention to the provisions of the new law and the pertinent sections of the law of 1834 (copies of which were included with the regulations). The regulations then spelled out in detail just what duties were imposed by these laws upon the military officers and the Indian agents, who were enjoined to be vigilant in the execution of their duties and were threatened with removal from office if they did not succeed.[65]

Federal laws and regulations to control the liquor traffic had effect only within the Indian country and not in the adjoining states. In an attempt to prevent the Indians from moving across the line to obtain liquor, Secretary of War Marcy wrote a strong letter on July 14, 1847, to the governors of Missouri, Arkansas, and Iowa, invoking their aid. The stringent laws of Congress, he pointed out, failed to reach the most prolific source of the evil, which lay within the limits of the nearby states. He described the evils resulting from the trade and noted that the insecurity of the frontier whites often was the result of Indian retaliation for such injuries.[66]

The efforts to prevent whiskey from reaching the Indians met with considerable success. But all the laws of Congress and the strenuous efforts of the Indian agents and military officers on the frontier to enforce them did not end drunkenness. The frontier was too extensive and the profits to the whiskey dealers too large to make complete prohibition possible. More reliance was urged upon a system of rewards and punishments operating directly on the Indians themselves.[67]

The general reports of progress that came from the reformers as the decade neared its close were surely optimistic despite the lack of perfect success. The government officials held firm to their views of the perfectibility of the Indians, of the red man's ability to attain the civilization of the whites. Whatever evidence pointed in that direction they eagerly latched onto. They were convinced that the advances in education among some of the tribes proved conclusively that all Indians were amenable to such attainments, immediately or in the near future. They were sure that their efforts had contributed to the good result, and they spoke in justification of the faith they had had. Only a few voices were raised in opposition, not to deny the possibilities nor even some of the accomplishments, but to point to the slowness of the progress.

Removal had caused tremendous disruptions in the Indian nations, yet many of the Indians made a rapid adjustment to their new homes. The Superintendent of the Western Territory wrote glowing reports of the progress and condition of the Choctaws, Chickasaws, Creeks, Seminoles, and Cherokees living under his jurisdiction. "Civilization is spreading through the Indian country," he reported as early as 1840, "and where but a few years past the forest was untouched, in many places good farms are to be seen; the whole face of the country evidently indicating a thrifty and prosperous people, possessing within themselves the means of raising fine stocks of horses, cattle, and hogs, and a country producing all the substantials of life with but a moderate portion of labor."[68] The Superintendent of Indian Affairs at St. Louis in 1846 reported rapid improvements among many of the tribes in agriculture and the general comforts of life. He listed the Shawnees, Wyandots, Delawares, Kickapoos, Munsees, Stockbridges, Ottawas, and Potawatomis as the tribes among whom the improvements were most visible, and he attributed the success to the influence of the missionaries and their schools.[69] The Choctaw chief Peter Pitchlynn, remonstrating in 1849 against a movement to establish a federated government for the tribes in the West, drew a pleasant picture of the advances of his nation:

> Our constitution is purely republican, the gospel ministry is well sustained, and our schools are of a high order. Our people are increasing in numbers. Peace dwells within our limits, and plenteousness within our borders.
>
> Schools, civilization upon Christian principles, agriculture, temperance and morality are the only politics we have among us; and adhering to these few primary and fundamental principles of human happiness, we have flourished and prospered: hence we want none other. We wish simply to be let alone, and permitted to pursue the even tenor of our way.[70]

By the end of the decade success seemed assured and was in fact proclaimed from on high. Secretary of War Marcy in December, 1848, reported: "No subject connected with our Indian affairs has so deeply interested the department and received so much of its anxious solicitude and attention, as that of education, and I am happy to be able to say that its efforts to advance this cause have been crowned with success. Among most of the tribes which have removed to and become settled in the Indian country, the blessings of education are beginning to be appreciated, and they generally manifest a willingness to co-operate with the government in diffusing these blessings." The schools, he concluded, afforded evidence that nearly all of the emigrated tribes were rapidly advancing in civilization and moral improvement, and he gave full credit to the Indian Department for the improved condition of the numerous tribes.[71] In the same year William Medill, then Commissioner of Indian Affairs, acknowledged the earlier decline and disappearance of the Indians. "Cannot this sad and depressing tendency of things be checked, and the past be at least measurably repaired by better results in the future?" he asked. His answer was cautious but reassuring. "It is believed they can," he wrote; "and, indeed, it has to some extent been done already, by the wise and beneficent system of policy put in operation some years since, and which, if steadily carried out, will soon give to our whole Indian system a very different and much more favorable aspect."[72]

The optimism of the next Commissioner of Indian Affairs, Orlando Brown, knew no bounds, but his report of 1849 differs only in degree and not in kind from the enthusiastic appraisals of his predecessors. "The dark clouds of ignorance and superstition in which these people have so long been enveloped seem at length in the case of many of them to be breaking away, and the light of Christianity and general knowledge to be dawning upon their moral and intellectual darkness," he wrote. Brown gave credit for the change to the government's policy of moving the Indians toward an agricultural existence, the introduction of the manual-labor schools, and instruction by the missionaries in "the best of all knowledge, religious truth—their duty towards God and their fellow beings." The result was "a great moral and social revolution" among some of the tribes, which he predicted would be spread to others by adoption of the same measures. Within a few years he believed that "in intelligence and resources, they would compare favorably with many portions of our white population, and instead of drooping and declining, as heretofore, they would be fully able to maintain themselves in prosperity and happiness under any circumstance of contact or connexion with our people." In the end he expected a large measure of success to "crown the philanthropic efforts of the government and of individuals to civilize and to christianize the Indian tribes." He no longer doubted that the Indians were capable of self-government. "They have proved their capacity for social happiness," he concluded, "by adopting written constitutions upon the model of our own, by establishing and sustaining schools, by successfully devoting themselves to agricultural pursuits, by respectable attainments in the learned professions and mechanic arts, and by adopting the manners and customs of our people, so far as they are applicable to their own condition."[73]

This was a bit too much, for we know that the Indians did not reach utopia. But it was quite in tune with the age, when zealous reformers saw no limit to the possibilities for ameliorating and perfecting the human condition, when the insane were to be cured, the slaves freed, the prisons cleansed, women's rights recognized, and Sunday Schools flourish. Certainly we can believe that they hoped for no less for the American Indian.

Why were not the hopes more fully realized? What darkened the visions of reform that seemed so bright to the officials of the 1840s?

Fundamentally, the work was a slower process than anyone at the time appreciated. Cultural transformation was not to be accomplished within a single generation, no matter how excellent the schools or how devoted the teachers.[74] The goals of the white society, which the missionaries and the men of the Indian Office accepted unquestioningly, did not seem so obviously good to many of the Indians. Perhaps if the isolation from white contacts behind the "permanent Indian frontier" had indeed been permanent, the happy beginnings depicted in the 1840s might have grown and blossomed in accordance with the visions. But this did not occur.

New problems came to absorb the interests and energies of the Indian Office, and new forces developed that cracked the fragile beginnings of effective Indian betterment. Manifest Destiny and the Mexican War renewed and reemphasized the expansion into Indian lands that the removal proponents had expected to be permanently closed. Emigrant whites moving to the Pacific Coast in unprecedented numbers brought a demand for an extinguishment of Indian titles to lands along their path and a greater concentration of the colonies of Indians in the West, which presaged the ultimate restriction of the Indians to small reservations. Wild tribes of the plains and Rockies, resisting the invasion of their lands by emigrants to Oregon and California, made the predominant concern of the Indian Office once again defense not civilization, and the Indians of Oregon and Texas required administrative attention that severely strained the facilities of the Indian Office. These new developments had their roots in the 1840s and grew to such dimensions that the peaceful attempts to advance the Indians in white civilization received less emphasis, though they by no means completely disappeared.[75]

Although the attempts in the 1840s to improve the condition of the Indians did not fulfill all the hopes of the reformers, we cannot dismiss them as inconsequential. Although the goals were frequently unrealistic, we cannot accuse the Indian commissioners, the agents, and the missionaries of insincerity or worse still of hypocrisy. Other reform movements, too, petered out, only to reappear with new vigor at a later time. Much of the work of those who sought Indian betterment was substantial and enduring, and it was a foundation upon which future generations of reformers built.

Notes

1. Arthur M. Schlesinger, *The American As Reformer* (Cambridge, Mass., 1950), 3. For surveys of the reforming spirit of the times, see Alice Felt Tyler, *Freedom's Ferment: Phases of American Social History to 1860* (Minneapolis, Minn., 1944), and Clifford S. Griffin, *Their Brothers' Keepers: Moral Stewardship in the United States, 1800–1865* (New Brunswick, N.J., 1960). The intellectual setting in which movements for bettering the conditions of the Indians must be placed is set forth in Perry Miller, *The Life of the Mind in America from the Revolution to the Civil War* (New York, N.Y., 1965). See especially his remarks on benevolence, 78–84. On reform in general see David Brion Davis, ed., *Ante-Bellum Reform* (New York, N.Y., 1967).

2. James D. Richardson, comp., *A Compilation of the Messages and Papers of the Presidents, 1789–1897* (10 vols., Washington, D.C., 1896–1899), II, 281–82.

3. *Ibid.*, 458.

4. Report of the Secretary of War, November 21, 1831, *House Executive Document* No. 2, 22 Cong., 1 Sess., serial 216, pp. 30–34.

5. Report of T. Hartley Crawford, November 25, 1839, *House Executive Document* No. 2, 26 Cong., 1 Sess., serial 363, p. 346.

6. Report of T. Hartley Crawford, November 28, 1840, *Senate Document* No. 1, 26 Cong., 2 Sess., serial 375, pp. 232–34.

7. Report of T. Hartley Crawford, November 16, 1842, *Senate Document* No. 1, 27 Cong., 3 Sess., serial 413, p. 379.

8. Report of Joel R. Poinsett, December 5, 1840, *Senate Document* No. 1, 26 Cong., 2 Sess., serial 375, p. 28; Report of John C. Spencer, November 26, 1842, *Senate Document* No. 1, 27 Cong., 3 Sess., serial 413, p. 190.

9. Report of T. Hartley Crawford, November 25, 1844, *Senate Document* No. 1, 28 Cong., 2 Sess., serial 449, p. 315.

10. Report of Thomas H. Harvey, October 8, 1844, *ibid.*, p. 435; Report of William Wilkins, November 30, 1844, *ibid.*, 127.

11. The phrase is from a chapter heading in Arthur A. Ekirch, Jr., *The Idea of Progress in America, 1815–1860* (New York, N.Y., 1944), 195.

12. Report of T. Hartley Crawford, November 25, 1839, *House Execu-*

tive Document No. 2, 26 Cong., 1 Sess., serial 363, p. 343; Report of Crawford, November 16, 1842, *Senate Document* No. 1, 27 Cong., 3 Sess., serial 413, p. 386. See also his report of November 28, 1840, *Senate Document* No. 1, 26 Cong., 2 Sess., serial 375, p. 242.

13. Report of T. Hartley Crawford, November 25, 1844, *Senate Document* No. 1, 28 Cong., 2 Sess., serial 449, p. 313.

14. Report of T. Hartley Crawford, November 28, 1840, *Senate Document* No. 1, 26 Cong., 2 Sess., serial 375, p. 243. Crawford got his information from a report of John B. Luce, November 11, 1840, *ibid.*, 387–88. See also the reports on the beginning of the school in Report of the Commissioner of Indian Affairs, 1839, Appendix No. 38, *House Executive Document* No. 2, 26 Cong., 1 Sess., serial 363, pp. 433–34.

15. Report of W. L. Marcy, December 5, 1846, *Senate Document* No. 1, 29 Cong., 2 Sess., serial 493, p. 60; Report of W. Medill, November 30, 1846, *ibid.*, 227.

16. Report of T. Hartley Crawford, November 25, 1839, *House Executive Document* No. 2, 26 Cong., 1 Sess., serial 363, p. 344.

17. Report of T. Hartley Crawford, November 25, 1841, *House Executive Document* No. 2, 27 Cong., 2 Sess., serial 401, p. 241.

18. Angie Debo, *The Rise and Fall of the Choctaw Republic* (Norman, Okla., 1934), 44–45; Carolyn T. Foreman, "The Choctaw Academy," *Chronicles of Oklahoma*, VI (December, 1928), 453–80; IX (December, 1931), 382–411; X (March, 1932), 77–114.

19. Report of T. Hartley Crawford, November 25, 1839, *House Executive Document* No. 2, 26 Cong., 1 Sess., serial 363, p. 344; Report of William Wilkins, November 30, 1844, *Senate Document* No. 1, 28 Cong., 2 Sess., serial 449, p. 127.

20. Report of W. L. Marcy, December 5, 1846, *Senate Document* No. 1, 29 Cong., 2 Sess., serial 493, p. 60; Report of W. Medill, November 30, 1846, *ibid.*, 227.

21. Report of W. Medill, November 30, 1847, *Senate Executive Document* No. 1, 30 Cong., 1 Sess., serial 503, p. 749. See also Report of W. L. Marcy, December 2, 1847, *ibid.*, 70.

22. A year-by-year listing of expenditures from the fund for the period 1820–1842 appears in *House Document* No. 203, 27 Cong., 3 Sess., serial 423. See also George D. Harmon, *Sixty Years of Indian Affairs: Political, Economic, and Diplomatic, 1789–1850* (Chapel Hill, N.C., 1941), Appendix, Table V, 378–79. Some information on the use of the fund usually appears in the annual reports of the Commissioner of Indian Affairs. For a discussion of the act, see Francis Paul Prucha, *American Indian Policy in the Formative Years: The Indian Trade and Intercourse Acts, 1790–1834* (Cambridge, Mass., 1962), 221–24.

23. Charles J. Kappler, ed., *Indian Affairs: Laws and Treaties* (2 vols., Washington, D.C., 1904), II, 315; P. P. Pitchlynn to William Armstrong, December 12, 1842, *Senate Document* No. 1, 28 Cong., 1 Sess., serial 431, pp. 367–68.

24. Kappler, *Laws and Treaties*, II, 451–52.

25. Harmon, *Sixty Years of Indian Affairs*, Appendix, Table VII, 381.

26. Kappler, *Laws and Treaties*, II, 553, 566.

27. Debo, *Choctaw Republic*, 60–61; Documents 69–72, attached to Report of T. Hartley Crawford, November 25, 1843, *Senate Document* No. 1, 28 Cong., 1 Sess., serial 431, pp. 367–72.

28. Report of W. Medill, November 30, 1847, *Senate Executive Document* No. 1, 30 Cong., 1 Sess., serial 503, p. 750.

29. Grant Foreman, *The Five Civilized Tribes* (Norman, Okla., 1934), 410.

30. Document 83, attached to Report of T. Hartley Crawford, November 16, 1842, *Senate Document* No. 1, 27 Cong., 3 Sess., serial 413, pp. 520–22; Report of Orlando Brown, November 30, 1849, *House Executive Document* No. 5, 31 Cong., 1 Sess., serial 570, p. 956.

31. Tyler, *Freedom's Ferment*, 31–32.

32. There was a controversy at the time among the missionaries about which should come first, civilization or Christianity, but the Indian Office did not enter into the dispute since it was agreed that both were ultimately needed. See Robert F. Berkhofer, Jr., *Salvation and the Savage: An Analysis of Protestant Missions and American Indian Response, 1787–1862* (Lexington, Ky., 1965), 3–9.

33. There is an excellent discussion of this cooperation in R. Pierce Beaver, *Church, State, and the American Indians: Two and a Half Centuries of Partnerships in Missions between Protestant Churches and Government* (St. Louis, Mo., 1966).

34. Report of T. Hartley Crawford, November 25, 1839, *House Executive Document* No. 2, 26 Cong., 1 Sess., serial 363, p. 343.

35. Report of Joel R. Poinsett, December 5, 1840, *Senate Document* No. 1, 26 Cong., 2 Sess., serial 375, p. 28.

36. Report of W. Medill, November 30, 1847, *Senate Executive Document* No. 1, 30 Cong., 1 Sess., serial 503, p. 749. See also Report of Orlando Brown, November 30, 1849, *House Executive Document* No. 5, 31 Cong., 1 Sess., serial 570, p. 937.

37. Report of Thomas H. Harvey, October 8, 1844, *Senate Document* No. 1, 28 Cong., 2 Sess., serial 449, p. 436. See also his report of September 10, 1845, *Senate Document* No. 1, 29 Cong., 1 Sess., serial 470, p. 532, and his report of September 5, 1846, *Senate Document* No. 1, 29 Cong., 2 Sess., serial 493, pp. 282–83.

38. See Epilogue, "The Harvest Unreaped," in Berkhofer, *Salvation and the Savage,* 152–60, for a critical appraisal of the missionaries' success up to 1860. Reports of the missionaries appear in such sources as the *Annual Report* of the American Board of Commissioners for Foreign Missions and in the Board's journal, *The Missionary Herald,* as well as in reports attached to the annual reports of the Commissioner of Indian Affairs.

39. Report of T. Hartley Crawford, November 25, 1841, *House Executive Document* No. 2, 27 Cong., 2 Sess., serial 401, pp. 238–39.

40. Report of James M. Porter, November 30, 1843, *Senate Document* No. 1, 28 Cong., 1 Sess., serial 431, pp. 58–59.

41. See for example the report of James Clarke, Iowa Superintendency, October 2, 1846, *Senate Document* No. 1, 29 Cong., 2 Sess., serial 493, p. 243.

42. *United States Statutes at Large,* IV, 737.

43. *Ibid.,* IX, 203–4.

44. W. Medill to Thomas H. Harvey, August 30, 1847, *Senate Executive Document* No. 1, 30 Cong., 1 Sess., serial 503, p. 756.

45. Report of W. Medill, November 30, 1848, *House Executive Document* No. 1, 30 Cong., 2 Sess., serial 537, p. 400. For the reaction of Thomas H. Harvey to the new legislation, see his report of October 29, 1847, in *Senate Executive Document* No. 1, 30 Cong., 1 Sess., serial 503, pp. 832–41. Commissioner Luke Lea in 1850, although conceding "the general wisdom and justice of the policy," argued that it tended to reduce the position of the chiefs, through whom the government dealt with the tribes. Report of Luke Lea, November 27, 1850, *Senate Executive Document* No. 1, 31 Cong., 2 Sess., serial 587, pp. 44–45.

46. Report of W. Medill, November 30, 1847, *Senate Executive Document* No. 1, 30 Cong., 1 Sess., serial 503, p. 746.

47. Report of W. Medill, November 30, 1848, *House Executive Document* No. 1, 30 Cong., 2 Sess., serial 537, p. 400. See, however, the remarks of D. D. Mitchell, Superintendent of Indian Affairs at St. Louis, October 13, 1849, in which he criticized the semiannual payment for small tribes, in *House Executive Document* No. 5, 31 Cong., 1 Sess., serial 570, p. 1068.

48. Report of W. Medill, November 30, 1848, *House Executive Document* No. 1, 30 Cong., 2 Sess., serial 537, pp. 393–94. See also Report of Orlando Brown, November 30, 1849, *House Executive Document* No. 5, 31 Cong., 1 Sess., serial 570, p. 958.

49. Report of John S. Spencer, November 26, 1842, *Senate Document* No. 1, 27 Cong., 3 Sess., serial 413, p. 192.

50. Report of T. Hartley Crawford, November 28, 1840, *Senate Document* No. 1, 26 Cong., 2 Sess., serial 375, p. 240.

51. *Ibid.,* 240–41.

52. Report of T. Hartley Crawford, November 16, 1842, *Senate Document* No. 1, 27 Cong., 3 Sess., serial 413, pp. 382–83. See also his report of November 25, 1841, *House Executive Document* No. 2, 27 Cong., 2 Sess., serial 401, pp. 239–40, and his report of November 25, 1843, *Senate Document* No. 1, 28 Cong., 1 Sess., serial 431, p. 266.

53. The bill (No. 430) was introduced on June 14, 1844, and was committed to the Committee of the Whole. *House Journal,* 28 Cong., 1 Sess., 1112.

54. Report of T. Hartley Crawford, November 25, 1844, *Senate Document* No. 1, 28 Cong., 2 Sess., serial 449, pp. 312–13.

55. *United States Statutes at Large,* IV, 729–30; Report of W. Medill, November 30, 1847, *Senate Executive Document* No. 1, 30 Cong., 1 Sess.,

serial 503, pp. 750–51. The "Regulations Concerning the Granting of Licenses to Trade with the Indians," dated November 9, 1847, and the forms of licenses and bonds to be used are printed in Appendix A, *ibid.,* 760–64.

56. Report of W. L. Marcy, December 1, 1848, *House Executive Document* No. 1, 30 Cong., 2 Sess., serial 537, pp. 83–84; Report of Orlando Brown, November 30, 1849, *House Executive Document* No. 5, 31 Cong., 1 Sess., serial 570, p. 958.

57. Report of T. Hartley Crawford, November 28, 1840, *Senate Document* No. 1, 26 Cong., 2 Sess., serial 375, pp. 233–34. The temperance crusade is discussed in Tyler, *Freedom's Ferment,* 308, 350.

58. Report of T. Hartley Crawford, November 28, 1840, *Senate Document* No. 1, 26 Cong., 2 Sess., serial 375, p. 241.

59. Report of T. Hartley Crawford, November 25, 1841, *House Executive Document* No. 2, 27 Cong., 2 Sess., serial 401, p. 243.

60. Report of T. Hartley Crawford, November 25, 1843, *Senate Document* No. 1, 28 Cong., 1 Sess., serial 431, p. 270–71.

61. *Ibid.,* 271; Report of D. D. Mitchell, September 29, 1843, *ibid.,* 387. See also Report of T. Hartley Crawford, November 25, 1844, *Senate Document* No. 1, 28 Cong., 2 Sess., serial 449, pp. 311–12.

62. Prucha, *American Indian Policy in the Formative Years,* 102–38, 267–68.

63. Report of J. M. Porter, November 30, 1843, *Senate Document* No. 1, 28 Cong., 1 Sess., serial 431, p. 59; Report of W. L. Marcy, November 29, 1845, *Senate Document* No. 1, 29 Cong., 1 Sess., serial 470, p. 205. A thorough discussion of the evils of the liquor traffic among the Indians is Otto F. Frederikson, *The Liquor Question Among the Indian Tribes in Kansas, 1804–1881* (Lawrence, Kans., 1932).

64. *United States Statutes at Large,* IX, 203.

65. Regulations, April 13, 1847, *Senate Executive Document* No. 1, 30 Cong., 1 Sess., serial 503, pp. 764–66.

66. W. L. Marcy to governors of Missouri, Arkansas, and Iowa, July 14, 1847, *ibid.,* 767–69.

67. Report of W. Medill, November 30, 1848, *House Executive Document* No. 1, 30 Cong., 2 Sess., serial 537, p. 402; Report of W. L. Marcy, December 1, 1848, *ibid.,* 83–84; Report of Orlando Brown, November 30, 1849, *House Executive Document* No. 5, 31 Cong., 1 Sess., serial 570, p. 939. See also Frederikson, *Liquor Question,* 55–64, on the Act of 1847 and its effect.

68. Report of William Armstrong, October 1, 1840, *Senate Document* No. 1, 26 Cong., 2 Sess., serial 375, p. 310. See also his reports for the subsequent years attached to the annual reports of the Commissioner of Indian Affairs.

69. Report of Thomas H. Harvey, September 5, 1846, *Senate Document* No. 1, 29 Cong., 2 Sess., serial 493, p. 282.

70. Remonstrance of Col. Peter Pitchlynn, January 20, 1849, *House Miscellaneous Document* No. 35, 30 Cong., 2 Sess., serial 544, p. 3.

71. Report of W. L. Marcy, December 1, 1848, *House Executive Document* No. 1, 30 Cong., 2 Sess., serial 537, p. 84.

72. Report of W. Medill, November 30, 1848, *ibid.*, 385–86.

73. Report of Orlando Brown, November 30, 1849, *House Executive Document* No. 5, 31 Cong., 1 Sess., serial 570, pp. 956–57.

74. See Berkhofer, *Salvation and the Savage*, 156–60, on the lack of a realistic theory of culture among the reformers.

75. See the discussion of the period as one of transition in James C. Malin, *Indian Policy and Westward Expansion* (Lawrence, Kans., 1921).

Stephen A. Douglas
and the
American Mission

Robert W. Johannsen, University of Illinois

The idea of mission has always been deeply imbedded in American thought and action, its roots extending back to the earliest settlement of the continent and its expression continuing down to the present day. Seldom, however, did it attain such wide acceptance as in the middle decades of the nineteenth century, when the belief that the American people had been chosen to fulfill certain high and lofty purposes became a dominant theme in their democratic faith. Nurtured by the circumstances of national growth and position, the idea of mission embraced concepts of progress and destiny. The expansion of democracy, the rise of technology, and the appearance of a large-scale movement to ameliorate the human condition gave credence to the idea. Born of revolution, free from the restraints of tradition, and enjoying a unique geographic position, the young United States seemed to embody the hopes and ideals of men everywhere. Isolated physically from the rest of the world and poised on the edge of a vast and empty continent, the youthful nation occupied an advantageous position for bringing its glorious destiny to realization. The United States, wrote one editor of the period, must "carry forward the noble mission entrusted to her of going before the nations of the world as the representative of the democratic principle and as the constant living exemplar of its results." Democracy, he pointed out, was the cause of Humanity. It was a challenge and a charge to a generation already stirred by a reforming zeal.[1]

Comprehensive in scope, including both idealistic and materialistic elements, the idea of mission provided a strong impulse to American politics and gave an evangelical character to much of the political expression. Some of its most dedicated disciples were men of action, the political activists who sought to realize their ideology of hope and optimism through direct, positive, and practical programs. Such an individual in the 1840s and 1850s was Stephen A. Douglas, who from his position at the center of national activity became a spokesman for national growth and hegemony and an advocate of the American mission in its broadest dimensions.

Two important influences shaped Douglas's faith during the formative years of his life. The popular image of Andrew Jackson captured his allegiance and he became imbued with the equalitarian ideas that the "Old Hero" seemed to represent. Of greater importance was the Western environment in which he served his political apprenticeship. "I have become a *Western* man," the twenty-year-old Douglas recorded shortly after his arrival in Illinois, "[and] have imbibed Western feelings principles and interests." Years later he recalled, "I came out here when I was a boy and found my mind liberalized and my opinions enlarged when I got on these broad prairies, with only the Heavens to bound my vision."[2] Combining his zeal for popular democracy with shrewd political acumen, Douglas embarked on a remarkably successful career in state and national politics, developing a fierce attachment to the institutions of American government and a fervent belief in his nation's future. For Douglas, as for others of his generation, it was a basic conservatism tempered by a missionary impulse. "From early youth," he proudly confessed, "I have indulged an enthusiasm, which seemed to others wild and romantic, in regard to the growth, expansion, and destiny of this republic."[3]

For Douglas, the American mission was intimately related to the development of democracy and democratic institutions. The American Revolution, which severed the ties with a declining and decadent Europe, and the Constitution, which established a flexible and adaptable federal system, were clues that the United States would perform a unique role in the world community. That this role would be played from the vantage point of a vast, rich, and empty continent further demonstrated that the nation's mission was part of an irresistible plan. North America, Douglas declared, had been "set aside as a nursery for the culture of republican principles." The nation was guided by a force larger than itself or its people, a force which Douglas sometimes referred to as the "spirit of the age" or as the "genius of progress which is to ennoble and exalt humanity" and more rarely as simply "Divine Providence."[4] Democracy, he told an audience in 1852, had a "mission to perform. It is the great mission of progress in the arts and sciences—in the science of politics and government—in the development and advancement of human rights throughout the world." Improvement began at home, and one of the first tasks was to develop "correct principles here," for only through the force of its own example could the nation expect to fulfill its mission. Laws and policies were temporary, to be altered as the times themselves change, but "democratic principles are immutable, and can never die so long as freedom survives." To see that freedom not only survived but prospered and expanded as well was the particular obligation of the American people. The responsibility was awesome, requiring constant exertion. Democratic principles were eternal, but "perpetual action and undying energy" were necessary to give them force and carry them into effect.[5] As agents of democracy, Americans became the instruments of civilization itself.

With this charge, Douglas believed, the prospects for national growth were limitless. American destiny could not be precisely defined, for to define it would be to limit it. "You cannot fix bounds to the onward march of this great and growing country," he stated. "You cannot fetter the limbs of the young giant. He will burst all your chains. He will expand, and grow, and increase, and extend civilization, christianity, and liberal principles."[6] No government had done more to elevate the condition of the people nor had any other nation so furthered the cause of civilization. "What nation on this globe," he asked, "has been so wonderfully and so bountifully blest as this people under our Constitution. We have progressed more rapidly in numbers, in wealth, in the extension of our territory, and in all things which make a people prosperous and happy, than any nation on earth. If our history can be taken as an evidence of a kind Divine Providence," Douglas concluded, "we are the favored nation of the world."[7] American character and opportunity guaranteed a glorious future. "With our broad expanse of country, our fertile soil, and our universal enterprise, who can predict the destiny and greatness of this people."[8]

The American mission was to provide the model for the world to emulate. Lovers of freedom and democracy everywhere, Douglas believed, had their eyes fixed on the United States. "Our success is the foundation of all their hopes."[9] He saw a world conflict between democracy and aristocracy in which the young nation, with its freshness and vigor, was pitted against all the reactionary forces of European monarchism. America's principal antagonist was England, "an old, decrepit nation, tottering and ready to fall to pieces." Douglas's patriotism was always marked by an outspoken and almost blind Anglophobia. "I cannot recognize England as our mother," he shouted. "If so, she is and ever has been a cruel and unnatural mother."[10] England was not only America's chief competitor, Douglas constantly reminded his listeners, but she also represented all the forces against which the United States must struggle if the national mission were ever to be fulfilled.

America's example, Douglas was convinced, already exerted a powerful influence on Europe, and the revolutions that convulsed western Europe in the late 1840s seemed to substantiate his belief. "A great movement is in progress," he announced, "which threatens the existence of every absolute government in Europe. It will be a struggle between liberal and absolute principles—between Republicanism and Despotism." Bound by its own revolutionary past and by its obligation to mankind, the United States could not "remain cold and indifferent spectators" to the upheavals. Douglas urged Congress to extend the hand of sympathy and fellowship to those who struggled against oppression. "I think that the bearing of this country should be such as to demonstrate to all mankind that America sympathizes with the popular movement against despotism, whenever and wherever made." When the Hungarian revolt was put down by Austria and Russia, he went beyond moral support, insisting that the United States had the right "to interfere or not, according to our convictions of duty."[11] The time had arrived when America should take her position among the nations of the world and "assert those principles which her destiny and her mission demand she should maintain."[12] As the revolutions failed, Douglas held out his hand to their leaders, asserting that America must also serve as "the asylum of the oppressed of all nations on earth."[13]

In order to dramatize the youth and vitality of the American mission, Douglas frequently contrasted the Old World with the New, to the great disadvantage of the former. Europe ever remained the seat of declining power and decadence, a land of princes and monarchs thwarting the popular will and stifling democratic aspirations. In the spring of 1853, he drew one of his most graphic comparisons:

> Europe is antiquated, decrepit, tottering on the verge of dissolution. When you visit her, the objects which enlist your highest admiration are the relics of past greatness; the broken columns erected to departed power. It is one vast grave-yard, where you find here a tomb indicating the burial of the arts; there a monument marking the spot where liberty expired; another to the memory of a great man, whose place has never been filled. The choicest products of her classic soil consist in relics, which remain as sad memorials of departed glory and fallen greatness! They bring up the memories of the dead, but inspire no hope for the living! Here everything is fresh, blooming, expanding, and advancing.[14]

A few months after he uttered these sentiments, Douglas left the United States for an extended visit to Europe, but nothing he saw

or heard altered his opinions. He quarreled with the ministers of
the British Queen over the matter of court dress and in the end
refused an audience with the monarch; he visited the Ottoman
Empire but found it inconvenient to confer with the Sultan; and
he snubbed the Pope.

Douglas returned to the United States more confident than
before that this "is the first nation upon the face of the globe." The
American mission demanded a vigorous foreign policy, adapted
to the "spirit of the age," designed "to enhance our own power and
greatness," and pursued without regard for the wishes of other
nations and without fear of reprisal. "We should act in fear of
God, performing our duty to ourselves and to mankind, and leave
the world to form its own opinion." In the wake of the European
revolutionary movements, he mapped the course of American
policy and defined the nation's role as a defender of democracy
throughout the world—sympathize with every liberal movement,
recognize the independence of all republics, form commercial
treaties with them, protest against "all infractions of the laws of
nations, and hold ourselves ready to do whatever our duty may
require when a case shall arise." While Douglas often spoke of
the "laws of nations," a vague notion of international polity which
he never defined, he made it increasingly clear that special rules
applied to the United States. He wanted no treaties that would
inhibit the American mission; in any case, such agreements could
hardly withstand the irresistible force of national growth. The
growth of the United States was inevitable, he exclaimed, and
"the barriers of any treaty would be irresistibly broken through by
natural causes, over which we had no control."[15] America's pursuit
of its destiny became a law of nature!

The responsibilities imposed on the American people, however, went beyond relations with other countries and the active
promotion of the American example. The American mission also
demanded excellence in the arts and sciences, in agriculture, in
commerce, and in manufacturing.[16] Douglas sang the praises of
the nation's inventive genius and saw in the developing technology of his time part of the unfolding destiny of which he spoke so
enthusiastically. The "power of great conceptions, the aspiration
and the will, the mental faculty and the manual skill" which
characterized the American progressive temperament had been

aroused "by the triumphant spirit of liberty which throbs in the great heart of our continent." He paid tribute to the mechanic, to whom the nation owed its rapid progress more than to any other class of citizens. "And why is it," Douglas asked, "that the American mechanic excels all others? It is because he has, under our institutions, a right to think freely and boldly."[17] New discoveries in the sciences and developments in the arts went hand in hand with technology, and Douglas never tired of enumerating America's achievements. The application of steam power to transportation on land and sea, improvement in the means of communication and the spread of intelligence, the recognition accorded American artists, and the mechanization of agriculture were cited as evidence of America's commitment to progress. Science, technology, and the arts were not the domain of an intellectual elite; they belonged to the people, and this, to Douglas, was the secret of American success.

Douglas not only pointed with pride to the results of American inventive genius but became himself an active promotor of technological development. Receptive to new ideas, he used his position in Congress to secure their acceptance. The rapid transmission of news by means of a magnetic telegraph captured his interest, and he became one of the most persistent supporters of the "oceanic telegraph" or Atlantic cable. The latter not only had its practical benefits but it would also bring honor and glory to "American genius and American daring." Steam power had revolutionized transportation, and Douglas was eager to place this technological advance in the service of national growth through a network of intersectional railroads. He was equally convinced that steam, if properly and speedily utilized, would bring mastery of the seas to the United States; and to this end, he urged the approval of government subsidies which would facilitate the construction of mail steamers. Not content with promoting transportation on land and sea, Douglas was fascinated with the possibilities of "aerial navigation." The construction of balloons that could be used for war purposes as well as for the transportation of passengers and mail, Douglas thought, was worthy of government support.[18]

"Two great objects of individual and general prosperity," began a document endorsed by Douglas in 1851, are "the development of the natural resources of our country, and the promotion of practical science." To accomplish the former, he sought unsuccessfully to secure grants of land to the states for the support of geological surveys, and for the latter he urged the introduction of practical science as a subject of primary instruction in the schools. "Agriculture and mechanism" were two leading objects of human pursuit; educational institutions should, therefore, be charged with instruction in those sciences most closely related to these pursuits. Geology, chemistry, geometry, and botany ought, he thought, to be "treated in a clear, specific, practical manner adapted to the use and capacity of the plain farmer, the mechanic, the laborer." When Jonathan Baldwin Turner proposed a system of national industrial universities which would provide instruction for farmers and mechanics, Douglas was among the first to support the project. Convinced that the United States would soon become the great center of the world's agricultural production, he urged the creation of an agricultural bureau in the government's executive branch and the establishment of a national agricultural society through which scientific information might be made available to the nation's farmers.[19] Douglas's concern for the promotion and dissemination of practical scientific knowledge was reflected in his long association with the Smithsonian Institution. Appointed a Regent in 1854, he remained active in its affairs until his death seven years later.[20]

Douglas was not unmindful of the importance of the arts and letters in the pursuit of national greatness, but the developments that excited him most were those that helped to tame the land, to bring civilization into the wilderness, and to promote economic and commercial supremacy. He was obsessed with practicality and utility. Steamships, railroads, the telegraph, mowers and reapers—these were the true monuments to the spirit of progress that animated the American people. "We in America," he proudly announced, "are accustomed to spend money for works of utility, not on those of mere ornament, pomp, and show."[21]

One of the sources of America's strength, Douglas believed, was in its people. Immigration produced a heterogeneous population, giving vitality to American society and infusing "into the national temperament those influences without which we might have become inert and stagnant." The United States was "a cross of all nations," its population "the most peculiar and superior people on the face of the earth." The gates, he urged, must never be closed to the immigrant.[22] Every American, whether native or foreign-born, was an agent in the nation's rapid advance "to maturity and perfection." Progress, Douglas contended, ultimately depended upon individual expression and aspiration. "Pride of character, self-love, the strongest passions of the human heart," he declared, "all impel a man forward and onward." Progress, "the desire for free institutions," must first find an abiding place in the hearts of the people. When the people shall come together, united in their quest for perfection, then the nation will make giant strides toward the fulfillment of its mission.[23]

The catalyst in America's surge toward its manifest destiny was what Douglas always called the "Great West," for it was his basic Western orientation and identification that gave reason and vitality to his concept of the American mission. To this young, dynamic politician the West was America. It was the one great feature that distinguished the United States from other nations, that gave the American dream its clearest impulse, and that insured its invincibility. The West provided the powerful cement that held the Union together and impelled it onward; it was the seat of progress and strength, providing space, resources, and opportunity to forward-looking Americans. The Great West constituted the hope of the nation and hence of the entire world.

Douglas's West was an ever-growing, expanding region. In area it embraced all that lay west of the Appalachians, extending to the shores of the Pacific and even beyond, but its heart and soul was always in the Mississippi Valley. It was a vantage point from which to observe the true course of national development and to recognize the true needs of national growth. "It so happens in this Confederacy," Douglas once complained, "that no man can see anything west of him. Whatever his locality may be, he thinks he must stand and look eastwards towards the rising sun." Men may stand at New York, Buffalo, Detroit, or Chicago, but always their look is eastward. "The consequence is," he concluded, "that the man furthest west has a better knowledge of the topographical and locality of the internal resources of this great Republic." But the West was also much more than an area and a vantage point. It was the stage on which the drama of American growth and progress was being acted out. Douglas could proclaim, as he did in 1854, "I belong to no section," only because the West to him was the nation and to be Western was to be national.[24]

In an era of rising sectional tensions, the role of the West became even more obvious and more imperative. "I am by no means certain," he noted in 1852, "but that the sectional strife, jealousy, and ambition engendered between the North and the South would ere this have dissolved this glorious Union had it not been for the Great West." Her population "intelligent and patriotic," drawn from "each of the great geographical divisions of the Union," her trade flowing through the Great Lakes to the North and down the Mississippi to the South, the West bore the lineaments of a great internal empire, bound tenaciously to both North and South. The Mississippi Valley was "the heart of the Republic, more extensive, powerful and glorious than any empire that the world ever beheld."[25] In a masterful statement, spoken during one of the nation's great political crises, Douglas summed up his position:

> . . . there is a power in this nation greater than either the North or the South—a growing, increasing, swelling power, that will be able to speak the law to this nation, and to execute the law as spoken. That power is the country known as the great West—the Valley of the Mississippi, one and indivisible from the gulf to the great lakes, and stretching, on the one side and the other, to the extreme sources of the Ohio and Missouri—from the Alleghanies to the Rocky mountains. There, sir, is the hope of this nation—the resting-place of the power that is not only to control, but to save, the Union. We furnish the water that makes the Mississippi, and we intend to follow, navigate, and use it until it loses itself in the briny ocean. So with the St. Lawrence. We intend to keep open and enjoy both of these great outlets to the ocean, and all between them we intend to take under our especial protection, and keep and preserve as one free, happy, and united people. This is the mission of the great Mississippi valley, the heart and soul of the nation and the continent.[26]

The nation's strength was in the West and it was upon the growth and development of the West that America's future greatness depended. When he first went to Congress in the mid 1840s, Douglas carried with him a dedication to Western development that influenced virtually all of his subsequent legislative activity. He lost no time in articulating a Western program to which he remained committed for the rest of his life. Presented first to Congress and later amplified in a letter to the railroad promoter Asa Whitney, Douglas's proposals involved (1) territorial expansion, (2) the development of improved transportation and communication in and through the West, (3) the encouragement of Western settlement, and (4) the extension of organized government to the West.[27] His efforts on behalf of these proposals were always justified in terms of American destiny and mission.

Territorial expansion, for Douglas, was not only a primary obligation but it was also a natural law which Americans were powerless to resist. "This is a young, vigorous, growing nation," he maintained. "Increase is the law of our existence and of our safety. Just as fast as our population increases our territory must expand. You cannot arrest this law. He is unwise who voluntarily places himself in the path of American destiny."[28] It was a "law of progress" that could not be stayed. "You may like it or you may dislike it," he told a Southern audience in 1858, but "you can never fulfill your destiny without it." The extension of territory, he had declared thirteen years before, would result "as natural consequences from causes over which we have no control."[29] Douglas eschewed passivity and called upon his fellow citizens to recognize the inevitable through a course of action. The expansion of America's boundaries and the extension of American influence, he contended, served a cause that was larger than the nation for it would be carried out in the name of progress, humanity, and civilization.[30]

As a fledgling Congressman, Douglas demanded that the limits of the United States be extended from ocean to ocean. "I would make this an *ocean-bound republic*, and have no more disputes about boundaries or red lines upon the maps." The area of freedom would be made as broad as the continent itself. The institutions of democratic government and technological advance were the handmaids of expansion. The American federal system, with its "great conservative and renovating principle" of states' rights, was "as well adapted to the whole American continent as it was to the thirteen original States of the Union." The development of steam power in transportation and the improvements in communication would bring the extremities of the continent closer together with respect to time than were the various parts of the republic at its formation. With such advantages, "we might extend our republic safely to the extreme parts of the continent, and even further if necessary."[31]

When he first urged American expansion, Douglas seemed content to limit the nation to the Pacific shore, unwilling, he said, to go beyond the boundaries which the "God of nature" had provided. In later years, he overcame his reluctance to expand beyond the sea and broadened his position: "When I speak of our country being well adapted to an ocean-bound republic, of course I mean to include the islands on this side of the main channel of the two great seas." The Caribbean Sea and the Gulf of Mexico, he added, are American waters, to be treated as "closed seas to the exclusion of all European powers."[32] Nor was he solely interested in expansion into contiguous areas. "I do not want Central America," Douglas once conceded, "but the time will come when our destiny, our institutions, our safety will compel us to have it." So also with the island of Cuba. "I do not care whether you want it or not. . . . we are compelled to take it, and we can't help it." Douglas prescribed a different set of ground rules, however, for expansion into areas that were already heavily populated. "I do not say that we ought, at one blow, to acquire a vast amount of new territory," he explained. Rather, the task was to "Americanize" these areas before the question of annexation could be met. The process, he warned, would be slow, gradual, and steady, but it was one which would serve the cause of civilization. "I would like to see the boundaries of the Republic extended gradually and steadily, as fast as we can Americanize the countries we acquire and make their inhabitants loyal American citizens when we get them."[33]

Douglas became a close student of Western geography and needs until, as he boasted, he understood the country between the Mississippi River and the Pacific Ocean quite as well as he knew the older states of the Union.[34] In both House and Senate he was selected to head the Committee on Territories, and in the Senate for a time he sat on the Foreign Relations Committee. He viewed his responsibilities broadly; everything that pertained to Western expansion and development, he insisted, came under his purview. His outspoken advocacy of expansion, with its constant and often tedious reference to manifest destiny, frequently invited ridicule from colleagues who contrasted Douglas's diminutive stature with the scope of his ideas. "He is fond of boasting," said Delaware's distinguished Senator Clayton, "that we are a *giant* Republic; and the Senator himself is said to be a 'little giant'; yes, sir, quite a *giant*, and everything that he talks about in these latter days is gigantic." Thomas Hart Benton, with whom Douglas tangled on more than one occasion, bellowed, "He thinks he can bestride this continent with one foot on the shore of the Atlantic, the other on the Pacific. But he can't do it—he can't do it. His legs are too short."[35]

When Douglas entered Congress, the question of Texas annexation was approaching its final stages of discussion, and Westerners were looking with increased longing at the Oregon country. Illinois was in the center of the agitation. The Texas issue, observed one local politician, was "a flame . . . burning from one end of the State to the other"; at the same time, Illinoisans were gripped by what some called "Oregon Fever."[36] Emigrant companies had been formed in the state, and many of its citizens were on their way to the Pacific Northwest. Oregon meetings were scheduled, in some of which Douglas participated, and the cry was raised for the immediate acquisition of that disputed territory. Douglas lost little time in placing himself at the head of both movements.

Texas annexation, it was argued, would strengthen the United States, but it would also achieve higher ends. By giving Texas "the protection of our laws, the benefits of our institutions and a full share of the blessings which flow from our happy form of Government," the nation would "increase the sum of human happiness."[37] In keeping with his broad view of national destiny, Douglas placed annexation on practical as well as idealistic grounds. Texas was a key to the defense of the Mississippi Valley; it would strengthen the market for American cotton abroad and would open a large new area (including northern Mexico) to American manufactures. National honor and faith required annexation; but it was also a measure "which appealed to all our interests, alike commercial, agricultural, and manufacturing."[38]

In December, 1844, Douglas submitted a series of resolutions providing for annexation which, after much parliamentary maneuvering, formed the basis for the joint resolutions that eventually passed the House and Senate. Looking back on his role, Douglas reaffirmed his position. Texas had been acquired "upon broad national grounds . . . considerations which addressed themselves to the patriotism and pride of every American—considerations connected with the extension of territory, of commerce, of navigation, of political power, of national security, and glory."[39] He expressed contempt for those who sought to distract the nation from its mission by relating Texas annexation to the issue of slavery. Their efforts, he concluded, were an "insidious attempt" to excite one part of the Union against another; Texas had been added to the United States for reasons that were "elevated far above, and totally disconnected from, the question of slavery."[40] For Douglas, it was an early encounter with a question that he felt was not only subordinate in importance but completely unrelated to the American drive toward its destiny.

Texas did not stand alone in Douglas's program for national expansion. Title to the whole of the Oregon country, he maintained, was "perfect and indisputable," and he called for "bold, immediate, speedy action" to bring that vast area within the nation's boundaries. Texas and Oregon were like man and wife— "when separated, the welfare and happiness of both were seriously injured; but when once united, they must be kept together forever." The same reasons that impelled the extension of American rule over Texas demanded the acquisition of Oregon. "Interest and patriotism—national glory and security—all unite in prompting us to embrace the 'present golden opportunity' to extend the principles of civil and religious liberty over a large portion of the continent."[41] Oregon's fertile soil and genial climate were superbly adapted to American agriculture, but the value of the Oregon country was not to be measured simply by "the number of miles upon the coast," nor did it depend solely on the character of the country and the quality of the soil. "The great point at issue," he said, "is for the freedom of the Pacific ocean, for the trade of China and of Japan, of the East Indies, and for the maritime ascendancy on all these waters."[42] In short, the Oregon question not only involved the responsibilities of the American mission in their most idealistic sense, but it also involved the highest commercial and economic interests of the country.

Douglas's arguments for Texas and Oregon were spurred by his fierce and almost irrational Anglophobia. England, the representative of reactionary monarchism in the world struggle for democracy, stood in the way of American destiny. A threat to the national mission, she was also America's chief competitor for economic and commercial supremacy. The villainous British lion crouched, he was convinced, ready to spring upon helpless Texas. Britain's aim was apparent even to a blind man: "It was to check the growth of republican institutions on this continent, and the rapidity with which we have progressed, not only in political power, but in trade and national glory."[43] He denounced those who would compromise the Oregon boundary at the forty-ninth parallel; and to those who proposed arbitration, Douglas replied that the American people, "being a peculiar people, with a peculiar system of government unlike that of the balance of the world, which excites the prejudices of other nations of the world against us," could not safely place their rights in the hands of others. Title to all of Oregon was indisputable, and Douglas would not be satisfied as long as Great Britain "shall hold possession of one acre on the northwest coast of America."[44]

Douglas's belligerent tirades alarmed many of his colleagues who feared that the nation might be drawn into a needless war with Great Britain. For Douglas, however, war as an instrument for advancing American destiny was only a last and unlikely resort. American expansion, he reiterated, was part of "the natural progress of things" and could be achieved "without war, without force, without violation of treaty, and without infringement of the rights of others," requiring only a bold, dynamic, and fearless policy that was commensurate with the dimensions of the national mission.[45] Why should America quail before British power? he asked. Britain had tried once before "to check the progress of this nation by a war" and had undoubtedly learned her lesson.[46] The Oregon controversy was settled peacefully and, as far as the expansionists were concerned, ignobly. Douglas suffered deep and bitter disappointment when the treaty establishing the boundary at the forty-ninth parallel was ratified in 1846. His zeal for expansion, however, was hardly dimmed, for by the time the dispute with Great Britain had been resolved, a new opportunity for advancing national destiny had opened.

Relations between the United States and Mexico had deteriorated long before the Texas issue reached its climax, and, for Douglas, conflict could not be avoided. Just as he counselled bold action as a deterrent to war in the case of the British, Douglas now argued that a firm policy against Mexico earlier would have rendered war unnecessary. Americans, however, had "allowed their sympathy for the weakness and degradation of a nominal sister republic to prevail over their sense of duty to the citizens and flag of our own country." Mexico, mistaking sympathy for weakness, "magnanimity for pusillanimity," had responded to the government's just complaints with contempt and defiance. Misplaced American sympathy had encouraged Mexican bellicosity. Douglas denied that the Mexican War was one of conquest. It was, on the contrary, a "war of self-defence, forced upon us by our enemy, and prosecuted on our part in vindication of our honor, and the integrity of our territory."[47]

Having found justification for the Mexican War, Douglas quickly discovered a place for it in the drama of progress and mission which Americans were acting out. As rumors of a clash on the Rio Grande raced through the West in the summer of 1845, Douglas advised President Polk, "The Northern Provinces of Mexico including California ought to belong to this Republic, and the day is not far distant when such a result will be accomplished. The present is an auspicious time."[48] These lands would presumably be annexed through the operation of the natural law of American expansion, but Douglas was ready to assist the forces of destiny with more immediate measures. An expedition should be raised immediately, he informed the President, to occupy New Mexico and California. When war was declared less than a year later, he was not slow to grasp its significance to the national mission. The acquisition of California, he explained, had been as important to him as Oregon; both were essential "to the fulfilment of our destiny as the first maritime nation upon the globe." Anyone "capable of comprehending our manifest destiny" could see that California "was soon to be a part of this great confederacy."[49]

The war with Mexico meant more than new lands and harbors; it was "a fervent, glorious, patriotic zeal to advance the great cause of freedom." The shouts of America's victorious armies would strike terror in the hearts of all enemies of republican institutions, demonstrating the superiority of American arms as well as of American democracy. Europe, already jealous "of our growing greatness and importance among the nations of the world," could not help but heed the lesson.[50]

Half a million square miles of territory were added to the United States as a result of the Mexican War, enough, it would seem, to thrill the hearts of every expansionist. California and New Mexico were acquired, and the United States more than doubled its Pacific coastline. But for Douglas, the Treaty of Guadalupe-Hidalgo proved as disappointing as the Oregon boundary settlement. Not enough territory had been taken, but more important the United States disavowed any further acquisitions in Mexico without that nation's prior consent. Who can say, Douglas asked, that "amid the general wreck and demoralization in Mexico" a regard for American rights and safety as well as the interests of humanity might not compel the United States to annex additional territory without Mexican consent?[51] The treaty, however, like the earlier one with Great Britain, was ratified despite Douglas's opposition.

In spite of his disappointments, Douglas looked back on the years of the Polk administration with great satisfaction and pride:

> When we trace the changes which have taken place within the last four years in our domestic policy—in the development of our national resources—in the expansion of our commerce—in the enlargement of our territory—in the augmentation of our power—and in the respect and awe with which the renown of our arms has impressed the world—the mind is startled and dazzled as if beholding at one panoramic view the mighty work of ages.[52]

Douglas's own role in this "mighty work" had labeled him as one of the most extreme and uncompromising of expansionists. His conception of manifest destiny reflected not only the often wild enthusiasms of the West but also a deep and more sober faith in the progress and future growth of the United States. His was not a narrowly conceived manifest destiny nor was it based solely on idealistic premises. Harbors and ports were as much a part of Douglas's conception of manifest destiny as was his determination to make the area of freedom as broad as the continent itself. At the same time, his concept of destiny involved much more than territorial expansion. The enlargement of the nation's boundaries was not an end in itself. National destiny and mission also required the development of the West, and to accomplish this Douglas turned his attention in other directions and to other projects.

At first urged as a means for strengthening the American claim to frontage on the Pacific, Douglas's Western program became even more meaningful and urgent once expansion had been accomplished. The grand project, which he described in detail as early as 1845, was the construction of a Pacific railroad, the first step in the ultimate development of "a continous line of rail roads to the Pacific ocean." Such a project, however, would be the "work of years"; in the meantime, he urged the immediate adoption of several measures that would insure the completion "of this great railroad communication within the period that the course of events will render necessary." The first of these was the extension of territorial government to the growing settlements on the Pacific and to the vast intervening country between Missouri and the Rockies. Secondly, a railroad route to the Pacific should be selected and surveyed. Finally, in order to encourage the settlement of the country through which the railroad would run, Douglas asked that Western lands be donated in 160-acre tracts "to the actual settler." These proposals, Douglas conceded, were "crude and undigested," but they revealed the dimensions of his plans for the West and formed a program that would occupy his attention during the remaining years of his public service.[53]

Douglas had early been captivated by the immense possibilities for national growth provided by railroad transportation. "No man," he once wrote, "can keep up with the spirit of this age who travels on anything slower than the locomotive."[54] Railroads, he believed, could serve the nation by binding the Union together. For years he dreamed of uniting the Mississippi Valley with a railroad that would link the Great Lakes with the Gulf of Mexico, allaying sectional antagonisms between the North and South and harmonizing the people of the West. His dream was finally realized with the construction of the Illinois Central Railroad. Similar purposes attended his advocacy of a Pacific railroad. First proposed before the expansion of the 1840s, he believed it would provide an irrevocable bond between the nation's heartland and the continent's far shore. As settlements on the Pacific grew, a railroad became essential to their continued allegiance to the United States. "People 3000 miles off," wrote one of Douglas's correspondents, "separated by dreary wastes & snowy mounts will never consent to be governed by the people of the Atlantic States unless some more rapid communication can be established."[55] As his plans for a Pacific railroad became entangled with sectional politics, Douglas became more insistent lest Congressional inaction encourage separatism in Oregon and California. "It is the first and highest duty of this nation," Douglas declared in 1853, "to see that this road is made." The integrity of the Union, and hence the thrust of its mission, depended upon the completion of the road. "When we have connected the Atlantic and the Pacific by a railroad, there is no power on earth, no question which is in existence . . . which can sever the bonds of the Union."[56]

Douglas considered the projected transcontinental railroad to be much more than a force for unity. It would also serve as the means by which the trans-Mississippi West would be peopled, converted "from a wilderness into one of the most densely populated and highly-cultivated portions of America." Railroads would play an active role in extending civilization to the unsettled West. The work of construction itself would attract laborers, storekeepers, and mechanics, thus creating "one of the best markets that can be opened to the agriculturists anywhere." Permanent settlers would soon follow the construction gangs, farms would be cultivated and towns founded. Enterprising miners would move into the mountains to tap the region's valuable mineral resources. The country would be rendered secure by this "quiet, silent occupation," and the West, settled by "a hardy and industrious population," would soon become the scene of great production as well as a large new market for manufactured goods and merchandise.[57] He refuted the charge that the land to be traversed by the Pacific railroad was nothing more than great impassable and uninhabitable deserts. The desert myth, Douglas suggested, had been perpetrated by explorers who compared the plains with the lands they had left in the Mississippi Valley, with the result that everything they saw seemed desolate. "It will not do," he declared, "to judge every section of the country by the one in which you have been raised." The vast deserts reputed to exist west of the Mississippi, he predicted, would disappear "before investigation and settlement, in the way that other deserts have."[58]

Douglas envisioned not one but a large number of railroad lines to the Pacific—"the valley of the Mississippi will require as many Rail Roads to the Pacific as to the Atlantic."[59] Practically, he proposed legislation for the construction of three lines, following northern, central, and southern routes. When it seemed likely that only one would succeed, he supported the central route in order to give North and South equal advantages. A bond of Union, the basis for settlement and economic strength in the trans-Mississippi West, the Pacific railroad would also connect America's growing commercial activity in the Pacific with the "great heart and center of the Republic." "If we intend to extend our commerce—if we intend to make the great ports of the world tributary to our wealth," Douglas insisted, "we must penetrate the Pacific, its islands, and its continent, where the great mass of the human family reside—where the articles that have built up the powerful nations of the world have always come from."[60] The Pacific railroad, he concluded, would enable "America to assume the position to which she is now entitled . . . the first commercial and maritime Power upon the face of the globe."[61] It was essential to America's destiny and mission.

"To those vast multitudes, who wish to change their condition, and select new homes," Douglas wrote in 1845, "the promised land is westward." The Pacific railroad would serve as an inducement to settlement, but "a further necessity for the road" would also be created by the natural tide of emigration.[62] In his anxiety to foster the settlement of the trans-Mississippi West, Douglas gave little thought to the fate of the area's Indian inhabitants. He denounced the idea of a permanent Indian reservation on the plains as a barbarian wall that would restrain "the onward march of civilization, christianity, and free government." The Indian must simply give way. Lashing out at those who expressed concern for the rights of the Indians, he urged that the government could not longer "keep that country a howling wilderness . . . roamed over by hostile savages."[63] One way to penetrate the Indian barrier, protect emigrants to the West, and at the same time lay the foundations for permanent settlement was the establishment of military colonies along the main routes of travel. Volunteers, to be paid as soldiers, would build posts of native materials and supply their own provisions by turning the land to cultivation. After three-years' service, each would be granted six hundred and forty acres of land.[64] After the plains had been rendered secure from Indian attack and provided the basis for settlement, the way would be open to the pioneer farmer. In his original plan for a Pacific railroad, Douglas proposed that alternate sections of land along the route be granted to the states and territories through which it ran, the proceeds to be applied to the costs of construction. Land in the other alternate sections could then be thrown open to settlement, and Douglas suggested that they be granted in one-hundred-and-sixty-acre parcels to actual settlers. From this early suggestion emerged his support for a free-homestead policy.

Douglas was not alone in his advocacy of a free-land policy, nor was he among the first to support such a proposal. By 1849, however, when he introduced his first homestead bill, the idea had become an integral part of his scheme for Western development. The true policy of the government, he declared, was "to grant the public lands, in limited quantities, to actual settlers who shall reside on it for some years." In urging the passage of his bill, he extolled the role of the pioneer farmer and denounced the activities of land speculators. "The man who goes into the wilderness, and makes the first settlement, who erects his house, who makes his improvements, who undergoes the privation to which pioneers are subject, is entitled to the preference over him who purchases the land merely for purposes of speculation."[65] Coupled with his later development of the principle of popular sovereignty for the Western territories, a free-homestead policy would be the instrument by which the West would be peopled by independent Northern farmers, thus guaranteeing freedom rather than slavery to the frontier, a facet of Douglas's thinking that has not always been appreciated. By the end of the 1850s he had become more convinced than ever of the merits of a free-land policy. The system that offered public lands at auction, placing the speculator on an equality with the actual settler, he declared in 1860, was "vicious and defective." The preemption and homestead policies should be applied to all public lands, allowing the title to remain in the national government until the actual settler should avail himself of their opportunities. "My policy," he maintained, "always has been to make every inhabitant of the new states and territories a land-holder, as far as it was possible to do so, by our legislation."[66]

Perhaps the most important element in Douglas's program for the West, certainly the one that consumed most of his energy as a member of Congress, was the extension of American laws and institutions to the frontier through the organization of territories. For Douglas, territorial organization was the logical partner of territorial expansion; his proposals for a Pacific railroad and for a free-land policy were intimately related to, indeed dependent upon, the establishment of territorial government in the trans-Mississippi West. At the same time, the extension of government to the nation's ever-expanding frontier fulfilled a vital require-ment in America's drive toward its inevitable destiny by increasing the scope of the democratic institutions to which Douglas was committed. The great advantage of the American form of govern-ment, he was fond of saying, was the flexibility of its federal sys-tem, adaptable to infinite expansion without endangering the liberties of the people. The admission of new states, each sover-eign within its own local sphere, strengthened the whole without weakening any of the parts. The territorial stage of government was an integral part of this process, to which Douglas would ex-tend the counterpart of states' rights for the territories, his prin-ciple of popular sovereignty.[67]

From the time Douglas first proposed the organization of Oregon and Nebraska territories as a young Congressman in the mid 1840s, he remained closely identified with the frontiersman's interest in the character of his local government. He was ap-pointed chairman of the Committee on Territories in both the House and the Senate, and he discharged the responsibilities of his position with single-minded devotion until his removal for political reasons late in 1858. "The preparation of the various bills necessary to give government to the people of the territories, and prepare them for admission as states," he told a group of Californians in 1851, "required labor and investigation. But it was a work of love—a labor in which duty and inclination ran in the same channel."[68] Between the end of the Mexican War and 1854, Douglas was instrumental in securing the organization of seven Western territories—Oregon, Minnesota, Utah, New Mexico, Washington, Kansas, and Nebraska. During the decade of the fifties he fought for several more that did not make it—Arizona, Colorado, Nevada, and Dakota. The establishment of territorial government in the West was, he repeated, a national necessity, as essential to the settlement and development of the area as it was to the initial expansion of the United States. During the debates over the organization of the Mexican Cession, Douglas evolved his doctrine of popular sovereignty, and from that time on it was irrevocably linked to his interest in the territories and in the West. His commitment to popular sovereignty was the deeper because he recognized in it a formula that would (he hoped) bridge the differences between the North and South on the slavery question, thus preserving the Union that was so essential to his national faith. Like the West with which it was identified, the doctrine became a force for national unity in a time of rampant sectionalism.

Popular sovereignty, to Douglas, was simple, pragmatic, and just. He once defined it as the "right of the people of an organized Territory, under the Constitution and laws of the United States, to govern themselves in respect to their own internal policy and domestic affairs."[69] From the point of view of the West, Douglas's espousal of popular sovereignty was a happy development, for it accorded with a long-standing frontier demand. Since the early days of the republic, frontier communities had leveled sharp and bitter attacks against the nation's territorial system, which vested virtually absolute control over the territories in the executive and legislative branches of the national government. Douglas's doctrine appeared as a long-overdue innovation that would diminish the odious "foreign" control and broaden the area of territorial self-government; to many Westerners Douglas became the champion of frontier rights.[70] The pioneers who emigrated to the Western territories "were as capable of self-government as their neighbors and kindred whom they left behind them," he said in 1850, "and there was no reason for believing that they have lost

any of their intelligence or patriotism by the wayside, while crossing the Isthmus or the Plains." Moreover, Douglas added, "after
their arrival in the country, when they had become familiar with
its topography, climate, productions, and resources, and had connected their destiny with it, they were fully as competent to judge
for themselves what kind of laws and institutions were best
adapted to their condition and interests, as we were who never
saw the country, and knew very little about it." To question their
competency, he insisted, was to deny their capacity for self-
government.[71]

Popular sovereignty, as one manifestation of democratic
development, played a dominant role in Douglas's concept of
American destiny and mission. With territorial expansion, territorial self-government was necessary to "the cause of freedom, of
humanity, and of republicanism."[72] It soon became clear that
expansion and popular sovereignty—manifest destiny and democracy—overshadowed all other aspects of Douglas's program. By
the end of the fifties, he had reduced his belief in the American
mission to its essentials. "I am in favor of expansion," he observed,
"as fast as consistent with our interest and the increase and development of our population and resources." But, he added, "I
am not in favor of that policy unless . . . the right of the people
to decide the question of slavery, and all other domestic questions,
for themselves shall be maintained." By following these pathways,
the United States would have a more glorious future than any
other nation in history. "Our Republic will endure for thousands
of years," and "progress will be the law of its destiny." This was
in 1858, and Lincoln's "House Divided" speech was fresh in his
mind. Lincoln, Douglas believed, suffered from a narrowness of
vision; his famous statement seemed to be a call for uniformity
and conformity in policy as well as institutions. With expansion,
Douglas countered, new states will be admitted to the Union and
with every new state the nation will gain strength. "The more
degrees of latitude and longitude embraced beneath our Constitution, the better." Variety was among America's greatest assets,
"making us the greatest planting as well as the greatest manufacturing, the greatest commercial as well as the greatest agricultural power on the globe."[73] Local self-government, he insisted,
must be scrupulously protected wherever it existed. It was an

"inherent, inalienable right of all American citizens . . . to govern themselves in respect to their local and domestic concerns," and Douglas would apply that principle to the territories as well as to the states. "Let it only be observed," he concluded, "and this people can live in peace forever." The Union, with all its heterogeneity, "can continue to exist in all time to come."[74]

America's mission and America's destiny were beyond the power of its people to alter or control. "Steady growth and gradual expansion is one of the laws of our national existence," Douglas maintained. "It is the decree of Providence." The North American continent had been reserved as a nursery for liberty and an asylum where the world's oppressed population might take shelter "under the shadows of the great tree of Liberty." "A wise man," he advised, "always conforms his action to a policy which he cannot prevent, and hence I say, Let America have a policy in harmony with her destiny. Let us be what our numbers and what our position require us to be—not only an example to the friends of liberty, but a terror to the oppressors of man throughout the world."[75] In all of this, the West played a leading and vital role. As the representative and the guardian of truly national interests, the West, to Douglas, was identified with the nation, a bulwark against the sectional storms that increased in fury; the American mission, to a very large extent, was a Western mission.

Stephen A. Douglas was not a systematic thinker in an abstract sense. He was a pragmatic, professional politician, frequently bumptious and full of bluster, subject to outbursts of oratory that were not always designed to clarify the issues under discussion. His politics, nevertheless, were founded on certain deeply and sincerely held principles, and one of these was his profound faith in America's future. His concern for Western development bordered at times on obsession; but, for Douglas, the West embodied all the hopes and aspirations that focused upon the young republic, and it was in the West that the nation's destiny was being revealed. Douglas was a representative of his times—captivated by technological advances, seized by naive enthusiasms, swayed by ill-defined and even indefinable concepts of national greatness, but he was always persuaded of the superiority of American institutions and passionately devoted to their advancement. In the end, however, the national destiny that Douglas pursued proved illusory. As deep as were his convictions, he found difficulty in adjusting them to the hard, cold political realities of the prewar years. Indeed, his devotion to the chimerical, even mythical, goal of national greatness may have blinded him to the more urgent requirements of his age. His energies were distracted by issues he clearly regarded as secondary to the major thrust of American policy, and his latter years were spent in a fruitless attempt to find their adjustment so that the nation could get on with its more important business. Douglas died a saddened and disappointed man. America's mission was not only unfulfilled but the Union itself, the great agent of progress, wavered in the balance. His program for the West had fallen short of achievement—American expansion had been blunted, the Pacific railroad and the free-land policy still awaited passage. Popular sovereignty had become hopelessly entangled in abstract discussion over the slavery question. Still, a brief look at Douglas's own picture of America, his faith in its mission and his hopes for its future, may provide us with a better understanding of his generation. It may also help us to appreciate the quality and the dimensions assumed by the ideas of progress, destiny, and mission during the exciting and often puzzling years of the mid nineteenth century.

Notes

1. *The United States Magazine and Democratic Review,* I (October, 1837), in Joseph L. Blau, ed., *Social Theories of Jacksonian Democracy: Representative Writings of the Period 1825–1850* (New York, N.Y., 1954), 32. Two pioneer studies of these ideas in early nineteenth-century America are Albert K. Weinberg, *Manifest Destiny: A Study of Nationalist Expansionism in American History* (Baltimore, Md., 1935), and Arthur A. Ekirch, Jr., *The Idea of Progress in America, 1815–1860* (New York, N.Y., 1944). A more recent study of the idea of progress which emphasizes its conservative character is Rush Welter, "The Idea of Progress in America: An Essay on Ideas and Method," *Journal of the History of Ideas,* XVI (June, 1955), 401–15. A general treatment of the idea of mission is Edward McNall Burns, *The American Idea of Mission: Concepts of National Purpose and Destiny* (New Brunswick, N.J., 1957); a recent study of the religious elements in the idea of mission is Ernest Lee Tuveson, *Redeemer Nation: The Idea of America's Millenial Role* (Chicago, Ill., 1968). Frederick Merk has examined the relationship between manifest destiny and territorial expansion in *Manifest Destiny and Mission in American History: A Reinterpretation* (New York,

N.Y., 1963); Norman Graebner, adopting a narrow view of manifest destiny, discounts its importance in territorial expansion in *Empire on the Pacific: A Study in American Continental Expansion* (New York, N.Y., 1955). See also Graebner's *Manifest Destiny* (Indianapolis, Ind., 1968) for a discussion of the relationship between manifest destiny and diplomacy. For a brief, incisive treatment of these ideas "in the total pattern of the American mind," see Russel B. Nye, *This Almost Chosen People: Essays in the History of American Ideas* (East Lansing, Mich., 1966).

2. Douglas to Julius N. Granger, December 15, 1833; Robert W. Johannsen, ed., *The Letters of Stephen A. Douglas* (Urbana, Ill., 1961), 3; Johannsen, ed., *The Lincoln-Douglas Debates of 1858* (New York, N.Y., 1965), 158.

3. Springfield *Illinois Daily Register,* April 8, 1851.

4. *Congressional Globe,* 28 Cong., 1 Sess., Appendix, 601 (June 3, 1844); *Washington Union,* January 9, 1853.

5. *Washington Union,* January 11, 1852.

6. *Cong. Globe,* 33 Cong., 1 Sess., Appendix, 337 (March 3, 1854).

7. Springfield *Illinois Daily Register,* February 5, 1852; *Washington States and Union,* October 11, 1860.

8. *Washington Union,* October 4, 1851.

9. *Cong. Globe,* 32 Cong., 1 Sess., 569 (March 30, 1848).

10. *Cong. Globe,* 32 Cong., 3 Sess., Appendix, 274, 275 (March 16, 1853).

11. *Cong. Globe,* 28 Cong., 2 Sess., 226 (January 31, 1845); 32 Cong., 1 Sess., 70 (December 11, 1851).

12. *Washington Union,* June 11, 1852.

13. *Cong. Globe,* 34 Cong., 3 Sess., 852 (February 24, 1857).

14. *Cong. Globe,* 32 Cong., 3 Sess., Appendix, 273 (March 16, 1853). For a discussion of the context in which Douglas developed his image of Europe, see Cushing Strout, *The American Image of the Old World* (New York, N.Y., 1963).

15. *Cong. Globe,* 32 Cong., 1 Sess., 71 (December 11, 1851); 32 Cong., 3 Sess., Appendix, 272, 274 (March 16, 1853).

16. *Cong. Globe,* 35 Cong., 1 Sess., 2746 (June 7, 1858).

17. *Washington Union,* January 9, 1853; *Cong. Globe,* 32 Cong., 2 Sess., 870 (February 26, 1853); *New York Herald,* September 3, 1852.

18. *Cong. Globe,* 34 Cong., 3 Sess., 420 (January 22, 1857); 30 Cong., 1 Sess., 964 (July 20, 1848); 31 Cong., 2 Sess., 132 (December 30, 1850).

19. *Washington Union,* March 13, 1851; *Cong. Globe,* 31 Cong., 1 Sess., 87 (December 27, 1849); Springfield *Illinois Daily Register,* November 6, 1851; *Cong. Globe,* 32 Cong., 1 Sess., 920 (March 30, 1852).

20. *Cong. Globe,* 29 Cong., 1 Sess., 749–50 (April 29, 1846); *New York Times,* January 13, 15, 16, 1855; William J. Rhees, ed., *The Smithsonian Institution: Journals of the Board of Regents, Reports of Committees, Statistics, etc.* (*Smithsonian Miscellaneous Collections,* XVIII; Washington, D.C., 1880), 179.

21. *National Intelligencer*, November 10, 1853.

22. Springfield *Illinois Daily Register*, November 6, 1851; *Washington Union*, January 31, 1852; *Cong. Globe*, 31 Cong., 1 Sess., 264 (January 30, 1850).

23. *Speech of Hon. Stephen A. Douglas, on the "Measures of Adjustment," Delivered in the City Hall, Chicago, October 23, 1850* (Washington, D.C., 1851), 14; *Cong. Globe*, 31 Cong., 1 Sess., Appendix, 372, 373 (March 14, 1850).

24. *Cong. Globe*, 34 Cong., 1 Sess., 1956 (August 6, 1856); Springfield *Illinois State Register*, April 8, 1851; *Cong. Globe*, 33 Cong., 1 Sess., Appendix, 788 (May 25, 1854).

25. *Washington Union*, January 11, 1852; Douglas to Committee of Invitation . . . , November 17, 1858, Johannsen, ed., *Letters*, 430.

26. *Cong. Globe*, 31 Cong., 1 Sess., Appendix, 365 (March 13, 1850).

27. Douglas to Asa Whitney, October 15, 1845, Johannsen, ed., *Letters*, 127–33.

28. *New York Herald*, January 1, 1859.

29. *Cong. Globe*, 34 Cong., 3 Sess., 852 (February 24, 1857); *New York Herald*, December 6, 1858; Springfield *Illinois State Register*, June 13, 1845.

30. *Cong. Globe*, 34 Cong., 1 Sess., 1072 (May 1, 1856).

31. *Cong. Globe*, 28 Cong., 2 Sess., Appendix, 68 (January 6, 1845); Springfield *Illinois State Register*, June 13, 1845; *Washington Union*, January 11, 1852; *Cong. Globe*, 28 Cong., 2 Sess., 225–26 (January 31, 1845).

32. *Cong. Globe*, 28 Cong., 2 Sess., 227 (January 31, 1845); *Washington Union*, January 11, June 11, 1852.

33. *New York Herald*, December 6, 1858, January 1, 1859; *Cong. Globe*, 35 Cong., 1 Sess., 223 (January 7, 1858).

34. Springfield *Illinois Daily Register*, April 8, 1851.

35. *Cong. Globe*, 32 Cong., 3 Sess., Appendix, 276 (March 16, 1853); Springfield *Illinois State Journal*, September 8, 1858.

36. John Reynolds to John J. Hardin, May 4, 1844, John J. Hardin Papers, Chicago Historical Society.

37. Springfield *Illinois State Register*, April 19, 1844.

38. *Cong. Globe*, 28 Cong., 1 Sess., Appendix, 601 (June 3, 1844); Springfield *Illinois State Register*, October 4, 1844; *Cong. Globe*, 29 Cong., 1 Sess., 559 (March 26, 1846).

39. *Cong. Globe*, 31 Cong., 1 Sess., Appendix, 365 (March 13, 1850).

40. *Cong. Globe*, 29 Cong., 1 Sess., 559 (March 26, 1846); 31 Cong., 1 Sess., Appendix, 365 (March 13, 1850).

41. *Cong. Globe*, 28 Cong., 1 Sess., Appendix, 599–602 (June 3, 1844); 28 Cong., 2 Sess., 226 (January 31, 1845).

42. *Cong. Globe*, 29 Cong., 1 Sess., 259 (January 27, 1846).

43. *Cong. Globe*, 28 Cong., 1 Sess., Appendix, 601 (June 3, 1844); 28 Cong., 2 Sess., 226 (January 31, 1845).

44. *Cong. Globe*, 29 Cong., 1 Sess., 259–60 (January 27, 1846).

45. *Cong. Globe,* 29 Cong., 1 Sess., 260 (January 27, 1846).

46. *Cong. Globe,* 28 Cong., 2 Sess., 226 (January 31, 1845); 28 Cong., 1 Sess., Appendix, 600 (June 3, 1844).

47. *Cong. Globe,* 30 Cong., 1 Sess., 221–22 (February 1, 1858).

48. Douglas to James K. Polk, August 25, 1845, Johannsen, ed., *Letters,* 119–20.

49. Springfield *Illinois Daily Register,* April 8, 1851, October 27, 1849.

50. *Cong. Globe,* 29 Cong., 1 Sess., Appendix, 903 (May 13, 1846); *Washington Union,* February 1, 1847; *Cong. Globe,* 30 Cong., 1 Sess., Appendix, 227 (February 1, 1848).

51. *Cong. Globe,* 32 Cong., 2 Sess., Appendix, 171–72 (February 14, 1853).

52. *Washington Union,* November 7, 1849.

53. Douglas to Asa Whitney, October 15, 1845, Johannsen, ed., *Letters,* 130–32.

54. Douglas to J. H. Crane, D. M. Johnson, and L. J. Eastin, December 17, 1853, Johannsen, ed., *Letters,* 270.

55. Charles Fletcher to Douglas, August 3, 1846, owned by Martin F. Douglas.

56. *Cong. Globe,* 32 Cong., 2 Sess., 508 (February 4, 1853).

57. *Ibid.;* Douglas to Whitney, October 15, 1845, Johannsen, ed., *Letters,* 130–31.

58. *Cong Globe,* 32 Cong., 2 Sess., 508–9 (February 4, 1853).

59. Douglas to Crane, Johnson, and Eastin, December 17, 1853, Johannsen, ed., *Letters,* 270–71.

60. *Cong. Globe,* 35 Cong., 1 Sess., 1644–46 (April 17, 1858).

61. *Cong. Globe,* 32 Cong., 2 Sess., 508 (February 4, 1853). For a discussion of somewhat similar views expressed by Thomas Hart Benton and Asa Whitney, with a brief but limited mention of Douglas, see Henry Nash Smith, *Virgin Land: The American West as Symbol and Myth* (Cambridge, Mass., 1950), 19–34.

62. Douglas to Whitney, October 15, 1845, Johannsen, ed., *Letters,* 131.

63. Douglas to Crane, Johnson, and Eastin, December 17, 1853, *ibid.,* 270; *Cong. Globe,* 33 Cong., 1 Sess., Appendix, 337 (March 3, 1854).

64. *Cong. Globe,* 32 Cong., 1 Sess., 1684, 1760 (July 8, 13, 1852).

65. *Cong Globe,* 31 Cong., 1 Sess., 263 (January 30, 1850).

66. Speech in Dubuqe, Iowa, October 11, 1860, quoted in Rita McKenna Carey, *The First Campaigner: Stephen A. Douglas* (New York, N.Y., 1964), 87–88.

67. Douglas's interest in the territories has too often been studied solely in its relation to the slavery question. For a discussion of his doctrine of popular sovereignty in a Western context, see the author's article, "Stephen A. Douglas, Popular Sovereignty and the Territories," *The Historian,* XXII (August, 1960), 378–95.

68. Springfield *Illinois Daily Register,* April 8, 1851.

69. J. Madison Cutts, *A Brief Treatise Upon Constitutional and Party Questions, and the History of Political Parties* (New York, N.Y., 1866), 124.

70. See Robert W. Johannsen, "The Kansas-Nebraska Act and Territorial Government in the United States," *Territorial Kansas: Studies Commemorating the Centennial* (Lawrence, Kans., 1954), 17–32.

71. *Speech of Hon. Stephen A. Douglas, on the "Measures of Adjustment," Delivered in the City Hall, Chicago, October 23, 1850* (Washington, D.C., 1851), 6.

72. *Ibid.*

73. *Speeches of Senator S. A. Douglas, on the Occasion of his Public Reception by the Citizens of New Orleans, Philadelphia, and Baltimore* (Washington, D.C., 1859), 10.

74. Speech at Columbus, Ohio, September 7, 1859, Harry V. Jaffa and Robert W. Johannsen, eds., *In the Name of the People: Speeches and Writings of Lincoln and Douglas in the Ohio Campaign of 1859* (Columbus, O., 1959), 147.

75. *Ibid.*, 148, 150.

Indian Allotments
Preceding
The Dawes Act

Paul W. Gates, Cornell University

To some historians of the West
the policy of breaking up Indian reserves by allotting them in
severalty seems to have had its origin in the Dawes Act of 1887
when a combination of land-hungry Westerners and impractical
Eastern idealists are said to have put this allotment act through
Congress. The fact that allotments had been made to Indians in
the colonial period, were resorted to increasingly in the early
years of nationhood, and long before 1887 had become a regular
feature of American policy toward the red men is quite neglected.
Many thousands of allotments for more than seventeen million
acres had been patented to Indians by 1887.[1]

Allotments and individual reserves, generally of 160 to 640
acres, early appeared in treaties with Indians—granted to chiefs,

subchiefs, and other headmen, to traders, agents, missionaries, half-breeds, and other influential people who had a part in wresting from the aborigines surrenders of their land.[2] That the allotments when patented quickly fell into the hands of traders and agents who had written provisions into the treaties providing for them is a clear indication of the purpose for which they were granted. Individual reserves were also another way of enabling the chiefs and headmen to settle their obligations to traders. Associated with provisions for these reserves were sections requiring that much of the money being paid for the cessions of land should go to John Jacob Astor and his partners in the American Fur Company, Pierre Chouteau, and the firm of W. G. & G. W. Ewing and other trading firms, to satisfy their claims.

The first of a long line of individual reserves or grants appears in a treaty of 1805 made with the Choctaws. This was a reserve of 5,120 acres in southwestern Alabama which was to be conveyed to the two daughters of Samuel Mitchell "by Molly, a Chaktaw woman." It was later partitioned and sold by the Mitchell family. A second reserve of 1,500 acres was to be conveyed to John M'Grew.[3] How threats and bribes were combined to induce compliance may be seen in negotiations involving Andrew Jackson that led to a treaty and a cession of land by the Chickasaws in 1816. Major Levi Colbert ("beloved chief") and Colonel George Colbert were promised three well located tracts of land on the Tennessee and Tombigbee rivers. These grants were confirmed and later sold back to the United States. Another tract of 640 acres was reserved for John M'Cleish and in 1816 confirmed to him and his heirs. In addition to rations and liquor provided during the negotiations, it was stipulated that in consideration of the conciliatory disposition evinced during the negotiations of this treaty, ten chiefs including Levi Colbert and an interpreter should be paid $150 each in goods or cash and to thirteen military leaders $100 each and to William Colbert should be provided a lifetime annuity of $100. Two years later the Chickasaws again were induced to surrender land, this time in western Tennessee; and in consideration of a "friendly and conciliatory disposition," twenty-one chiefs including Levi and George Colbert were to be given $100 or $150 each.[4]

In two treaties of 1817 and 1819 with the Cherokees—who

were under the greatest pressure to remove west of the Mississippi, as were all the Five Civilized Tribes—the allotment plan and the cession of land in trust were resorted to. These were to become the means of extensive abuses in the future. These allotments and trust lands were never to become a part of the public domain and subject to the land laws. Every Cherokee head of a family who might wish to become a citizen was to be given an allotment of 640 acres to include his improvements "in which they will have a life estate with a reversion in fee simple to their children." In the event of the allottees' removal, their lands were to revert to the United States. Grants in fee simple of 640 acres were made to thirty-eight named persons, and one grant of 1,280 acres was made to Major John Walker. Some ninety thousand acres in Alabama were ceded "in trust for the Cherokee nation as a school fund."[5]

The difficulties into which the federal officials fell in trying to administer the individual reserves and allotments provided for in the Cherokee treaty of 1819 scarcely argued for a continuation of this practice. Some 311 Indians accepted allotments, but neither Georgia nor North Carolina would concede the right of the federal government to convey them, and instead compensation had to be given the Indians in the Treaty of New Echota of 1835, by which the Cherokees ceded all their tribal lands remaining in Alabama, Georgia, Tennessee, and North Carolina. In return, they received a fee title to seven million acres in present Oklahoma, $5 million for the surrender of their land and $600,000 to pay for allotments denied them, for other claims, and for the cost of migrating to their new reserve.[6]

The Choctaws were the next of the Civilized Tribes to give way before the inexorable pressure of the settlers intruding into their lands, the states extending their jurisdiction over them, and the federal officials threatening, cajoling, bribing, and dividing them into conflicting groups. In return for the cession in 1820 of a choice tract of west-central Mississippi, including a portion of the Yazoo Delta, a tract of equal size in present western Arkansas was promised, and a blanket, kettle, rifle gun, bullet moulds and nippers, and ammunition sufficient for hunting and defense for one year were given to each member who would emigrate. Also 145,920 acres were to be sold for the benefit of Indian schools.

Members of the tribe who had made settlements within the surrendered area and wished to remain on them were each to have 640 acres surrounding their homes. Members preferring to move from their improved land were to be paid its full value.[7]

It soon appeared that the Arkansas tract had already been taken up in part by settlers, and in 1825 the Choctaws again had to go through the same dreary charade of being urged, bribed, or compelled to surrender a tract for the promise of another in the West. Federal officials, including John C. Calhoun, are described as systematically corrupting and intoxicating the Indians during the negotiations leading to the treaty of 1825. Those Indians who preferred to remain on their 640-acre allotments were given the right to sell them in fee simple with the approval of the President.[8] Previously inalienable allotments were opened to sale, subject to the consent of an officer of the government. This was the route most later allotments were to take.[9]

Land-hungry Mississippians were not satisfied by the slow removal of the Indians and the long withholding of parts of the state from settlement. To speed the migration of the Indians, the state extended its laws to persons and property within the remaining reserves, thereby compelling the United States to take more drastic steps against the unwilling natives. A treaty forced upon the Choctaws at Dancing Rabbit Creek in 1830 by systematic bullying by Secretary of War Eaton provided for a new country for them west of Arkansas Territory to which they were given title in fee simple in exchange for another huge cession in central Mississippi and Alabama.[10]

The Choctaws were rashly promised that "no Territory or State shall ever have a right to pass laws for the Government of the Choctaw Nation . . . , and that no part of the land granted them shall ever be embraced in any Territory or State." Members who preferred to remain on their 640-acre allotments east of the Mississippi and who should live on them for five years were to have a fee-simple title. In addition to the 640-acres each head of a family was entitled to, he might have 320 acres for each unmarried child over ten years of age and 160 acres for each dependent child under ten. Finally, 20,420 acres were to be divided among twelve chiefs, and 458,600 acres as cultivation claims were to be allowed to 1,600 heads of families, who were entitled to sell them

to the government for fifty cents an acre.[11] One could well say
that rarely was the treaty-making power so used to convince the
headmen that they could profit by signing personally and quickly,
no matter how badly past policies were repudiated. Supplemen-
tary articles to the treaty provided for additional allotments
amounting to 54,880 acres to named individuals. If the varieties
of claims and allotments seems complicated, the management and
disposition of the allotments and trust lands involved the government in even more intricate questions.[12]

Negotiations with the Chickasaws in 1832 and 1834 produced
treaties whereby the Indians ceded in trust all their lands east of
the Mississippi after making allotments of lands to members of the
tribe and white men who had cooperated with them. Allottments
were to range from 320 acres for orphans to 640 acres for each unmarried person over twenty-one, 1,280 acres for families of two
to five persons, 1,920 acres for families of six to ten, and 2,560
acres for families of more than ten. Ownership of one to nine
slaves entitled one to 320 acres extra, and for more than ten slaves,
640 acres. The allotments were to be granted in fee simple, but
were subject to alienation only with the approval of two chiefs
and an officer of the government. In addition to these allotments,
four sections each were to be given to "their beloved and faithful
old Chief" Levi Colbert and to George and Martin Colbert and
three other headmen. Twelve and a half sections were granted
other influential Indians and white men.[13]

After the survey of the cession, the selection of the allotments,
and special reserves, the remaining lands were to be offered for
sale as trust lands and not public domain, at $1.25 an acre.
Fearing that combinations of buyers might prevent competitive
bidding, as was a common practice at public-land sales, the
Chickasaws insisted that no such combination should be permitted without, however, determining how the usual buyers club
law could be avoided. Unsold lands continued to be subject to
purchase after the auction at $1.25 an acre for a year, when their
price was to be reduced to $1.00 an acre; during the next year they
could be sold at $.50 an acre, in the fourth year at $.25, and
thereafter at $.125. After the deduction of all costs of survey and
sale, the income was to be available for the Indians.

The reader will not be surprised to learn that within a short time the bulk of the allotments had passed into the hands of speculating individuals, partnerships, and land companies whose acquisitions ranged as high as 210,658 acres for the American Land Company, 206,787 for the New York and Mississippi Land Company, and 334,602 for Edward Orne, who represented three other land companies. Mary Young found that the first thirty-three buyers acquired ownership of 1,576,484 acres of allotments. An additional 461,437 acres were sold in amounts of 1,000 to 10,000 acres.[14]

The trust lands were offered in 1836 when 1,304,150 acres were sold for an average of $1.66 an acre. The graduated prices allowed by the treaty brought yearly average prices down to $.18 in 1840 and $.13 in 1850. What is more important, a combination of speculators got much of the land just as they and others had engrossed so many of the allotments. Sixty-one buyers acquired 1,380,311 acres in amounts of 10,000 or more. Buyers whose purchases exceeded 2,000 acres acquired 1,990,592 acres. Of the 6,718,856-acre cession of Chickasaw lands, at least two-thirds of the allotments and trust lands passed to large buyers. On none of the land were squatters given protection through preemption.[15]

Step by step the Creek Indians, once the possessors of the greater portion of Georgia, surrendered their claim between 1790 and 1827, retaining only a five-million-acre tract west of the Chattahoochee in Alabama. Then in 1832 they, too, were compelled to cede this reserve, but outright, not in trust. However, the treaty provided for ninety full-section reserves to as many principal chiefs and half-section allotments for every head of a family and twenty sections in trust to be sold for the benefit of orphan members of the tribe. Altogether, 2,187,200 acres were allotted. As in other treaties providing for allotments and in accordance with the wishes of the local people, there was no indication that the grants were intended to aid the natives in becoming permanent residents of their tract. Alienation of the allotments was made easier than was the case with individual reserves of other Indians, and there was a scramble by white speculators to buy them. So badly gouged and cheated were the Creeks, despite some slight efforts by the government to assure that a fair price was paid, that it was even proposed to have the allotments bought up by the government and possibly made a part of the public domain. Mary Young lists twenty-four groups and individuals who obtained 1,443,002 acres of Creeks allotments, the largest acquisition being 477,089 acres. Purchasers of 2,000 to 10,000 acres obtained an additional 276,986 acres. The disposal of the allotments to speculating groups brought little return to the Indians as well as great confusion over the right and fairness of the conveyances to the officials involved and surely to the ultimate developers of the land.[16]

North of the Ohio, individual reserves and allotments first appeared in Indian treaties in 1817, setting precedents not easy to overlook in later negotiations. In his instructions to Lewis Cass concerning proposals for discussions with the Indians, George Graham, Acting Secretary of War, suggested that those natives who wished to remain in Ohio might be given "a life estate" in individual reserves "which should descend to his children in fee . . . and that those who do not wish to remain on those terms should have a body of land allotted to them on the west of the Mississippi." Graham added somewhat indiscreetly that there was little expectation that any large cession of land could be obtained for the prices previously paid.[17]

Lewis Cass and Duncan McArthur, the two negotiators who met with the Wyandot, Seneca, Delaware, Shawnee, Potawatomi, Ottawa, and Chippewa tribes, had reason to be apprehensive that they went too far in providing individual reserves and in promising annuities for the cession they secured. In return for the surrender of 3,880,320 acres in northwestern Ohio, northeastern Indiana, and southern Michigan, the tribes were to receive small increases in their annuities. These were slight enough to be considered "unconscionable" by the Indian Claims Commission nearly a century and a half later. The questionable parts of the treaty were the provisions for limited reserves, individual and group, amounting to 271,800 acres, which were to be patented in fee simple with the power of conveying them. In the prose of Cass and McArthur, the persons to whom the reserves were to be given were "almost all . . . Indians by blood." In all cases "it was the urgent wish of the Indians that land should be granted to these persons. To have refused these requests would have embodied against us an interest and created obstacles, which no effort of ours would have defeated or surmounted." It is likely that the traders who expected to gain ownership of the reserves threatened to prevent any cession until the individual reserves were included in the treaty.[18] It was later charged that some of the individual reserves provided for in this treaty and in a treaty with the Chippewas of 1819 were intended for whites who had assumed Indian names and fraudulently claimed Indian children, thus being entitled to consideration. Cass's marked reliance on the word of traders had apparently led him into a serious error.[19]

Congressmen expressed strong doubts about the "unprecedented" privilege of allowing the grantees of individual reserves to sell them to whomever they wished. It was "at variance with the general principles on which intercourse with Indians had been conducted," said the Committee on Public Lands. If alienable reserves were allowed, there would soon be pressure to have reservations allotted to members of the tribes, and the very basis of government policy toward the Indians would be weakened. Secretary of War Calhoun said that the Senate would "probably ratify no treaty which recognizes in the Indian the right of acquiring individual property with the power of selling, except to the United States."[20] Because of the strong opposition of Congress, a second treaty was arranged with the tribes whereby a number of group reservations were enlarged but their status was changed. They were to be held "in the same manner as Indian reservations have been heretofore held," that is as occupancy rights that could only be sold to the government, and individual reserves were made alienable only with the approval of the President. For a time thereafter, a similar restriction was written into other treaties. It came to mean approval by the Office of Indian Affairs, and this, in notable instances, was not difficult to secure.[21] George Graham, Commissioner of the General Land Office, said in 1825 that there was "generally no objection to the Sale of the Lands reserved to Indians," but he thought care should be taken to assure that a fair price was obtained.[22]

Once the importance of including individual reserves in treaties was conceded by the Indian Office, it was found almost impossible to win concessions from the more advanced tribes without them. Such groups were already influenced by and deeply obligated to traders who were turning to land speculations as the fur trade declined. This was notably true of the negotiations with tribes of the Ohio Valley and the border lands of the Great Lakes. Examples are treaties with the Potawatomis, the Weas, and the Delawares in which seventeen individual reserves containing 11,360 acres alienable only with the approval of the President were granted. In a treaty with the Miami tribe of Indiana, whereby a large part of central Indiana and a small tract in Ohio were ceded, there appeared a variation in favor of a chief who was notoriously influenced by traders. Individual Miamis were to be given 31,360 acres of which 25,600 were alienable only with the "approbation of the President," but 5,760 acres, granted to Principal Chief Jean Baptiste Richardville, were conveyed in fee simple without any restriction on alienation. All the reserves were located close to prospective town sites along the Wabash and St. Mary's rivers.[23] In two treaties of 1819 and 1821 with the Saginaw Bay Chippewas and the combined Chippewa, Ottawa, and Potawatomi tribes, by which nearly half the lower peninsula of Michigan was ceded, twenty-one small reserves containing 162,000 acres were withheld and forty-five tracts containing 26,240 acres were assigned to individuals. They were "never to be leased or conveyed by the grantees or their heirs . . . without the permission of the President."[24]

The Chouteau family of St. Louis was long and profitably associated with the Osage Indians, whose claim to land in present Kansas, Missouri, and Arkansas exceeded eighteen million acres. In 1825 the Osages were persuaded to cede some ten million acres of their huge claim, in return for which they were to be paid an annuity of $7,000 in merchandise or money for twenty years and were to be provided with supplies upon ratification. A debt of $1,000, said to be owed to Augustus Chouteau, was to be paid, and forty-two square-mile tracts were reserved for half-breeds, including James G. and Alexander Chouteau. Fifty-four tracts of 640 acres each (34,560) were to be set aside as trust lands and sold for the support of schools for the Osages. In the same year the Kansas Indians agreed that François Chouteau was to be paid $500.[25] These were small sums, however, in comparison with those later conceded the Chouteau family and associates.

The Miami treaty of 1826 called for special reserves in Indiana of 17,600 acres of which 2,240 acres were for Jean or John

B. Richardville, making his personal ownership 8,000 acres. Other members of the Richardville family received 2,560 acres in the two Miami treaties. Four sections, or 2,560 acres, were assigned to Lagrow, a Miami chief. Seven days after the treaty was signed, it was arranged that the land was to go to John Tipton upon the death of Lagrow. Lagrow died just two months later, and when news of the conveyance to Tipton, who had been the chief person negotiating the treaty, became known, it created a scandal. The validity of the transaction was questioned, but President Jackson seems to have approved it. Eight years later Tipton paid Lagrow's heirs $4,000 for the 2,560 acres to quiet gossip, though probably not to satisfy his conscience.[26] Persons like Tipton were shrewd enough to locate the individual reserves on spots where towns and cities were likely to develop.

Article 7 of the Miami treaty also provided for the purchase by the United States of 6,720 acres which had been granted to individuals in the treaty of 1818. For this acreage $25,708 was to be paid, or $3.83 an acre. One wonders if these eight-year-old reserves purchased at this price were then sold as public lands at $1.25 an acre.[27]

As Governor of Michigan Territory and Superintendent of Indian Affairs for the Michigan-Indiana area (1813–1831) and later as Secretary of War (1831–1836), Lewis Cass played a leading role in the administration of Indian relations. He had negotiated nineteen Indian treaties[28] and had long since learned that cessions of land could only be obtained if individual reserves were granted and provisions were made for the payment of the Indians' trader debts. In 1826 Cass had a part in drafting the treaties with the Chippewas, the Potawatomis, and the Miamis whereby large tracts of strategically located as well as rich lands suitable for agriculture were surrendered, large sums in money or goods paid, the annuities increased, and many individual reserves granted. In the Chippewa treaty of 1826 the half-breeds were promised section reserves on the St. Mary's River in Michigan. The reserves were to be laid out "in the ancient French manner" of six- to ten-arpents frontage on the river and forty-arpents deep. Also some seventy-seven allotments amounting to 49,280 acres were assigned mostly to the Indian wives and children of white traders and trappers, presumably without power of alienation.[29]

In 1826 the Potawatomis ceded a 130-mile tract bordering the Wabash. To the members of the Burnett family, who had been assigned 5,120 acres in the treaty of 1821, an additional 4,480 acres were now granted. To other chiefs, half-breeds, and orphans were given 15,840 acres, and to fifty-eight "scholars in the Carey Mission School" of Isaac McCoy were given 160 acres each. All individual reserves were alienable only with approval of the President.[30]

Cass next negotiated a treaty with the Potawatomis in 1828, which provided eighteen individual reserves totaling 10,240 acres and authorized the purchase of an individual reserve of 640 acres granted by the treaty of 1821 for $1,000. Other treaties that came under Cass's jurisdiction provided for 8,960 acres in individual reserves in Michigan to the Chippewas, Ottawas, and Potawatomis and 26,880 acres of reserves partly in the mineral district of Illinois and Wisconsin to the Winnebagos.[31]

Trust lands appear again in a treaty of 1830 with the Delawares, in which 23,040 acres of "the best land" within a larger cession in southeast Missouri were to be sold to raise a fund for the support of schools.[32]

Although there was strong opposition to granting alienable reserves to full-blooded Indians, except for the Chickasaws, Choctaws, and Creeks of the South, there was less objection at the time to giving reserves to half-breeds. In a treaty of 1830 with the Sac and Fox and three Sioux bands—Omaha, Iowa, and Missouri—two tracts were set aside "to bestow upon half breeds." The tracts were to be held "by the same title, and in the same manner that other Indian Titles are held," but the President was authorized to convey to any of the half-breeds up to 640 acres in fee simple. Because the Sioux half-breeds refused to have anything to do with the 200,000-acre reserve in Minnesota, it was bought back by the United States for $150,000 in 1851. After the allotment of most of the second reserve in Nebraska, the balance of 6,500 acres was sold between 1878 and 1882 for $21,531.[33]

In the Winnebago treaties of 1829 and 1832 wherein large areas in Wisconsin and Illinois were surrendered, 30,720 acres in individual reserves were granted, of which the families of Pierre and John B. Pacquette received 9,600 acres, Catherine Myott received 1,280 acres, and her daughter received 640 acres.[34] One of the elder Myott's sections was conveyed to Henry Gratiot, who signed the treaty in which it had been allowed, and the other was acquired by Nicholas Boilvin, son of a long-time Indian agent at Prairie du Chien. The conveyance of these individual reservations shows that they were floating rights which could be located anywhere within the cession. The Boilvin tract was used to lay out a town. There is no indication that official approval was needed to sell the tracts.[35]

Between 1831 and 1842 the Ohio Indians were divested of title to their remaining lands, amounting to 419,384 acres plus 4,996 acres in Michigan. The Sandusky Senecas, the Senecas and Shawnee of Lewistown, the Shawnee, the Ottawas, and the Wyandots were promised in exchange five reservations containing 449,000 acres in the eastern front of the Indian country to which Eastern tribes were being moved. Since all but the Wyandots held their Ohio reservations in fee, their Kansas reserves were also granted in fee, but the Wyandot reserve was not so granted. Actually, the 109,144-acre tract promised them in 1842 was never turned over to them, and instead they were compelled to buy 23,040 acres at the junction of the Kansas and Missouri rivers from the Delawares for two dollars an acre. This included the site of present Kansas City, Kansas. In 1850 the Wyandots were paid $185,000 for the reserve they never received, which equalled $1.25 an acre, or all that the United States could hope to derive from the sale of the land.[36]

Three hundred thousand acres of the 419,384 acres thus ceded by the Seneca, Shawnee, Ottawa, and Wyandot Indians were surrendered in trust with the stipulation that they were to be sold to the highest bidder. After the deduction of the costs of survey and sale, the sums advanced to the natives, and $1.25 an acre for the 40,000 acres conveyed by the Sandusky Senecas and $.70 an acre for the other lands, the balance was to be held for the respective tribes.

In the treaty of 1833 with the Ottawas the six Indian grantees were denied the power of alienation without presidential approval; the other grantees presumably were to have that power. By the Wyandot treaty of 1836 seven chiefs were allowed the full

price the government received for a section each in the reserve
being ceded. Extraordinarily valuable floating rights of 640 acres
to be patented in fee simple were granted thirty-five leaders of
the tribe by a treaty of 1842. They could be located on "any land
west of the Missouri set apart for Indian use, not already claimed
or occupied by any person or tribe." Like the better known Valen-
tine scrip of a later time, because of the ease and speed with
which it could be laid on prospective town sites, these floats were
used by speculators to enter the land on which Lawrence, Em-
poria, Manhattan, and Topeka were later established.[37]

Altogether there were thirty-two individual reserves granted
by these treaties to thirty-seven mixed-bloods, orphans, chiefs, and
whites in Ohio for a total of 21,960 acres. All were made alienable
sooner or later, including those of Indians. There is little evidence
that they remained the property of the grantees for long.

Traders working with the Potawatomi and Miami tribes
whose homes were in the Kankakee and upper Wabash valleys
succeeded in having the largest quantity of individual and group
reserves made in this early period, if we accept the record of
allotments made for the Civilized Tribes of Alabama and Mississippi. In the previously cited treaties of 1818, 1826, and 1828 with
the Potawatomis, provision was made for 39,840 acres of reserves;
and in treaties of 1818 and 1826 with the Miami tribe 45,280 acres
were similarly reserved. Treaties of 1832 gave the Potawatomis
an additional 179,200 acres as reserves, making their total, mostly
in Indiana, 219,040 acres. The Potawatomis were also promised a
reserve in fee simple on the Osage River in the Indian country
"sufficient in extent, and adapted to their habits and wants."[38] The
ink was scarcely dry on the 1832 treaties with the Potawatomis
before the latter were being urged to sell their reserves, and in a
series of treaties 97,280 acres were bought for $.62 to $1.25 an acre,
or an average of $1.06 an acre. At these rates there was no pros-
pect of the government recovering its investment from the lands;
only the traders had profited.

In the drafting of the treaties with the Miami Indians in 1834,
1838, and 1840, when the last of their tribal possessions were
surrendered, the practice of making individual reserves reached
its most absurd extent. Instructions of July 19, 1833, from the War
Department to the agent in charge of negotiations with the Mi-

amis stressed that as many as forty individual reserves could be given, if necessary, and prescribed a top figure of $.50 an acre for a Miami cession. Actually, in the resulting treaty of 1834, only twenty-five individual reserves were granted, but the price paid for the cession was a dollar an acre.[39]

John B. Richardville, principal chief of the Miamis, who already had received 8,000 acres in individual reserves, was given an additional 20,320 acres, and all his holdings were to be conveyed to him in fee. He was also to have $31,800. Francis Godfroy, already the grantee of 4,480 acres, was given 6,400 more and $17,612. The three Miami treaties brought the total reserves granted them to 112,800 acres. A total of $1,133,000 was to be paid for the cessions of these three treaties, a sum far larger than the United States could expect to recover from their sale. The Miami were also promised a reservation in the Indian country of 500,000 acres which was to be guaranteed "to them forever."[40]

So generously paid were the Potawatomi and Miami Indians for their Indiana land that they became among the best-endowed of all Indians. In 1853 the per capita return to the Miamis in the form of annuities and other payments was $87, that of the Eel River Miamis was $68, in both cases exceeding that of all other tribes. The per capita payments of annuities and other grants to the Potawatomis were exceeded by those paid three other tribes (the Sac and Fox of Missouri, the Sac and Fox of Mississippi, and the Winnebagos), but the total paid the Potawatomis, $91,804, was only exceeded by that of the Winnebagos, $97,485.[41]

Some Indian officials were becoming increasingly troubled by the fact that individual reserves were being granted so extensively. It is not clear, however, whether their concern stemmed from knowledge that for the most part the reserves quickly fell into the hands of traders and others exploiting the ignorance of the natives. After Lewis Cass (that warm friend, and some would say pliant tool, of the traders) became Secretary of War, he instructed commissioners to treat with the Potawatomis for cessions of their land in 1833 as follows:

> Decline, in the first instances, to grant any reservations either to the Indians or others, and endeavor to prevail upon them all to remove. Should you find this impracticable, and that

granting some reservations will be unavoidable, that course may then be taken in the usual manner and upon the usual conditions. But I am very anxious that individual reservations should be circumscribed within the narrowest possible limits. The whites and the half-breeds press upon the Indians, and induce them to ask for these gratuities, to which they have no just pretensions; and for which neither the United States nor the Indians receive any real consideration. The practice, though it has long prevailed, is a bad one and should be avoided as far as possible.[42]

A combination of able and aggressive traders stationed at Fort Wayne and Logansport, Indiana, who worked at times closely with Senator John Tipton, completely ignored all such instructions in securing cessions from the Miami and Potawatomi Indians without any sharp disapproval from Cass, but elsewhere in the upper Mississippi Valley individual reserves were halted or kept to a minimum.[43]

The government's reluctance to grant individual reserves is best displayed in the negotiations for three treaties with the combined Chippewa, Ottawa, and Potawatomi Indians of 1833 and with the Ottawas and Chippewas of 1836, whereby some five million acres in Illinois and Wisconsin and from one-third to one-half of Michigan were surrendered to the United States. It was found that the traders who had close relations with these Indians and whose support was essential could be satisfied if provisions were included in the treaties for the payment of the debts of the Indians, real or imaginary, and sums of money equivalent to what the traders might have expected to get from individual reserves. Both these conditions were well met. In the two treaties with the combined tribes $100,000 was provided for "sundry individuals, in behalf of whom reservations were asked, which the Commissioners refused to grant." One hundred and fifty thousand dollars was provided to satisfy the claims of traders and $600,000 for miscellaneous purposes, including an annuity. Three lists of claimants and persons to whom the tribes wished to grant favors were included in the treaty, in all 351 individuals, groups, or companies, some of which were listed for multiple claims. Milo M. Quaife, historian of Chicago, speaks of "the striking display of

greed and dishonesty" of many of those who strove to have doubtful claims included.[44] Largest of the claims were those of the
American Fur Company ($20,300) and of members of the Kinzie
family ($23,216), who had previously had $7,485 paid them under
treaties of 1828 and 1829. Many of the payments were for claims
that Quaife thinks should rightly have been assumed by the
United States, not by the Indians. He expressed surprise that
numerous beneficiaries on the three lists signed the treaties, being
apparently unaware that government negotiators had long worked
with and through traders who received direct and indirect boons
from the treaties, which they had aided in extorting from the
natives and which they had signed as witnesses. The combined
tribes were given a reservation of five million acres in western
Iowa in exchange for their lands in Illinois, Wisconsin, and
Michigan.

During the negotiations leading to a treaty of 1836 with the
combined Ottawa and Chippewa, the traders demanded individual reserves and inclusion in the treaties of specific provisions
for the payment of stipulated claims. Rix Robinson, agent of the
American Fur Company, was heavily in debt to the company, and
the only way he could square his obligations was to get them
paid by the Indians. Ramsay Crooks of the American Fur Company in his numerous instructions to Robinson, who was with the
Indians throughout the discussions leading to the treaty, continu-
ally emphasized that payment for Robinson's claim must be included in any treaty of cession. Individual reserves, with their
chances of hidden profits, were much wanted, and the tribes were
anxious to provide them for their half-breeds; but "the President
having determined" not to allow any, it was agreed that $300,000
was to be allowed for the payment of debts, $150,000 should be
divided among the half-breeds, and $48,180 should be paid the
half-breed children of traders in place of 19,040 acres of individual
reserves, previously assigned. Included in the latter was the sum
of $23,040 for the family of Rix Robinson, most of which, if not
all, went to the American Fur Company. Another claim of $5,600
was included for an employee of the company and his family. The
employee had become blind, and Crooks used his influence to get
a position for him as an interpreter and aid for other members of
his family, thereby passing the burden to the government.[45]

Michigan Chippewas were denied the right to assign individual reserves but were allowed to cede 107,720 acres in trust in 1836 and 1837 with a stipulation that specifically exempted this land from preemption. Because the Indians feared that a combination of purchasers would prevent them from getting the actual value of their land when sold at auction, it was stipulated that for the first two years they were to be sold at no less than $5 an acre and any land remaining thereafter was to be held at $2.50. After five years, remnants of the land could be sold at $.75.[46]

Floating reserves, free to be located within broad areas or whose boundaries were not clearly defined, were much sought after by speculators, as were also reserves specifically located on sites almost certain to be valuable for town locations. In 1825 twenty-seven Kansas half-breeds were assigned full-section reserves on the north side of the Kansas River, which became the object of much intrigue by speculators because of their choice location. Similarly, we have seen how the Wyandot floats of 640 acres each were in great demand because of the priority given them in the selection and entry of land. One unusual reserve was included in a treaty of 1835 with the Caddo Indians of Louisiana, unusual because of its size and because individual reserves were not common in Louisiana or Arkansas. The reserve was for four square leagues—23,040 acres. The grantee, Francois Grappe, a black man, had never been known to have any interest in this land, though it was later estimated to be as much as 34,500 acres because of the way it was blocked out. It was laid on rich alluvial soil bordering the Red River and was subsequently estimated to be worth somewhere between $100,000 and $900,000. The basis for the reserve was an alleged donation of the land by the Indians some thirty-four years earlier. After ratification of the treaty and the approval of the patent, accusations of gross fraud led to a congressional investigation which in 1841 brought out the fact that the tract had been acquired by the commissioner in charge of negotiating the treaty and that in all likelihood arrangements for the purchase from Grappe had been made beforehand. Witnesses also testified that the tract had been improved by white planters, who had a good title dating back to the Spanish period, and furthermore that it was not a part of the Caddo reservation and that the Indians had no right to include it in their cession. The

House Committee on Indian Affairs considered the conduct of the commissioner "unfortunate" and "highly imprudent," scored the testimony in his behalf as utterly worthless, deplored the many fabrications of documents, and was deeply troubled by evidence that the commissioner had not only abused the treaty-making power and suppressed evidence contrary to his interest but had also grossly cheated the Indians in the rations and supplies the government had intended for them. The committee concluded that the district attorney should bring suit to recover the tract, which it declared had been "improperly or fraudulently" included in the treaty.[47] There was a close parallel between the Caddo fraud and the Lagrow reserve which John Tipton had acquired. One may well wonder how Cass could have favored, or the Senate ratified, the Caddo reserve, the largest included in any of the treaties in a period in which reserves were being frowned upon.

One may conclude that thus far, individual reserves to chiefs, orphans, Indian children of white traders, and political hangers-on were not planned with any real thought of enabling the Indians to move from communal or tribal ownership. Instead, they were used in the South as a means of eliminating the Indians by giving them property whose value and use they had no conception of other than as a means to a few drinks. The authors of the allotment policies in the treaties with the Creeks, Choctaws, Chickasaws, and Cherokees were aware that the lands would shortly be in the possession of whites. In the North, the individual reserves offered a means by which the support of traders could be obtained for cessions of land and the removal of the Indians, which would mean the end of their profitable business with the natives. Also, the reserves and stipulations for payment of debts in the treaties would permit the chiefs and headmen to rid themselves of those obligations that the traders had permitted, if they had not actually encouraged, them to accumulate. If the debts were listed in the treaties and it was stipulated that they were to be paid out of the large sums authorized for this purchase, the traders were sure of collecting. Few of the treaties did so list the sums to be paid, but those that did are useful in showing how business was conducted with the Indians and the way in which they were exploited.

Largest of the traders' claims to be paid was that of $133,997 to Pratte, Chouteau & Co., and members of the prolific Chouteau family. Second largest was the $76,587 paid to the firm of W. G. & G. W. Ewing and family. It was G. W. Ewing who informed Senator Tipton of Indiana that the Potawatomi Indians would never leave the Wabash until his firm was paid the full debt owed it.[48] The third largest of the sums paid for Indian debts went to John Jacob Astor and the American Fur Company, $59,961. Actually, the total received by the Astor–American Fur Company was far larger, for they had a major share in the Pratte, Chouteau & Co.; $20,961 assigned to others in the Chicago treaty of 1829 was collected by Astor, and other sums appearing under other names were either for Astor or for the company. G. W. Ewing also had at least $37,000 of claims confirmed in addition to those included in treaties.[49]

The *Wisconsin Herald* of September 27, 1845, a paper published in Prairie du Chien, where more gold and silver was distributed in the form of annuities to Indians than in any other place north of St. Louis, described the scramble by whites to get their hands on the funds being paid the Indians:

> Everybody claimed kin with the Indians and could bring proof of his genealogy about annuity day. How this money was watched all the way from Washington. Speculators, sharpers, gamblers and knaves followed it, and were in Prairie du Chien thick as buzzards when the annuities were to be paid. Princely was the sum disbursed, but thousands . . . stood eager to share it, and the money passed away like the dew.

By 1853 the Indians had surrendered their lands east of the Mississippi and in the first tier of states west of that river with the exception of northern Minnesota and small reservations elsewhere and had moved to the Indian country west of Missouri and Arkansas. In 1844, 85,473 tribesmen lived in the Indian country, much the larger number being in the region west of Arkansas. In 1854, 8,002 intruded Indians were reported in Kansas.[50] There, on clearly defined reservations they dwelt in misery, partly sustained by inadequate government aid and denied the freedom from white intrusions that their treaties had guaranteed them. Westward-moving Mormon refugees seeking relief from religious persecution, pioneers and traders looking for new opportunities in Oregon and New Mexico, and the rush of gold seekers to California in 1849 meant new trouble for the intruded Indians, as did the demand for their removal from the better lands in the Nebraska Territory that had been promised them in perpetuity.

The induced or forced migration of Eastern tribes to the west of the Mississippi began before definite plans for an Indian country had been adopted. Cherokee and Choctaw Indians were assigned reservations in Arkansas, and Delawares and Kickapoos were given tracts in Missouri; but by 1825 the granting of reservations in states or territories was halted. Thereafter, with a few exceptions, Indians were moved into unorganized areas west of Missouri and the Territory of Arkansas.

In 1830 Congressional policy was somewhat crystallized by an act of May 28, which restricted removals to areas that were not included in a state or organized territory but for which the Indian title had been extinguished.[51] This effectively defined the Indian country of present Oklahoma, eastern Kansas, and southeastern Nebraska and Iowa and Minnesota. To induce the Indians to give up their more eastern reserves, the President was authorized solemnly to assure them that "the United States will forever secure and guarantee to them, . . . the country so exchanged . . . and if they prefer it . . . will cause a patent of grant to be made and executed to them for the same." Then followed negotiations with the Senecas and Shawnees; the Kickapoos; the federated Kaskaskia, Peorias, Piankeshaws, and Weas; the Iowas, the Chippewas, and Wyandots, which provided for their removal across the Missouri line; and with the Creeks, Choctaws, Seminoles, Chickasaws, and the Seneca-Shawnees for their removal to reservations in what was to become Indian Territory.

The area west of Arkansas and Missouri contained much first-rate arable land that was suitable for grain and livestock production and capable of sustaining a large population. By 1850 many Westerners had come to the conclusion that an earlier generation had made a major error in designating the region permanent Indian country.

All of Indian Territory, except the panhandle, and the entire front of Kansas were in the possession of some 85,000 intruded Indians. They had been promised their reservations "in full and complete possession . . . as their land and home forever." What then was the prospect of creating new territories and states out of the Indian country? Congressmen knew the way and proceeded to follow it. First, in 1853 they added to the annual appropriation bill for the Office of Indian Affairs a section authorizing the Commissioner of Indian Affairs to negotiate with the Indians west of Missouri and Iowa for the extinguishment of their titles "in whole or in part" and appropriated $50,000 to further that end. Meeting no favorable response, the Commissioner had to report failure in his first effort.[52] Notwithstanding this failure and its plighted word, Congress next adopted the Kansas-Nebraska Act on May 30, 1854, for the creation of two territories and the opening of them to settlement. True, the rights of the Indians were to be preserved, and their reservations were excluded from the territories "until the tribes gave their assent" to such inclusion.

The passage of the Kansas-Nebraska Act was the signal for thousands of land-hungry people, looking for the economic opportunities that new territories provided, to rush across the Missouri line into Kansas. They disregarded Indian ownership, marked out their claims, built improvements that would justify preempting the land, established local government and put it into operation. The carpetbag officials whom the Pierce administration sent in to "rule" and officers of the Army united with the land seekers to break down the morale of the Indians and compel them to remove. Officers at Fort Leavenworth permitted the creation of a town on the Delaware lands and participated in the speculation without making any protest, though all was contrary to law. This lawless example led hundreds of Missourians to penetrate into the Delaware tract and into other reservations, disregarding the admonishments and warnings of Indian officials. The territorial governor took up office on Indian lands, and the legislature authorized polling places and held its session on Shawnee lands and extended county organization over some reservations, all in violation of the treaties and the territory's organic act. Protests to the Secretary of War and to the President were all to no avail; no one save the Indian Commissioner paid any attention to the rights guaranteed the Indians, and he was later to be displaced by a commissioner who was more sympathetic to Western attitudes.

Everywhere "trespass and depredations of every conceivable

kind" were committed against the Indians. They were "personally maltreated, their property stolen, their timber destroyed," and all their rights jeopardized. There seemed no alternative to surrender and removal.[53]

In the twenty-four days before Franklin Pierce signed the Kansas-Nebraska Act, the Commissioner of Indian Affairs had wrested from the reluctant Indians along the eastern border of the Indian country six treaties surrendering portions of their reserves in trust and portions outright, and providing that other parts were either to be retained in tribal ownerships for a time or were to be distributed in allotments to chiefs, headmen, heads of families, and half-breeds. The swarms of land seekers that swept across the Missouri border found no public lands in easy reach but met up with Indian trust lands, allotments, floating allotments, diminished reserves, and reserves still intact. On all of these lands settlement or intrusion by whites was illegal. The conflicts that emerged between the Indian occupants and owners on the one side and the intruders on the other, and the desperate struggles between contending whites for town sites, railroad terminals, county seats, the territorial capital, and land claims I have discussed as a major theme in the Kansas conflict in *Fifty Million Acres: Conflicts over Kansas Land Policy, 1854-1890*.[54]

A summary of the management and disposal of the Kansas Indian lands shows that few tracts in eastern and southern Kansas ever became a part of the public domain but instead were either allotted (at least 525,000 acres) or sold in trust for the benefit of the Indians (10,888,000 acres). On none of this land was homestead to apply, nor could military warrants with their reduction in cost to settlers be accepted for entries. To this extent had Congress permitted setting aside the public-land laws for most of eastern and southern Kansas.

The inclusion of allotments to chiefs, heads of families, and half-breeds had shown land-hungry elements how to hasten the opening of Indian lands and overcome the reluctance of the natives to surrendering their tribal reserves. With the opening of Kansas and Nebraska territories the allotment of Indian lands in severalty became a regular feature of the treaties being negotiated with tribes in the two new territories and in Minnesota, Oregon, Dakota, Colorado, Utah, Montana, Arizona, Idaho, and Wyoming territories and in Michigan. In the seven years following 1854, forty treaties included provisions for surveying the reservations and alloting the lands to individual Indians in amounts from 80 to 320 acres. Fourteen of the treaties applied to Kansas tribes, five to Washington tribes, and smaller numbers to tribes in other territories. In 1867 Indian commissioners included in treaties provisions allowing patents of 160 acres to Indians who had 50 acres fenced, plowed, and in crops (Sisseton and Wahpeton Sioux) or patents to each 40 acres of which 10 acres were cultivated, up to 160 acres (Chippewa of Minnesota). Provisions for assigning land to interested Indians, issuing certificates showing their exclusive possession, and for listing the certificates in the land books of the tribes were included in treaties with the Cheyenne and Arapaho, the Crow, the Sioux, the Navajo, the Shoshone, and the Ute Indians in 1867 and 1868.[55]

Indians in Michigan, Wisconsin, Minnesota, Nebraska, and Kansas were either given alienable titles or titles that could be and were made alienable by officials of the Department of the Interior, but the treaties with the "wild" Indians farther west offered no promise of alienation short of twenty-five years. In these latter cases the title in the allotments was only possessory and could only be conveyed to the United States or to the tribe, or in the event of disease of the allottee, his right could pass on to heirs though it remained inalienable. It was less possible for officials to speed the process of patenting these allotments, as they had done so extensively with allotments in Kansas, Indiana, and Michigan; and these allotments were not subject to taxation, mortgage, or lease.

Commissioners of Indian Affairs Manypenny, in 1855, Dole, in 1863, and E. P. Smith, in 1873, emphasized allotments as a means of inducing the redmen to make improvements on their tracts and to become farmers. The commissioners regarded the policy as the only one that offered a hope of ending tribal ownership and gradually assimilating the Indians into the acquisitive white culture of the frontier.[56] The Board of Indian Commissioners, which was appointed to scrutinize the operations of the Indian Office and to bring to public attention any mismanagement it uncovered, recommended in its first report in 1870 a general allotment policy. In the words of Angie Debo, it thereafter "regarded the extent of allotment as the measure of progress in

Indian advancement." It urged, however, that titles should be inalienable for two or three generations.[57] Carl Schurz, Secretary of the Interior from 1877 to 1881, threw his influence behind allotment, as did Senator Henry L. Dawes and other so-called humanitarians. Yet the evidence that the allotments failed to effect this objective was already clear wherever they had been given. The Kansas story should have been sufficient to deter experimenting with an allotment policy. The record of allotments in Michigan is perhaps less well known.

By treaties of 1855 and 1864 with the Ottawas and Chippewas parts of six townships in Michigan were set aside for allotments of 80 acres each, and some 1,735 Indians were given patents by 1871. E. A. Hayt, Commissioner of Indian Affairs in the Hayes administration, related the sad story of the victimization of the owners despite their relatively advanced state. So certain were the Indians that they would be removed, despite their allotments, that they were disinclined to improve or in any way make use of their land, an attitude expressed in the reports of the Indian Office. A major portion "fell victims to the greed of unscrupulous white men, and, one by one," parted with or were defrauded of their lands. "Every means that human ingenuity can devise, legal or illegal, has been resorted to for the purpose of obtaining possession" of the lands. Many sold their allotments for as little as $.25 an acre when they were worth $5 to $25 an acre. Collusion between the agents and the purchasers, liberal use of whiskey, the application of unequal taxes, and mortgaging, all contributed to lead the Indians to sign away their rights. In 1875 it was estimated that not one in ten of the allotments was still held by the Indians. Hayt's analysis shows that the Michigan record was almost a duplication of the Kansas frauds of a few years earlier.[58] Ten years later the local agent concluded that giving Indians titles they could convey resulted "in the almost entire dispossession of their land by bartering them away without scarcely any equivalent therefore." He asserted that allotments of the lands and their transfer to whites was part of "a well-laid scheme contemplated many years ago, ripened and consummated openly . . . without the intervention of the Government" whose duty it was to protect the Indians against the wiles of the exploiters "who have grown wealthy by their ill-gotten gains, taken from the people whom they now despise."[59]

At least 11,763 patents for allotments had been issued by 1886, in Kansas, Nebraska, and other states of the Upper Mississippi Valley.[60] This does not include the many thousands given the Creeks, Cherokees, Choctaws, and Chickasaws in Alabama and Mississippi. There was little or nothing in the record of allotments, however, to encourage the belief that they promised a humane and practical solution of the Indian problem. Yet since further concentration of the redmen in Indian Territory and in one or two other large reservations was unacceptable to the West, as Loring Priest has admirably pointed out, allotment was increasingly stressed as the only long-range solution, the more so as the errors of the past were glossed over or forgotten.[61] Former Commissioner Manypenny might well have been listened to in 1885 when he declared that had he been able to foresee how completely the allotment policy would be discredited, "I would be compelled to admit that I had committed a high crime" by pursuing it in Kansas.[62]

Neither Congress nor the authorities in the Indian Office were prepared to oppose the allotment policy when legislation to establish it generally was considered. It is true that the Coeur d'Alene, Yankton Sioux, Potawatomi, Kickapoo, Wyandot, Iowa, and the Five Civilized Tribes had made known their opposition so strongly that the Commissioner mentioned their views in his report, somewhat reluctantly, it appears. Other natives, however, he reported as anxiously awaiting the allotment of their reserves. J. P. Kinney marshaled some evidence showing that Indians domiciled on allotments in New Mexico, Minnesota, Nebraska, and elsewhere were making progress toward independence and full ownership of their tracts; but his information is drawn from the reports of agents who were committed to the policy. In 1883 "over fifty" Santee Sioux were reported to have obtained patents for their allotments; but all such information is from strong supporters of allotments, and no later information is given concerning the retention of ownership once the fee title had passed. Information concerning the progress of allotments among the other Plains tribes before 1887 is not accessible.[63] Most supporters of allotments agreed that extensive experience with them indicated that final ownership should be long delayed, except for those making unusual progress.

Henry Moore Teller, for many years Senator from Colorado, who commonly reflected Western and particularly Colorado sentiment on most questions, as Secretary of the Interior from 1881 to 1885 favored a different policy toward Indian lands, not, however, because of any humane concern for the Indians, for he callously neglected Indian rights and needs. He was both aware of, and frankly admitted, the fact that the great mass of Indians were violently opposed to allotment, an admission that required some courage at that time. To satisfy the land hunger of the West, Teller favored drastic reduction of the reserves and the opening of the surplus lands to settlers only. At the same time he would give the tribes a fee-simple title to their diminished reserves, which, he thought, would remove from them the fear of the loss of their lands and their consequent unwillingness to develop or in any way improve them. While Teller took a strong stand in opposition to allotment, his Commissioner of Indian Affairs, Hiram Price, supported the allotment policy as strongly as his chief opposed it. He maintained that "the best results" had followed from allotment and declared, "I shall, therefore, adhere to the policy of allotting lands wherever the same can legally be done and the condition of the Indians is such as to warrant it." Like his predecessors in the Indian Office, he reported that many Indians were clamoring for allotments.[64]

Senator Joseph N. Dolph of Oregon was one of the few Western members of Congress who foresaw the evils in the allotment policy. He predicted in 1887, when the measure to provide for forced allotting of Indian lands was under consideration, that they would be swiftly disposed of to whites, the proceeds squandered, and the Indians would not be prepared for self support and would again be dependent on government benevolence.[65]

The West, Congress, the Indian Office, and some of the true friends of the Indians wanted a general allotment act which would require its application to all Indians or to all but those in the Indian Territory, where opposition was intense. Such a combination was too powerful to resist. The Dawes General Allotment Act became law on February 8, 1887.[66] It followed previous measures in the size of allotments and the twenty-five-year period before fee-simple titles could be obtained, and provided for the sale of surplus lands only to actual settlers. Whatever the motives of those who worked for the enactment of the measure, its success in achieving its avowed object—the gradual assimilation of the Indian population—was dependent on sympathetic, honest, and understanding administration; and that the Dawes Act did nothing to assure. One need not wonder why the Act has come in for penetrating criticism in later years in the light of the demoralizing effect its incidence had upon the economy of the Indians.

Notes

1. *House Executive Documents,* 45 Cong., 3 Sess., vol. IX, serial 1850, pp. 443–44.

2. J. P. Kinney, *A Continent Lost, A Civilization Won* (Baltimore, Md., 1937), 185.

3. Treaty of November 16, 1805, Charles J. Kappler, *Indian Affairs, Laws and Treaties* (3 vols., Washington, D.C., 1903), II, 63; Charles C. Royce, *Indian Land Cessions,* Bureau of American Ethnology, *Eighteenth Annual Report,* 1900, 673.

4. Kappler, *Indian Affairs,* II, 93–94, 122.

5. *Ibid.,* II. 99, 124.

6. *Ibid.,* II, 324.

7. *Ibid.,* II, 133.

8. Angie Debo, *The Rise and Fall of the Choctaw Republic* (Norman, Okla., 1934), 50.

9. Kappler, *Indian Affairs,* II, 150. The amount of land to be sold for the benefit of schools was reduced to 34,560 acres, and the balance was commuted to a money payment.

10. Debo, *Choctaw Republic,* 54.

11. Kappler, *Indian Affairs,* II, 222.

12. Mary Elizabeth Young. *Redskins, Ruffleshirts and Rednecks: Indian Allotments in Alabama and Mississippi, 1830–1860* (Norman, Okla., 1961), 47 ff.

13. Kappler, *Indian Affairs,* II, 259, 312.

14. Young, *Indian Allotments,* 131–32.

15. James W. Silver, "Land Speculation Profits in the Chickasaw Cession," *Journal of Southern History,* X (February, 1944), 86; Young, *Indian Allotments,* 165–66.

16. *Ibid.,* 73–113.

17. *American State Papers, Indian Affairs,* II, 136.

18. *Ibid.,* 139.

19. John Biddle to John McLean, Detroit, November 14, 1822, in Clarence Carter, ed., *Territorial Papers*, XI, 295, 323, 371, 585. After hearing charges of fraud, Cass actually recommended that the individual reserves be sold despite the ratification of the treaty.

20. *American State Papers, Indian Affairs*, II, 149, 174.

21. *Ibid.*, 149, 166; Kappler, *Indian Affairs*, II, 114. *Territorial Papers*, XI, 353, shows that one Indian was permitted to sell one of his two sections to pay his debts, but in 1823 was denied permission to sell the other. In 1825 permission to sell the second was granted.

22. *Territorial Papers*, XI, 659.

23. Kappler, *Indian Affairs*, II, 119. For Richardville's reserves see maps in *History of Allen County, Indiana* (Fort Wayne, Ind., 1880).

24. Kappler, *Indian Affairs*, II, 140, 142, 148. A treaty of 1823 with the Florida tribe and another of 1824 with the Quapaw Indians of Arkansas provided for two full-section reserves, two quarter-section reserves, and ten half-quarter reserves to half-bloods in Arkansas.

25. *Ibid.*, 154, 158.

26. *Ibid.*, 199. Nellie A. Robertson and Dorothy Riker, eds., *The John Tipton Papers* (3 vols., Indianapolis, Ind., 1942), I, 611–12.

27. *American State Papers, Indian Affairs*, II, 684; Kappler, *Indian Affairs*, II, 200.

28. Wm. T. Young, *Life and Public Services of General Lewis Cass* (Detroit, Mich., 1852), 83.

29. Kappler, *Indian Affairs*, II, 194.

30. *Ibid.*, 197.

31. *Ibid.*, 211, 214, 216.

32. *Ibid.*, 218.

33. *Ibid.*, 219, 439; Addison E. Sheldon, *Land Systems and Land Policies in Nebraska* (*Publications*, Nebraska State Historical Society, XXI, 1936), 209, 333; Royce, *Indian Land Cessions*, 727.

34. Kappler, *Indian Affairs*, II, 216, 253.

35. The conveyance from Myott to Boilvin, which also mentions the previous sale of the other section to Gratiot, is in *History of Winnebago County, Ill.* (Chicago, Ill., 1877), 239–42. Pacquette children also were given $3,000 in a treaty of 1837 with the Winnebagos, and Catherine Myott was given $1,000. To the children of John B. Pacquette were given 3,845 acres in the treaty of 1829.

36. Kappler, *Indian Affairs*, II, 233, 235, 238, 242, 288, 341, 395, 436, 793; Royce, *Indian Land Cessions*, 777.

37. Kappler, *Indian Affairs*, II, 396; Annie Heloise Abel, "Indian Reservations in Kansas and the Extinguishment of Their Title," Kansas State Historical Society, *Transactions*, VIII (1904), 86.

38. Kappler, *Indian Affairs*, II, 362.

39. Letter to John Robb, Acting Secretary of War, July 15, 1823, to George Porter, *Senate Documents*, 23 Cong., 1 Sess., vol. IX, serial 246, no. 512, pp. 733–34.

40. Kappler, *Indian Affairs*, II, 315, 384, 393.

41. *Congressional Globe*, 32 Cong., 2 Sess., February 23, 1853, p. 806.

42. "Correspondence on the Subject of the Emigration of Indians. . . ." *Senate Documents*, 23 Cong., 1 Sess., vol. IX, serial 246, no. 512, p. 652. Cass's place in American Indian relations is summarized in Francis P. Prucha, *Lewis Cass and American Indian Policy* (Detroit, Mich., 1967).

43. In 1832–1833 three treaties with the Winnebago, Sac and Fox, and Kaskaskia Indians provided for a few reservations, the largest being for members of the Pacquette family for 3,200 acres in the Winnebago cession of southwestern Wisconsin or northwestern Illinois.

44. Milo M. Quaife, *Chicago and the Old Northwest, 1673–1835* (Chicago, Ill., 1913), 346 ff.

45. See the attention to the claim of Rix Robinson in the letters by and to Ramsay Crooks in Grace Lee Nute, "Calendar of the American Fur Company's Papers," American Historical Association, *Annual Report*, 1944, vol. II, passim. The total obligations the United States assumed for the cession were more than $1 million. Kappler, *Indian Affairs*, II, 334 ff.

46. *Ibid.*, 343, 358, 372, 382.

47. *House Documents*, 27 Cong., 2 Sess., vol. I, serial 401, no. 25, pp. 1–48; *House Report*, 27 Cong., 2 Sess., vol. V, serial 411, no. 1035, pp. 1–129.

48. Robertson and Riker, *John Tipton Papers*, I, 41–42n.

49. The "Calendar of the American Fur Company's Papers" and Kenneth Porter, *John Jacob Astor* (2 vols., Cambridge, Mass., 1931), II, 851 and passim, are very helpful in unraveling the intricacies of the various partnerships of Astor with others in the Great Lakes region. *Senate Documents*, 25 Cong., 3 Sess., vol. V, serial 342, no. 302; and *Senate Documents*, 26 Cong., 1 Sess., vol. IV, serial 357, no. 164.

50. Commissioner of Indian Affairs, *Annual Report*, 1844, 21, and *Annual Report*, 1855, 255–56.

51. *Register of Debates in Congress*, vol. VI, part 2, appendix, p. xxxii.

52. Kappler, *Indian Affairs*, II, 241, 287, 414; *Congressional Globe*, 39 Cong., 2 Sess., part 2, p. 359; George W. Manypenny, Commissioner of Indian Affairs, *Annual Report*, 1853, *House Documents*, 33 Cong., 1 Sess., vol. I, part 1, serial 710, no. 1, pp. 249 ff.

53. Manypenny was displaced by James W. Denver. Manypenny's account may be seen in his *Annual Reports* for 1853–1856 and in his own *Our Indian Wards* (Chicago, Ill., 1880).

54. Paul W. Gates, *Fifty Million Acres: Conflicts over Kansas Land Policy, 1854–1890* (Ithaca, N.Y., 1954).

55. Kappler, *Indian Affairs*, II, 735, 754, 762, 766, 776, 779, 798. Loring Benson Priest, *Uncle Sam's Stepchildren: The Reformation of United States Indian Policy, 1865–1887* (New Brunswick, N.J., 1942), 182, shows that not until 1884 did Congress appropriate funds to aid the Indians—presumably the wild Indians—in selecting their allotments and moving them toward title.

56. Kinney, *A Continent Lost*, 188, shows that the acting commissioner maintained in 1880 that the demand for "lands in severalty by the reservation

Indians is almost universal." He apparently made no effort to determine what elements were responsible for giving this impression nor to analyze the results of allotment in the past.

57. Debo, *And Still The Waters Run* (Princeton, N.J., 1940), 21; Board of Indian Commissioners, *Report*, 1870, 10.

58. Commissioner of Indian Affairs, *Annual Report*, 1878, vii–ix, 75.

59. Mark W. Stevens, Indian agent at Mackinac, September 1, 1887, in Commissioner of Indian Affairs, *Annual Report*, 1887, 126. A writer in *Nation*, XLII (March 11, 25, 1886), 215–59, sharply blamed United States officials for permitting "the jackals and hyenas of humanity" to despoil the Indians of their allotments.

60. The House Committee on Territories summarized briefly and un-critically in 1879 the experience gained in granting citizenship and allotting tribal lands in Kansas, Michigan, Wisconsin, and Minnesota as earlier described by Indian agents. *House Report*, 45 Cong., 3 Sess., vol. 2, serial 1867, no. 185.

61. Priest, *Uncle Sam's Stepchildren*, 178.

62. *The Council Fire*, VIII (Washington, January, 1885), 25.

63. Kinney, *A Continent Lost*, 187, 193; Indian Rights Association, *First Annual Report*, 1883 (Philadelphia, Pa., 1884), 15.

64. *House Executive Documents*, 47 Cong., 2 Sess., vol. 10, serial 2099, pp. vi–vii, and vol. 11, serial 2100, pp. 34–35, and *House Executive Documents*, 48 Cong., 1 Sess., vol. 10, serial 2190, pp. xiv–xv, and vol. 11, serial 2191, p. 12.

65. *Congressional Record*, 49 Cong., 2 Sess., January 25, 1887, p. 974. Much needed are fresh studies of the Dawes Act, the Burke Act of 1906, the Wheeler-Howard Act of 1934, and the Termination legislation of the Eisenhower administration.

66. Howard R. Lamar in *The Far Southwest, 1846–1912: A Territorial History* (New Haven, Conn., 1966), 15, writes that the Dawes Act "promised a new deal for the red man."

Squaw Men on the Kiowa, Comanche, and Apache Reservation: Advance Agents of Civilization or Disturbers of the Peace?

William T. Hagan,
State University of New York, Fredonia

One of the fixtures of reservation life in the late nineteenth century was the squaw man. In the preceding three centuries many white men had formed alliances of some degree of formality and permanence with Indian women. Within the last several years the phenomenon has attracted some attention. John Ewers probed an aspect of the relationship in his scholarly article "Mothers of the Mixed-Bloods: The Marginal Woman in the History of the Upper Missouri."[1] More recently, Walter O'Meara exploited the sensational possibilities of the subject in *Daughters of the Country.*[2] Neither study comes past mid nineteenth century, and Ewers's is confined geographically to the Upper Missouri. O'Meara ranges more widely but has produced principally an account of the relations of fur traders and trappers with Indian women of Canada and the northern United States.

Two earlier writers to treat the subject were Stanley Vestal (Walter S. Campbell) and Clark Wissler. Vestal delivered himself of the verdict: "One suspects that the term 'squaw-man' was invented by some spinster from the East, who came west to find a husband, only to discover that the Indian women had married all the best men."[3] It is not quite that simple, as Wissler made clear thirty years ago in a chapter entitled "The Enigma of the Squaw Man" in his *Indian Cavalcade*.[4]

The term squaw man apparently did not come into general use until the 1850s. Its derivation is unknown, but it was widely employed throughout the second half of the nineteenth century in a derogatory sense. In a popular play by that name first produced in 1905, audiences were entertained by the story of an expatriate English gentleman who took an Indian wife in the American West. One of the play's highlights is when the squaw man reveals his predicament to a fellow Englishman who has happened on him. "Socially ostracized," is how this squaw man described his situation, explaining, "You see we have our social distinctions, even out here."[5]

In objecting to the stigma of the term squaw man, Vestal made the point that "the foremost men" of our pioneer period had married Indian women, citing the cases of William Bent, Kit Carson, and Jim Bridger.[6] He might have added the names of hundreds of men from earlier frontiers, with John Rolfe heading the list, followed by such luminaries as William Johnson, Lachlan McGillivray, and Henry Schoolcraft.

Aside from the romantic attraction Indian women held for white men, there were practical reasons for their making such domestic arrangements. A helpmate who could do the camp chores, make snowshoes and moccasins, and help prepare furs for market was a real asset to a trapper or trader. An alliance with the family of a chief helped a trader both dispose of his goods and collect the debts owed him. Or the relationship might have significance in international affairs. The English regarded Pocahontas's betrothal to John Rolfe as putting the seal on the alliance with her father, Powhatan;[7] and in the lull following Queen Anne's War the Board of Trade took note of French success in this regard and recommended marriages between Indians and English settlers.[8]

Thus by 1850 the practice of intermarriage was long established, and while not completely socially acceptable, had not yet
produced that term of opprobrium "squaw man." And new types
of relationships were developing, ones of greater duration than
were typical of the fur trade. These were established in the back-
wash of the frontier among relatively advanced tribes like the Five
Civilized. According to a census taken in 1825, nearly one hundred and fifty white men had married among the Cherokees and,
even more remarkable, about half that many white women had
chosen Cherokee mates and life with the tribe.[9]

The problems presented responsible officials by the introduction of such large numbers of whites into the Indian country became apparent within a few years. In the late 1830s the agent for
the Five Civilized Tribes deplored the lack of legislation empowering him to cope with the influx of whites, pointing out that
they were generally fugitives from the law or others not "calculated to advance the interests of the Indians."[10] The incidence of
such remarks in agents' correspondence increased rapidly in the
1840s and 1850s. The suggestion that Indian annuities had attracted some of the intermarried whites was voiced by D. D.
Mitchell, superintendent at St. Louis. "It will readily be seen that
such men add nothing to the stock of Indian morality!" observed
Mitchell, and he particularly charged them with contributing to
the liquor problem among the tribesmen.[11] Other agents were
concerned about the influence the intermarried white man could
exert in tribal politics. Thomas Twiss, a West Pointer turned
Indian agent on the upper Platte who himself had an Indian wife,
was one of the most vehement in his denunciation of whites living
among Indians. He maintained many were fugitives from justice
and "addicted to all of the lowest and most degrading vices." But
worst of all, Twiss felt, was the tendency of these white men to
conspire against the agent and "allure them [the Indians] on to
ruin step by step."[12]

Not all observers were so alarmed as Mitchell and Twiss at
the influence of intermarried whites. A few looked upon them as
catalysts for the civilization process. Potawatomi agent Richard
S. Elliott went so far as to claim that, "Whatever advances the
Pottawatomies have made towards civilization have been promoted in a greater degree by the intermixture of whites with the

tribe, than any other cause." As he saw it, emulation was at the heart of the improvement, the houses and farms of intermarried whites challenging the Indians to progress.[13]

Two others who saw it this way were Thomas Fitzpatrick and James H. Norwood, both stationed among Plains Indians.[14] However, the views of these three agents ran counter to those generally held, and two of the three, Fitzpatrick and Norwood, never held administrative responsibility for a real reservation.

Reservations of a sort had appeared as soon as the first waves of settlers had bypassed remnants of Eastern tribes, remnants which lingered on as enclaves in white society. But the reservation system, whose vestiges we see today, was a product of the obvious impossibility of maintaining in the West a huge, thinly populated "Indian country" in the face of a burgeoning, aggressive white population. A solution seemed to be to pare the Indian holdings to satisfy the demands of whites while leaving enough land to serve as the setting for the transformation of the Indian from savage hunter to civilized farmer.[15]

The concept of the reservation as a civilizing institution had among its basic elements the necessity for isolating the Indians during this critical period.[16] Experience had shown that Indians on the borders of white settlements usually contacted a class of whites interested in exploiting and corrupting, not civilizing, them. Thus, to work their magic, reservations had to be forbidden to whites other than agency employees. By the Kiowa and Comanche Treaty of October 21, 1867, which provided the legal framework for the reservation experience that those Indians had had for more than a quarter-century, the United States solemnly pledged "that no persons except those herein authorized so to do and except such officers, agents, and employes of the Government as may be authorized to enter upon Indian reservation in discharge of duties enjoined by law, shall be permitted to pass over, settle upon, or reside in the territory described in this article."[17]

However, at the time this treaty was signed, a few white men had already established connections with the Penateka band of Comanches. These first contacts had occurred on the Comanche Reservation on the Clear Fork of the Brazos in Texas. There the few hundred who been persuaded to give up the life of plains nomads were exposed to the rudiments of civilization.

Recognition of the inability to do much with the fraction of the tribe on the reservation while most Comanches followed the buffalo, led to plans as early as 1855 to secure a larger reservation which would support all the Comanches.[18] Before this could be worked out in detail, the Texans, their long-standing opposition to any Indians exacerbated by raids on frontier settlers, virtually drove the Comanches and several smaller tribes from the state. These Indians were then located in a district the government leased from the Chickasaws and Choctaws.

The Civil War delayed plans to locate all the Comanches in the Leased District, but this was finally provided for in 1867 by the previously mentioned treaty. Under its terms the Comanches, and the Kiowas who had joined them in earlier negotiations with the United States, accepted a three-million-acre reservation as their future home. In a separate document the Comanches and Kiowas agreed to incorporate the Kiowa Apaches and share their reservation, annuities, and government services with the latter tribe.[19]

Eight years were to pass before all the Comanches, Kiowas, and Kiowa Apaches were located on the new reservation. The last bands did not settle down until June, 1875, and then only after army columns and the declining buffalo herds had combined to make life on the plains impossible. The agent for this reservation was also made responsible for the neighboring one set aside for the Wichitas and several other small tribes. In 1878 the headquarters for the Kiowa, Comanche, and Apache Agency was moved to Anadarko from Fort Sill, and the administration of the two agencies was merged completely, making it the Kiowa, Comanche, and Wichita Agency.[20]

By the time the agency was located at Anadarko, squaw men, as they were now known, were becoming conspicuous in agency affairs. Three stand out by 1878, William G. Williams, J. J. Sturm, and William Chandler. Williams and Sturm had married Caddo women, and Chandler was the husband of a Mexican captive of the Comanches. All three men had entered the reservation as employees of the government, from whose ranks most squaw men came.

Agency employment usually attracted single men, for which there was a ready explanation. Life at the Kiowa, Comanche, and Wichita Agency held few attractions for a man with family responsibilities. In the early 1870s it was about two hundred miles from the nearest railroad, and the triweekly stage from that point took two full, bone-jarring days and nights to reach the agency, that is if the creeks and rivers were not flooding, in which case the trip might drag out to a week or two. The isolation was made even less acceptable by conditions for the employees. Until the late 1880s, when several cottages were built, there usually was no separate housing for employees other than the agent himself. Families might have two rooms in a dilapidated structure, which they would share with other agency staff members. Nor were the salaries sufficient to support a family, most agency employees receiving annual pay in the $400–$600 range, with perhaps $250 of that going for board. Given this situation, it is not strange that the possibility of making homes with the reservation's women proved attractive to agency employees.[21]

The connection of Sturm and Williams with government service dated back to the days when the Caddoes were living on a separate reservation. Sturm was an agency farmer on the Brazos reserve in Texas in 1857,[22] and Williams entered government service in 1863, after the Caddoes had moved to the Leased District.[23] Chandler, who was part Cherokee or Creek, first met the Indians among whom he was to make a home when he began to supply beef to the government for the reservations on the Brazos. When the Indians moved from Texas, he moved with them and in time became an agency interpreter. Meanwhile, he had married Tomasa, a young Mexican captive for whom he had paid two dollars and a chicken.[24]

Within a few months after the opening of the agency at Fort Sill, the question of the rights of white men on the reservation arose. The names of Chandler, Sturm, Williams, Horace P. Jones, and Philip McCusker were submitted to the Commissioner of Indian Affairs as candidates for adoption by tribes associated with the agency.[25] Neither Jones nor McCusker had Indian wives, but all five were represented as men who had long resided with the Indians and whose presence among them was beneficial. The response of the commissioner was typically cautious where legal questions might be involved. He vetoed the adoption procedure, indicating that there was ample precedent for white men—particularly those with Indian wives—being permitted to reside with tribes. But if they were not legally adopted members of the tribe, it was also easy to expel them from the reservation if they misbehaved.[26]

What must have been behind the interest of the five in adoption became apparent within two years, when Joseph Chandler applied for a grant of land under the 1867 treaty.[27] A clause of this agreement, designed to encourage the transition from hunter to farmer, had provided that the head of a Kiowa, Comanche, or Apache family might receive a deed to as much as 320 acres of the reservation if he were prepared to "commence farming." Although the deed was made out to Chandler, the commissioner subsequently held that since he was not a Comanche, the title to the land could only rest in his wife Tomasa.[28]

As complaints about squaw men came in from agents throughout the service,[29] an effort was made in 1876 by Representative Julius H. Seelye of Massachusetts to amend the Indian Appropriation Bill. He sought to forbid "the issue of rations or supplies of any kind to any white men living with Indian women, or to any Indian women or their children who are married to or living with such white men," and to ensure "that no such white men shall claim any rights on any Indian reservation by reason of such real or pretended marriages." After a short debate featuring, on the one hand, references to "miscegenation" and "lazy and loose white men" and, on the other, testimonials to the wisdom of encouraging the "intermingling" of the races, the amendment was defeated.[30]

By the time of the debate Joseph Chandler was dead, but Sturm and Williams lived on to be joined by a new crop of squaw men. One of these, George W. Conover, came to the Indian Territory with the Army and remained there when he was discharged in 1870, entering the agency service. In 1873, while employed by the government as a laborer at forty dollars per month, he quit that job to work briefly for a cattleman and then entered the employ of Chandler's widow, Tomasa. For nearly two years he helped her manage her 320 acres, meanwhile working for a time for an agency trader, purchasing hides from the Indians. He and Tomasa were married in 1875.[31] By 1878 the now Mrs. Conover had the largest herd of cattle of any of the reservation inhabitants.[32] At least some of the residents of the reservation clearly were awakening to the opportunities in the cattle business. In this, squaw men seem to have been foremost.

As it took money to stock a ranch, and few squaw men had much of that commodity, one possibility was to use any range rights that a squaw man might be able to claim or inveigle, to graze the cattle of another party. This Sturm attempted to do in 1878 on the Wichita Reservation, only to be denied permission by the commissioner. But that official did indicate that Sturm might run his own cattle on the reservation.[33]

The Wichita Reservation contained nearly three-quarters of a million acres, and the Kiowa, Comanche, and Apache about three million, most of both reservations offering good grazing for cattle. The sight of this grass going to waste was too great a temptation to white men. The same thing happened at this agency as happened elsewhere when such conditions existed. The squaw men, in the words of the commissioner in 1879, "assume that . . . they have all the rights of full-blooded Indians, and they endeavor to exercise these rights not only in the possession of cattle themselves, but also in ranging and pasturing . . . large herds belonging to other white men."[34]

That a new era was approaching for squaw men of the Kiowa, Comanche, and Wichita Agency was apparent by 1885. The incumbent agent was P. B. Hunt, who had taken over the office in the spring of 1878. For the first few years the intermarried whites seem to have been no particular problem to him. Some were dependable subordinates contributing their bit to the smooth functioning of the agency, others were rather harmless reservation hangers-on who inspired a mixture of contempt and pity.

In his annual report of 1884, however, Hunt spoke with some bitterness of his recent experience. "I had been nearly five years in office before I met with the common experience of a U.S. Indian Agent's trouble with squaw men." "There are some good men among this class," he acknowledged, "but there are others, whose character and influence are so bad that it is futile to expect peace as long as they are permitted to remain among the Indians."[35]

Hunt's ire had been aroused by William G. Williams, James M. Davis, and C. R. McKinney, all three married to Caddo women but attempting to exploit their connections, not only with the Wichita Reservation of which their wives were legal residents, but also the Kiowa, Comanche, and Apache Reservation administered by the same agent.

Williams transgressed by purchasing twenty-two head of cattle from Comanches at prices significantly lower than Agent Hunt deemed proper.[36] The agent directed his Indian police to seize the cattle and return them to their original owners, but Hunt did not require that the Indians return Williams's money to him, presumably using this as a means of punishing the squaw man. The commissioner first sustained Hunt's action by directing that Williams be ordered from the reservation if he repeated the offense. But after the squaw man got a Congressman to intercede for him, the commissioner directed that either the cattle or the money be restored to Williams. Hunt was furious. He felt his efforts to encourage the Indians to build up herds would be in vain if his rule forbidding Indians to sell cattle to white men was thus undercut. The agent could not point to legislation sustaining the position he had taken, but he was very concerned about the impact on the two reservations if the squaw man successfully appealed his decision. Particularly disturbing was the position taken by the commissioner that only he could order the removal of an offending white man. "To make public your letter," wrote Hunt with some heat, "will destroy what little discipline we have here and will start white men to running 'rough shod' over the reservation." He commented despairingly that "if a white man gets . . . an Indian woman to become his wife, then that man is a fixture in the reservation and it makes no difference what he may do he can only be removed by the Commissioner of Indian Affairs . . . and . . . the Agent is a mere figure head."[37]

Even as Hunt's concern for protecting the Indians' herds had produced problems for him, so would his efforts to protect Indian land. This situation involved the other two squaw men, C. R. McKinney and his father-in-law, J. M. Davis, both married to Caddoes and originally located on the Wichita Reservation.[38] Hunt had erred initially by doing McKinney a favor. In 1880 he had permitted the squaw man to move onto the Kiowa, Comanche, and Apache Reservation to be nearer to a job that he held in the Chickasaw Nation. Then, without the agent's permission, Davis had quietly joined his son-in-law, and the two men and their families lived there uneventfully for three years. But with the increase in herds on the reservation, fences began to go up, and one that the agent authorized deprived McKinney of a portion of a range he had been using. McKinney boldly proceeded to complain to Washington, citing the labor and money he had expended in improving the property and charging the agent with discrimination. Particularly galling to Hunt, who received a copy of McKinney's complaint, was the squaw man's claim to "have as much right here as he [Hunt] has."[39]

As had been the case in the Williams affair, Hunt was asked to provide a full report on the incident, which had the effect of putting him on the defensive. To strengthen his position, Hunt called a council of chiefs and headmen and elicited from them the request that the agent order both McKinney and Davis off their reservation. (He had not seen fit to ask their permission to let McKinney on in the first place.) The commissioner approved, but only after subjecting Hunt to the always embarrassing experience of an investigation by a special agent. McKinney and Davis were permitted to sell their improvements if they could find a purchaser, but he had to be on the Kiowa, Comanche, and Apache Reservation. When one of them sold fence rails, the purchaser was denied permission to remove them to the Wichita Reservation. Only a river might divide them and the same agent might preside over both, but the line between the two reservations was strictly maintained for some purposes.[40]

Considering the embarrassment, challenge to his authority, and added paper work that Williams, McKinney, and Davis had caused him, Hunt might be pardoned for taking a dim view of squaw men: "And as some of [them] seem to believe that the fact that their having once cohabited with a squaw secures to them not only the much cherished right—'the right to live on an Indian reservation'—but also the right to do pretty much as they please, some decision is required defining their status."[41] Some progress toward defining the rights and privileges of intermarried whites at the Kiowa, Comanche, and Wichita Agency was made under the colorful ex–Texas Ranger J. Lee Hall, who succeeded Hunt in 1885.

Hall had been in office but a few weeks when he queried the commissioner about the right of squaw men to employ other whites or rent them land on the reservation.[42] The commissioner did not respond immediately, but he was being pressed by other parties for action on the squaw-man problem. An inspector had reported the Kiowa, Comanche, and Apache Reservation overrun by undesirable whites, and the agent for the adjoining Cheyenne and Arapahoe Reservation was complaining of similar troubles.[43] The commissioner, when he did reply to Hall's query, discussed the general problem at length. Describing it as "one of the most complex features in the Indian service" and "a mixed evil," the commissioner harked back to the isolation concept which was basic to the reservation as an instrument of civilization. "Bad" white men could be ordered off the reservations immediately, the commissioner decreed, calling on the military for aid if necessary. No squaw man could rent land to another white man, and any white laborers a squaw man might hire must be approved by the agent. But the commissioner was forced to admit that there was little that could be done if the intermarried whites behaved. Nevertheless, the agent must see that they did not "enrich them-selves at the expense of other members of the tribe," nor "monop-olize large tracts of the best land on the reservation." The com-missioner requested Hall and the Cheyenne and Arapahoe agent to provide him with statistics about whites present at their agencies.[44]

The reports by the two agents revealed the extent of the problem. Hall identified fifteen squaw men on the reservations under his jurisdiction, and twenty-four were counted on the Chey-enne and Arapahoe Reservation. Of Hall's fifteen, four were Mexi-can and two were employed at the agency. Among them the four Mexicans farmed only 140 acres, held twelve head of cattle, and employed five helpers on their farms. The two agency employees did no farming and held no cattle. Neither of these categories posed serious problems in administering the reservations. But the other nine squaw men made up for it. Although not all were involved in each of these activities, among them they ran a total of 4,575 head of cattle on the reservations, farmed 1,370 acres, and employed twenty-four whites and five Indians.[45]

Of the nine, four we have already encountered: Conover, Williams, Sturm, and Davis. The other five were H. P. Pruner, W. F. Deitrich, E. L. Clark, Robert L. Curtis, and Emmet Cox.[46] They provide an interesting cross section of the type. They had been on the reservation an average of about nine years each.

Three (Pruner, Clark, Cox) were at some time or other employees of the agency. One (Cox) came with the Texas cattlemen when they began to lease range, and another (Clark) as a soldier stationed at Fort Sill. Four of the five married into prominent Indian families, Cox being successively a son-in-law of Comanche chiefs Quirts-quip and Quanah Parker, Deitrich marrying a daughter of Mrs. Conover, Pruner wedding the daughter of the Delaware chief Black Beaver, and Clark choosing as a wife a daughter of Moxie, a Comanche band chief.

As husbands of Indian residents of the agency, the fifteen white men had some justification for being there, troublesome as they might be on occasion. The most that could be done about them was to insist that they be legally married to their consorts and to propose legislation that would make the requirement binding. Explicit in the discussion of the topic was the conclusion that any increase in the ranks of the squaw men would be unfortunate.[47] As Agent Hall summarized it: "My opinion of 'Squaw Men' does not differ from most of other Indian Agents; that the presence of such men as are willing to marry Indian Women is not conducive to their moral advancement." Nor did Hall leave much room for romance in such arrangements: "There are no white men who marry Indian Women, especially amongst the lest civilized tribes, but do so from mercenary motives . . . the privilege of occupying land and raising live stock within the Indian reserve."[48] This view of the motivations of intermarried whites was one generally held in the Indian Service, from the top down. Hall's superior, the Secretary of the Interior, lumped squaw men with mixed-bloods, the "chief interest in the Indians of both" being "to drive sharp bargains . . . and to make money out of his [sic] ignorance, unsuspecting confidence, and characteristic liberality and hospitality."[49]

Addressing himself to an additional cause of concern, the increasing number of white farm laborers and herders in the employ of squaw men, Hall advised that preference for these positions go to married applicants. That perhaps would serve to discourage the steady increase in the number of intermarried whites. But as has been previously noted, reservation life did not attract family men, and all that the authorities in Washington could do was to require that the agents clear with them the admission of white farm laborers or herders to the reservation. Theoretically, these white men could be employed only if the applicant for such assistance was incapable of maintaining his own property. In actual fact, agents were quite lenient in interpreting the rules, and Washington officials generally accepted their recommendations, although they complained as the number of white men on reservations steadily increased.

Washington did take a strong stand on the legal sanction for the union of Indians and whites. The commissioner advised Hall that the Secretary of the Interior and he agreed that white men living with Indian women should be married to them "according to civilized use" or be removed from the reservation.[50] As the commissioner had described it in his letter to the secretary, "The institution of proper and lawful marriage would be a great step in the way of the ultimate civilization of the Indians, and a safeguard in perpetuating title to lands held in severalty."[51]

That the Indians were not as impressed by the formality of the white man's ceremony was apparent in an incident involving one Charles Rider and an Indian girl, Eva Pickard. Rider asked Hall's permission to marry the girl, and Hall insisted that Rider get the consent of her fellow tribesmen. They refused, and Hall ordered Rider off the reservation. Not so easily denied, the white man took Eva with him and got a minister to marry them. Hall warned the agitated Indians that the marriage was legal, but they ignored him, located the girl, and forced her to return to the reservation. Eva seems to have been rather passive throughout the adventure, although once back with her people, she refused to rejoin her husband.[52]

Although the Indians had disposed of Rider as a reservation problem, the general situation remained the same. An effort to ease it was made by the Fiftieth Congress. Originating in a recommendation of Secretary of the Interior, L. Q. C. Lamar, a bill to restrict the rights of squaw men was introduced by Senator Henry L. Dawes of Massachusetts, Chairman of the Senate Committee on Indian Affairs, who was best known for his championing of severalty. Discussions of the bill in both houses evoked some highly derogatory remarks about whites who settled among the Indians. In contrast with the discussion of the proposed legislation in 1876, no one came to their defense. A typical comment was that by Representative John H. Rogers of Arkansas which termed many of the squaw men "fugitives from justice" or "those who do not wish to pay their debts" or those "who are willing to sacrifice everything like civilization for the purpose of getting beyond the law and gaining head-rights among the Indian tribes."[53]

The important provision of the law approved August 9, 1888, banned the acquisition by the intermarried white man of "any right to any tribal property, privilege, or interest" in the tribe of his wife.[54] This was essentially the position the Indian Office had been taking for several years,[55] and the law provided more of a legal bulwark for current policy than a new departure. Certainly it didn't remove the burden from the agents.

Between the end of Hall's administration in 1887 and the opening of the Kiowa, Comanche, and Apache Reservation in 1901, nine different men presided over the destinies of the Indians. All of them faced the problem of the squaw men, and their responses could be anticipated in terms of their general approach to their responsibilities. Those agents who eschewed innovation and were willing to live-and-let-live had the least trouble with intermarried whites. But an agent who conceived of himself as the real guardian of the Indians, or who resented the pressures both subtle and overt that squaw men could bring to bear on him, would soon be fighting to save his job or his authority.

But even then there would be a distinct note of ambivalence in the comments on the intermarried whites. There were occasions when agents did battle in their behalf. A trusted subordinate with ten to twenty years' experience on a reservation, with family ties among the Indians, and with the ability to speak at least one of the several Indian languages used at the agency could be a godsend to an agent fresh from the grocery business in Maryland or a lumberyard in Missouri. The cases of Thomas F. Woodard and John Nestell exhibit some of the possibilities.

Nestell had come to the agency about 1875.[56] Entering the government service, he held increasingly responsible positions, being superintendent and overseer by 1888. Implicated in charges that led to the dismissal of Agent Hall, he resigned that post. Meanwhile, he had married a Mexican captive of the Kiowas and continued to reside on the reservation. After the passage of a few months he apparently was rehired in another capacity and continued in government employment for several years, despite sporadic efforts on the part of Washington officials to get rid of him. An agent who entered office several years after the J. Lee Hall affair defended Nestell as a Union veteran and one who held "the confidence of all the people of this reservation." At least to the Commissioner of Indian Affairs the agent professed to believe that Nestell's previous troubles had been a peccadillo involving a few spools of barbed wire.[57]

Nestall was a good clerk; Woodard was an even rarer but absolutely essential commodity, a good interpreter.[58] As a young man of twenty-two, Woodard had come to the Wichita Reservation with a newly appointed agent. Over the years he had held a variety of positions on the agency staff and had lived informally with a Kiowa girl. The latter activity got him into trouble in 1889, when the Commissioner of Indian Affairs ordered his discharge after an inspector charged Woodard with immorality. The agent rallied to his defense, stating that Woodard had married the woman since the inspector's visit and that "his influence among the Kiowas and Comanches was simply wonderful as they trust him implicitly, and rely more on his word, than that of any other man on the reservation." The previous summer Woodard had helped calm the Kiowas in a dispute over their religious practices, a dispute which might have required the use of troops had it gone further. The agent also added that Woodard was a "man of sober habits," a Mason, a churchgoer, and, last but not least, "the most reliable interpreter on the reservation."[59]

Such a man clearly was more valuable than the $500 he received a year as interpreter. And it is apparent that Woodard had other sources of income. As a squaw man he had access to free range for his cattle, and with the collusion of the agent there were other possibilities as well. Hauling from the railroad the many tons of freight the agency received every year was one of the earliest types of employment for Indians. Presumably, they received preference over white freighters, yet in one quarter in 1894, Woodard was paid $481 out of $788 the agent expended for the hauling of freight. And he earned it under his Indian name, "Wah-che-kah," which, however, did not escape the careful scrutiny of an inspector.[60]

Another example of the collusive relationship that could exist

between squaw men and agents was revealed in connection with
the negotiation of the Jerome Agreement in 1892.[61] This was the
instrument for applying severalty to the Kiowa, Comanche, and
Apache Reservation and required the approval of three-fourths of
the adult males. As there was considerable opposition to the
agreement, its negotiators, aided and abetted by the agent,
dredged up every signer possible. Two signatures turned out to
be the Indian names of squaw men Thomas F. Woodard and E. L.
Clark.[62] Elsewhere in the document both were listed by their
proper names as squaw men who should receive allotments on the
same basis as the regular members of the tribes. To add the final
touch to this classic example of conflict of interest, Clark was also
one of the official interpreters for the negotiations! The agent,
needless to say, was fully cognizant of the several faceted roles of
Woodard and Clark in the negotiation of the Jerome Agreement.

The foregoing suggests that an agent's view of a squaw man
related most closely to whether the man was working with the
agent or against him; per se there was nothing wrong with squaw
men from an agent's point of view.

Officials in Washington could be much more objective, as
they were not forced to rely upon the good will and cooperation
of intermarried whites to ensure smooth operation of an agency.
When one of the short-term occupants of the agent's position at
Anadarko registered a mild complaint about squaw men, suggesting that many of the cattle grazed by them really belonged to
others who were paying the white men for access to the range, he
felt it necessary to describe the squaw men as "an industrious class
of citizens" with whom his relations had been "pleasant."[63] But
the Commissioner of Indian Affairs responded that they had no
rights themselves to hold cattle upon a reservation and should be
removed immediately if they attempted it. Their wives, of course,
could, but the commissioner suggested a guide for determining
how many—divide the reservation's Indian population into the
number of cattle the range should be able to support, and the
resultant figure would be the number a single Indian could graze
free. Any in excess of that figure should be charged for at the
same rate that applied to others who leased grazing land from
the tribes.[64]

Nevertheless, the problem persisted and would be a bone of

contention between conscientious agents and squaw men. Two years later a new agent made a comparable protest and received the same reply.[65] The issue came to a head under still another agent, Captain Frank D. Baldwin.

Baldwin was not a fugitive from a lumberyard or a grocery store. On special detail from the Army, he was one of the young men who had entered service during the Civil War and had then passed long years at frontier posts on the plains. Baldwin had been cited for gallantry in action against both the Northern and Southern Plains Indians, winning the Medal of Honor in a battle with Comanches. He at least thought he knew Indians, and Baldwin had the army officer's dim view of the type of white men attracted to reservations.

In the seven years since Hall had left office, seven agents had presided over the destinies of the Indians of the Kiowa, Comanche, and Wichita Agency. Inevitably, the employees who managed to hold on through this succession of agents, together with the squaw men and traders who were relatively permanent fixtures on the two reservations, exercised even more influence than usual in agency matters. A man of Baldwin's temperament could not permit this.

Captain Baldwin assumed responsibility for the agency in December, 1894, and hardly a month had passed before he had been initiated into the complexities of agency politics. Representatives of the Conservative Comanche faction complained to the Commissioner of Indian Affairs about several things, among them the squaw men who were leasing Indian land to other white men and engrossing most of the farm implements sent to the agency for distribution to all its residents. Leaders among the complainants were an odd trio—Big Looking Glass, White Wolf, and William Tivis.[66]

Both Big Looking Glass and White Wolf were band chiefs in their sixties, men prominent in Comanche affairs since prereservation days. In contrast, William Tivis was a young man who had spent about one-third of his years at the Carlisle Indian School under the tutelage of Captain Richard H. Pratt. The thing that brought them together was opposition to the prevailing Progressive faction in agency affairs headed by Quanah Parker of the

Comanches and Ahpeahtone of the Kiowas, a faction normally allied with the agent and the government.[67]

The Conservative complaints about squaw men did lead Captain Baldwin to investigate the position of intermarried whites under his jurisdiction. In a week-long tour of his agency the Captain discovered that squaw men had been "most liberally supplied" with farm implements and also that they were "occupying the very best part of this reservation."[68] As he began to press the whites about their reservation holdings, they fought back, and the war was on. J. J. Sturm, one of the oldest squaw men on the reservation, pled his case directly to the Secretary of the Interior.[69] Another senior resident, George Conover, employed an attorney.[70] By the fall of 1895, less than a year after Baldwin had taken office, the Kiowa, Comanche, and Wichita Agency had become the scene of a test of strength between the agent and squaw men. Or perhaps, "some squaw men" would be more appropriate, as Baldwin, like other agents before him, found some intermarried whites useful and cooperative. His fire was centered on only six of perhaps twenty to twenty-five squaw men at his agency. His particular targets were Thomas Woodard, J. J. Sturm, William F. Deitrich, and George Conover (all of whom have been discussed previously), James Jones, and James D. Myers.

James D. Myers appeared at the agency as an employee of a cattleman only shortly before Baldwin assumed charge.[71] According to the agent, Myers married an Indian girl after declaring he was tired of paying for a grazing lease and was now going to get free grass for his cattle.[72] James Jones was originally an agency employee and held various posts on the agency staff, from herder to chief of police, until he married a Kiowa girl nearly twenty years after arriving at Fort Sill.[73]

Baldwin accused the squaw men of a variety of transgressions: getting more than their fair share of tools and wire issued to the Indians, paying the Indians ridiculously low prices for their cattle, cutting hay from reservation pastures, pasturing the cattle of themselves and other white men at the expense of the Indians, and contributing to factionalism among the tribes. "When the time comes when they cannot cheat and defraud the Indians," Baldwin wrote the commissioner, "then they will starve to death, they won't work."[74] Of the charges Baldwin brought against the squaw men, the most serious were the ones relating to their use of reservation pastures and their incitement of factionalism.

During the mid 1890s, the Kiowas, Comanches, and Apaches were leasing about half of their three-million-acre reservation to cattlemen. From the "grass fund" the agent distributed annually to the Indians about $80,000 "grass money."[75] As their total annuity from the 1867 treaty was $30,000 and their only other cash income came from occasionally hauling freight to the agency or selling a beef to the government for the ration issue, the amount of land they leased at six cents per acre was a matter of real concern to them. The Indians of the Wichita Reservation were even more dependent on this grass money. Nevertheless, the tribesmen usually suffered in silence as the squaw men appropriated thousands of acres to their personal benefit while never failing to line up at the time of per capita payments to collect grass money for their wives and children.

In 1895 Captain Baldwin was operating on the basis of a precedent established by his predecessors and allowing any Indian or squaw man twenty acres of pasture for each head of stock he held on the reservation. Both he and the commissioner regarded this as excessive,[76] and Baldwin was later to cut this to ten acres per animal.[77] The commissioner also advised limiting the number of acres any individual could hold to what he would be entitled to in a per capita division of the reservation. In the case of the Kiowas, Comanches, and Apaches this meant about one thousand acres each. But a squaw man could also use the shares of his wife and children and end up controlling several thousand acres. This much Baldwin was prepared to countenance; it was when the white man became *too* greedy that Baldwin reacted.

Frequently it was difficult to determine exactly how much land the intermarried white held. And by this time several of them were leasing large pastures, although the agent suspected they were occupying more than they were paying for and subleasing their holdings at substantial profits. Baldwin uncovered an example of the latter in George Conover.

When the agent required the squaw men to report on their holdings, Conover had established his at not more than 23,000 acres. Baldwin was confident the tract actually exceeded 30,000 acres and forced him to pay for an additional 5,000 acres, which meant an additional $300 in the grass fund. But as time passed there were other interesting revelations. A survey of the pasture revealed that Conover was holding not 23,000 acres, nor even the 28,000 Baldwin held him for officially, but 36,640 acres. This could not have come as a total surprise to Conover, although it may have been to the cattleman to whom he had subleased it. The cattleman had understood he was acquiring range rights to 40,000 acres. Conover had collected $2,600 from the cattleman, while paying the Indians only $300, a nice profit for being the husband of a woman and the father of children on the Comanche tribal rolls.[78] It is little wonder that when Baldwin threatened to interfere with the profitable position Conover had carved out for himself, Conover hired a lawyer with influence in Washington.

William F. Deitrich and Thomas Woodard were detected by the agent in similar activities. Baldwin charged they were making a profit of $1,500 by subleasing a pasture assigned to them. Woodard had compounded his crime by making room for his lessee by shifting his own herd of 500 head of cattle to other reservation range for which he paid nothing.[79] Baldwin flatly accused him and Deitrich of "defrauding the Indians of $1,500; and you are stealing the products of the soil that belongs to them in common." Never one to mince words, the agent said that he had given them enough rope and that they had demonstrated that "your only interest in these Indians is what you can make by dishonest ways out of them." Baldwin also informed them that he was aware of their joining Conover in retaining an attorney.[80]

It is hard to say what disturbed Captain Baldwin the most about the squaw men's activities. He exhibited righteous indignation at the exploitation of Indian resources, but the challenge to his authority may have produced the greater reaction. An agent might have to clear with Washington the purchase of a milk cow or the erection of a shed for it, but to people in Indian country he often seemed the total autocrat with a private court and police force to back his decisions. Certainly, as P. B. Hunt had demonstrated, he resented any suggestion that he did not run his agency and that it might be profitable to appeal an agent's decisions to Washington. Even a weak agent would object to this, and Captain Baldwin certainly was not that. And as a member of the peacetime army, his talents for controversy had been honed by the constant jockeying for position that went on among career officers.

Captain Baldwin reacted predictably to the report that some of the squaw men had hired an attorney. Conover, Woodard, and Deitrich had secured the services of William C. Shelley, who had held a position in the Washington office of the Indian Service before signing a contract with the Kiowas, Comanches, and Apaches to defend them against the numerous depredation claims being filed. Again Baldwin would have been unhappy with any attorney the squaw men retained, but he felt, understandably, that Shelley might have difficulty defending the Indians's interests while in the pay of the intermarried whites. The agent also was severely irked by the attorney's name-dropping. Shelley, in his visits to the Indians, left the impression that he retained personal ties with the Washington office and had access to correspondence relating to the Kiowa, Comanche, and Wichita Agency.[81] The tenor of letters written by Special Agent G. B. Pray to Commissioner of Indian Affairs W. A. Jones in 1897 and 1898 does suggest that Shelley had special ties with them.[82] Jones's predecessor, however, had exhibited no favoritism and chided the attorney for conduct about which Baldwin had complained.[83]

Baldwin's zeal for Indian welfare, reenforced by his often harsh and abusive language, brought him quickly at odds not only with the squaw men, but also with some of the men licensed to trade at the agency. The traders, another powerful interest group, intimidated the typical agent by their long-established ties with Indian leaders and their Washington contacts. But Baldwin was not the typical agent, and he embarked on policies that soon produced a hostile coalition of squaw men, traders, and Indians. Four of the eight trading firms at the agency were represented in this active opposition to the agent, with Dudley P. Brown and C. A. Cleveland in the van. Brown had secured a license to trade during the regime of his uncle P. B. Hunt and was a good friend and drinking companion of Captain Baldwin during the captain's early months on the reservation.[84] Cleveland's uncle, who was the first trader at Fort Sill, had also influenced Cleveland's relationship with the agency. Cleveland was employed by him until opening his own store at Anadarko in 1879.[85]

As virtually all of the annuity and grass money ended up in their hands before Baldwin took over the agency, the traders understandably opposed any change in this situation. But Baldwin proposed to divert some of the Indian income to good causes: the construction of houses and a new school, and the purchase of young cattle to build up the Indian herds. But every dollar that went for those purposes escaped the traders. Nor were some of them happy with the agent's decision to make annuity and grass payments at several points besides Anadarko—which hurt store operators at Anadarko. Baldwin also intervened to prevent D. P. Brown from garnisheeing the funds of Indians, ending up in court with them, and he forced the traders to increase by 50 percent the price paid Indians for cow hides. He climaxed his activities in this area by condoning, if not encouraging, his charges to seek better bargains in the towns now appearing on the borders of the agency.[86] The traders, particularly those at Anadarko, had good cause for hoping to see Baldwin returned to active duty with the Army.

To front for them, the squaw men and traders hostile to Baldwin had no trouble recruiting Indians from the Conservative faction in agency politics. The Kiowas Lone Wolf and Big Tree and the Comanche Big Looking Glass were generally found in opposition to government policies, and Lone Wolf and Big Tree had been hurt financially by the agent's reforms. Squaw man James Jones testified that in the early 1890s he had not paid a cent into the grass funds for a pasture he had leased to a cattleman for $900 a year. But he had paid Lone Wolf $25 a month on the side, and had provided Lone Wolf, and others who had enough influence to cause him trouble, an occasional beef.[87]

The George Conovers, D. P. Browns, and Lone Wolfs soon taught Baldwin the penalty for interfering with their vested interests. Indian delegations were inspired to travel to Washington to complain about their agent; charges of misconduct were filed by Attorney Shelley; and various inspectors, special agents, and even a Commissioner of Indian Affairs descended upon the embattled Baldwin.

The captain called on his allies, including Quanah Parker and Ahpeahtone among the Indians, Captain Hugh L. Scott (and through him General Nelson Miles),[88] and squaw men Emmet Cox and Frank Farwell. Cox, as previously noted, was the son-in-law first of Chief Quirts-quip and next of Chief Quanah Parker and had profited from his family ties. He held a trading license, but not at Anadarko, and also was one of the largest leasers among the squaw men.[89] Cox sometimes served in the highly sensitive post of interpreter. As one of the "good" squaw men, he was a real asset to Baldwin, and the latter did his best to help Cox retain his trading license and operate his store where he wished.[90]

Farwell, addressed as Captain by his associates, had married a Comanche girl a few years after coming to the agency as an employee.[91] During Baldwin's tenure, Captain Farwell served as chief of the Indian police and loyally supported his superior. In turn, Baldwin endorsed his application for adoption into the Comanche tribe, which would have made him eligible for a per capita share in any land distribution under the Jerome Agreement.[92]

Apparently Farwell and Cox and his other supporters enabled Agent Baldwin to maintain an edge over his opponents until the change in administration in March, 1897. The new commissioner, W. A. Jones, visited the agency himself. Baldwin later wrote the commissioner: "It is very evident to me that you are fully under control of that gang of people who have heretofore defrauded and cheated these Indians."[93] This was strong language for an agent to use with a commissioner, and Baldwin's position was rapidly becoming precarious.

The commissioner had struck at Baldwin's influence with the Indians by forcing Quanah Parker and Ahpeahtone from the Court of Indian Offenses and replacing them with Conservatives aligned with the Lone Wolf–Big Looking Glass faction.[94] The same faction dispatched a petition to Washington designed to accomplish Quanah's removal as the ranking Comanche chief, and a month later several of them appeared in Washington to testify before the Senate Committee on Indian Affairs.[95] This delegation headed by Big Looking Glass was matched by a Progressive one led to Washington by Quanah and Ahpeahtone. In conference with the commissioner, the Progressives denounced Shelley, the Lone Wolf–Big Looking Glass faction, and squaw men Conover, Deitrich, Jones, and Woodard, but failed to achieve the reinstatement of Quanah and Ahpeahtone.[96] The only success Baldwin's party achieved was the prevention of the extension of Shelley's contract,[97] but this occurred only after the beginning of the Spanish-

American War had led to the transfer of Captain Baldwin back to regular duty. War or no war, in April, 1898, Baldwin's days as head of the Kiowa, Comanche, and Wichita Agency had been numbered.

Baldwin's troubled tenure had been an impressive demonstration of the influence squaw men could exercise at an agency. Baldwin also had publicized the various techniques by which the intermarried whites bettered themselves financially. Indeed, this had been the origin of the trouble, as an inspector reported early in the controversy:

> There has been some friction between him and certain squaw men, and three or four of the old chiefs, growing out of the fact that he has undertaken to change some of their past ways, which he thought unjust to the other Indians. He has cut down some of their pasture and cut off the tribute money heretofore received by the chiefs, and brought all the money into the public treasury for an equal division among all the Indians.[98]

Within three years of Captain Baldwin's departure, a modified version of the long-delayed Jerome Agreement would be approved by Congress, and another change in agents would take place. Baldwin's immediate successor was a political appointee, William T. Walker, whose career in small-town journalism poorly prepared him for the hot seat the Captain had vacated. Walker lasted about a year, being replaced by retired Lieutenant Colonel James F. Randlett, who already had revealed talent for reservation administration at the Unitah and Ouray Agency.

Walker's brief tenure saw the agency quiet down, apparently because he did not exhibit the same willingness as Baldwin to challenge the squaw men and traders. Indicative of the new climate at the agency was the approval of the applications of several of the squaw men, who had managed to be adopted by the Kiowas or Comanches, for 320-acre headrights under the 1867 treaty. Despite the obvious injustice in permitting a few adopted whites to obtain twice the amount of land to be made available to each person on the tribal rolls under the Jerome Agreement, George Conover, W. F. Deitrich, Thomas F. Woodard, Emmet Cox, and others were permitted to do just that.[99]

Meanwhile, those who had exploited their favored position to secure free range continued to do so. Until the opening of the reservation in the summer of 1901, squaw men held pastures of about five thousand acres each, free of charge.[100] Theoretically this amount was available to any Indian on the tribal rolls of the Kiowas, Comanches, and Apaches; but very few had the cattle, or the connections with white men who did, to profit from the situation. Nor if every Indian had availed himself of the opportunity, would there have been enough good grass land to go around.

As the era of the closed reservation drew to an end in western Oklahoma, squaw men continued to do the things that agents had complained about interminably. James Myers was accused by Randlett of acting as agent for Baldwin's old enemy D. P. Brown in the purchase of young cattle from the Indians.[101] On the nearly five hundred thousand acres of range that the Kiowa, Comanche, and Apache Indians continued to hold in common until late 1906, squaw men were the most conspicuous users of the special rate for Indian cattle. For example, of the nine individuals holding permits for one pasture in late 1902, squaw men with the familiar names Deitrich, Woodard, Farwell, Cox, and Clark were grazing 1,700 cattle; the three Indians on the list were holding a total of only 320 head.[102]

Protests about the favored position of squaw men were now coming from a new source, the thousands of white settlers who thronged the Anadarko–Fort Sill area hoping to draw homesteads when the surplus lands of the Kiowa, Comanche, and Apache Reservation were distributed. For the approximately thirteen thousand homesteads available, there were more than one hundred and sixty-seven thousand applicants. Odds like this meant mostly disappointed home seekers, and some of them chose to challenge the allotment procedure by which squaw men and their families had received homesteads. But an investigation of the agency turned up only one instance of a squaw man securing more land for members of his family than they were entitled to.[103] Intermarried whites did not have to resort to fraud to do well, as was indicated by a bit of doggerel entitled "The Squaw Man" appearing in a local newspaper:

I wish I'd been a squaw man
  And had raised a papoose band
To draw beefsteak and rations
  And acres of choice land.

. . . .

I could live in royal splendor,
  As happy as a king;
For Uncle Sam would deal to me
  My share of everything.

And when the day was ended,
  Before my prayers were said,
I would thank the Heavenly Father,
  That with my daily bread
He'd give me good sense enough
  A red skin wife to wed.

Whose only charm to win me
  Is not beauty thin skin deep,
For beauty fades,
  But U.S. money always full the larders keep.

Not I, to choose the palefaces fair
  When each increase in band
Would bring to him fresh toil and care
  To me fresh beef and land.

. . . .

She may not have rare beauty
  She will do her part each day,
To help you cause the hungry world
  To ever stand at bay.

You may not draw the rations
  Or have the alloted land,
But you may have contentment
  With your little pale face band.[104]

But even as the verse appeared in a paper published within what had been the boundaries of the Kiowa, Comanche, and Apache Reservation, the conditions that had produced the squaw man were passing. He had flourished on the closed reservation where being an intermarried white carried with it a privileged position. It was exploiting this advantage that earned him the hostility and the envy of his fellow white man and the demeaning title "squaw man."

Although the term had come to be applied uniformly to inter-married white men, for the record, those among the Kiowas, Comanches, and Apaches were good or bad depending upon their relationship with the current agent. As the case of Thomas Woodard revealed, the squaw man might be the recipient of high praise from one agent, only to be denounced by the next. However, as Captain Baldwin's experience demonstrated, any agent was in for trouble who took too seriously his guardianship of the Indians and struck at the privileged position of the squaw men. They had too much influence to be disposed of casually.

Relative to the question my subtitle poses, the record seems to suggest that squaw men were indeed disturbers of the peace. Countless agents across the West protested their activities, Washington officials deplored them, and Congress echoed to attacks on squaw men. On the Kiowa, Comanche, and Apache Reservation they shamelessly profited from their connections with the tribes and made life miserable for any government official or Indian who opposed them.

Yet, it is sad but true that they also were advance agents of civilization. The more active, energetic, and grasping they were, the more they represented the ideal type toward which the Indian was supposed to evolve. Before 1850 the frontier had known many generations of white men who had taken Indian wives. But pity and contempt were dominant in the reactions of their fellow whites, rather than the envy and hostility the squaw men inspired. They were portents of the future. Their careers at the expense of the Indian foreshadowed the oppression of the Indian as the reservation was dissolved under him and he was cast out to make his way in an alien society.

Squaw men were at the heart of reservation politics and factionalism. They helped supply the continuity to reservation affairs that the ephemeral agents could never provide in their brief tenures. Thus, regardless of how we react to the squaw men, they cannot be ignored if we wish to understand reservation life in the second half of the nineteenth century.

Notes

Abbreviations Employed in Footnotes:

AR	Annual Report.
CIA	Commissioner of Indian Affairs.
ID-LS	Indian Division—Letters Sent, Department of the Interior, National Archives, Record Group 75.
IOLB	Indian Office Letter Book, National Archives, Record Group 75.
KLB	Kiowa Letter Book, Oklahoma Historical Society.
LB	Letter Book.
MC	Micro-copy, National Archives, Record Group 75.
OHS	Oklahoma Historical Society.
OIA-LR	Office of Indian Affairs—Letters Received, National Archives, Record Group, 75.
RG 75	Record Group 75, National Archives.
ser.	Volume in United States Government Publications Serial Set.

1. In K. Ross Toole *et al.*, eds., *Probing the American West* (Santa Fe, N.M., 1962), 62–70.

2. Walter O'Meara, *Daughters of the Country* (New York, N.Y., 1968).

3. Stanley Vestal, *New Sources of Indian History, 1850–1891* (Norman, Okla., 1934), 313.

4. Clark Wissler, *Indian Cavalcade* (New York, N.Y., 1938), 217–36.

5. Burns Mantle and Garrison P. Sherwood, eds., *The Best Plays of 1899–1909* (New York, N.Y., 1933), 233. The first movie produced by Jessie L. Lasky, with Cecil B. de Mille as a co-director was *'Twixt Love and Duty*, which was based on the play. A novel, also based on the play, Julie Opp Faversham's *The Squaw Man* (New York, N.Y., 1906), appeared in 1906.

6. Vestal, *New Sources*, 313.

7. Grace Steele Woodward, *Pocahontas* (Norman, Okla., 1969), 165–70.

8. E. B. O'Callaghan, ed., *Documents Relative to the Colonial History of the State of New York* (15 vols., Albany, N.Y., 1856–1887), V, 625.

9. Clark Wissler, *The American Indian* (New York, N.Y., 1931), 128.

10. AR of William Armstrong, 1838 (ser. 344, p. 438).

11. AR of Mitchell, 1843 (ser. 481, p. 387).

12. AR of Twiss, 1856 (ser. 875, p. 640).

13. AR of Elliott, 1845 (ser. 470, p. 552).

14. AR of Fitzpatrick, 1851 (ser. 636, p. 336); AR of Norwood, 1852 (ser. 658, p. 359).

15. For a good statement of this policy, see AR of CIA Charles E. Mix, 1858 (ser. 974, p. 357).

16. As CIA J. W. Denver put it in 1857: "No white person should be permitted to obtain any kind of possession or foothold within the limits of the reservations, nor even to enter them, except in the employ or by permission of the government" (ser. 942, p. 293).

17. Charles J. Kappler, ed., *Indian Affairs: Laws and Treaties* (2 vols., Washington, D.C., 1904), II, 978.

18. Robert S. Neighbors to Major General D. E. Twiggs, July 17, 1857 (ser. 919, p. 554).

19. Kappler, *Indian Affairs*, II, 982–84.

20. The 1879 population figures were: Comanches, 1,552; Kiowas, 1,138; Apaches, 315; Wichitas, 209; Wacoes, 49; Towaconies, 155; Keechies, 75; Caddoes, 543; Delawares, 81 (ser. 1910, p. 168).

21. Conditions for employees are referred to in P. B. Hunt to CIA, July 23, 1883, typed copy at OHS; AR of E. E. White, 1888 (ser. 2637, p. 95); Hugh Brown to CIA, January 23, 1894, in KLB 40, pp. 182–83; W. D. Myers to A. B. Kelly, July 29, 1889, in KLB 31, pp. 176–77.

22. Statement by J. J. Sturm, February 24, 1883, typed copy at OHS.

23. Hall's list of whites on the reservation, in OIA-LR, 1886, 7421.

24. Grant Foreman, *Indian-Pioneer History* (OHS), XXV, 449.

25. General W. B. Hazen to Superintendent Hoag, January 5, 1870, MC Roll 376.

26. CIA to General W. B. Hazen, February 9, 1870, IOLB 94, pp. 242–43.

27. Acting CIA to P. B. Hunt, August 12, 1878, Land LB 51, p. 420, RG 75.

28. CIA to W. D. Myers, March 30, 1889, Land LB 182, p. 399, RG 75.

29. For example, see Agent for Northern District of California, 1862 (ser. 1157, p. 455); Agent for the Upper Platte, 1864 (ser. 1220, pp. 531–32); Mackinac Agent, 1864 (ser. 1220, p. 589); Navajo Agent, 1875 (ser. 1680, pp. 832–33).

30. *Congressional Record*, U.S. House of Representatives, 44th Cong, 1 Sess., 3568.

31. J. F. Randlett to CIA, June 17, 1902, KLB 99, pp. 20–21; George W. Conover, *Sixty Years in Southwest Oklahoma* (Anadarko, Okla., 1927), 15 ff.

32. Census by Agent, February 14, 1878, Cattle Grazing File, OHS.

33. CIA to A. C. Williams, March 22, 1878, Cattle Grazing File, OHS.

34. AR of CIA E. A. Hayt, 1879 (ser. 1910, p. 104).

35. AR of Hunt, 1884 (ser. 2287, p. 124).

36. For the Williams affair, see Acting CIA to Hunt, June 4, 1883, Civilization LB 39, p. 487, RG 75; P. B. Hunt to CIA, December 7, 1883,

typed copy at OHS; CIA to Hunt, December 19, 1883, Land LB 120, pp. 155–58, RG 75.

37. Hunt to CIA, December 27, 1883, typed copy at OHS.

38. For the McKinney-Davis affair, see copy of C. R. McKinney to Luther H. Pike, December 20, 1883, in Cattle Grazing File, OHS; Hunt to CIA, February 29, 1884, KLB 15, pp. 484–88; Acting CIA to Hunt, June 17, 1884, Land LB 126, pp. 441–42, RG 75; Acting CIA to Hunt, August 14, 1884, Land LB 128, pp. 416–17, RG 75.

39. Copy of C. R. McKinney to Luther H. Pike, December 20, 1883, in Cattle Grazing File, OHS.

40. Acting CIA to J. Lee Hall, October 13, 1885, Land LB 141, pp. 93–94, RG 75.

41. AR of Hunt, 1884 (ser. 2287, p. 124).

42. Hall to CIA, September 15, 1885, in KLB 21, p. 13.

43. Acting CIA to Hall, October 6, 1885, in Agents and Agency File, OHS.

44. Acting CIA to Hall, October 8, 1885, Land LB 140, pp. 470–76, RG 75.

45. CIA to Secretary of the Interior, March 5, 1886, Land LB 145, pp. 263–79, RG 75; CIA to Hall, April 14, 1886, in Squaw-man File, OHS.

46. For biographical data on Pruner, see J. F. Randlett to CIA, March 10, 1900, in KLB 83, pp. 291–94; Foreman, *Indian-Pioneer History*, LXXX, 494, OHS. For Deitrich, see: Randlett to CIA, March, 1900, in KLB 83, pp. 333–34; J. J. Methvin, *In the Limelight* (Anadarko, Okla., 1928), 113. For Clark, see Charles E. Campbell, "Down Among the Red Men," *Kansas Historical Collections*, XVII, 640; Hugh D. Corwin, *Comanche and Kiowa Captives in Oklahoma and Texas* (Guthrie, Okla., 1959), 103. For Curtis, see CIA to G. P. Pray, September 15, 1898, in Cattle and Grazing File, OHS. For Emmet Cox, see Foreman, *Indian-Pioneer History*, C, 282; Hunt to Sam Simpson, August 25, 1883, in KLB 16, p. 68. There is information on all five in Hall's list of whites on the reservation, in OIA-LR, 1886, 7421, RG 75.

47. For example, see Acting Secretary of the Interior to CIA, March 9, 1886, in OIA-LR, 1886, 7421.

48. Hall to CIA, January 21, 1886, in OIA-LR, 1886, 7421.

49. AR of Secretary of the Interior L. Q. C. Lamar, 1887 (ser. 2542, p. 8).

50. CIA to Hall, April 14, 1886, in Squaw-man File, OHS.

51. Quoting a former Commissioner. CIA to Secretary of the Interior, March 5, 1886, Land LB 145, pp. 263–69, RG 75.

52. Hall to CIA, April 14, 1886, quoted in Martha Buntin, "History of the Kiowa, Comanche, and Wichita Indian Agency" (M.A. thesis, University of Oklahoma, 1931), 86–87.

53. *Congressional Record*, U.S. House of Representatives, 50 Cong., 1 Sess., 6885–86.

54. 25 United States Code, section 818 (1964).

55. For example, see Acting CIA to Hall, October 8, 1885, Land LB

140, pp. 470–76, RG 75; CIA to Secretary of the Interior, March 5, 1886, Land LB 145, pp. 263–79, RG 75.

56. For biographical data on Nestell, see George D. Day to CIA, February 3, 1892, in KLB 38, pp. 86–89; T. D. Marcum to Secretary of the Interior, October 14, 1887, in OIA-LR, 1887, 27959; CIA to E. E. White, February 1, 1888, Accounts LB 91, p. 5, RG 75.

57. George D. Day to CIA, February 3, 1892, in KLB 38, pp. 86–89.

58. For biographical data on Woodard, see Charles E. Adams to CIA, November 7, 1889, in KLB 32, pp. 26–31; Adams to CIA, September 12, 1890, KLB 33, pp. 414–19; Foreman, *Indian-Pioneer History*, XCI, 248.

59. Charles E. Adams to CIA, November 7, 1889, in KLB 33, pp. 414–19.

60. W. H. Able to CIA, n.d., OIA-LR, 1894, 25353.

61. For the modified version enacted into law, see Kappler, *Indian Affairs*, I, 708–13.

62. This was discovered by investigators for the law firm representing the Kiowas, Comanches, and Apaches in their suit against the government. See *Petitioners Request for Findings of Fact*, Docket #32, National Archives.

63. Charles E. Adams to CIA, March 19, 1891, KLB 35, pp. 488–90.

64. Acting CIA to Adams, March 27, 1891, Land LB 213, pp. 446–48, RG 75.

65. Hugh Brown to CIA, October 31, 1893, KLB 40, p. 105, OHS; CIA to Brown, November 6, 1893, Land LB 268, pp. 68–69, RG 75.

66. CIA to Baldwin, January 17, 1895, Land LB 295, pp. 455–56, RG 75.

67. Quanah was the son of a Comanche chief and a white captive, Cynthia Parker. Ahpeahtone had won a measure of fame in 1890 by visiting the Paiute messiah, Wovoka.

68. Baldwin to CIA, KLB 44, pp. 234–37.

69. Sturm to Secretary of the Interior, June 17, 1895, OIA-LR, 1895, 34589.

70. Acting CIA to Baldwin, May 3, 1895, Estates File, OHS.

71. Foreman, *Indian-Pioneer History*, LXXIV, 327.

72. Baldwin to CIA, KLB 55, pp. 357–59.

73. Foreman, *Indian-Pioneer History*, XXII, 183–84.

74. Baldwin to CIA, KLB 58, pp. 100–102.

75. CIA to Secretary of the Interior, March 21, 1894, Land LB 276, pp. 446–50, RG 75.

76. CIA to Baldwin, December 23, 1895, Land LB 320, pp. 428–30; Baldwin to CIA, December 28, 1895, OIA-LR, 1896, 1828.

77. Testimony by Deitrich and Woodard, April 26, 1897, in Cattle Grazing File, OHS.

78. Baldwin to CIA, May 13, 1896, KLB 51, pp. 116–23; Baldwin to CIA, December 28, 1895, OIA-LR, 1896, 1828.

79. Baldwin to Woodard, June 3, 1896, KLB 52, p. 2.

80. Baldwin to Woodard and Deitrich, June 3, 1896, KLB 52, pp. 5–7.

81. Baldwin to CIA, July 2, 1896, KLB 51, pp. 222–27.

82. For example, see Pray to CIA, May 25, 1898, OIA-LR, 1898, 24520.

83. Secretary of the Interior to Shelley, May 20, 1896, ID-LS, v. 88, p. 459.

84. J. Lee Hall to CIA, November 2, 1885, KLB 23, pp. 3–4; G. W. Conover to Shelley, April 21, 1896, OIA-LR, 1896, 16116.

85. Methvin, In the Limelight, 54–55.

86. Baldwin to CIA, January 7, 1897, KLB 55, pp. 42–44; Baldwin to CIA, November 5, 1897, KLB 58, pp. 100–102.

87. Examination of James N. Jones, April 28, 1899, in Cattle Grazing File, OHS.

88. Baldwin to H. L. Scott, January 10, 1898, KLB 60, pp. 59–63; Baldwin to Scott, January 6, 1898, KLB 60, p. 4 (a telegram). Scott had served several years at Fort Sill and knew the Indian situation well.

89. In 1901, Cox held a 14,302-acre pasture.

90. Baldwin to CIA, September 3, 1897, KLB 55, p. 469; Baldwin to CIA, March 9, 1898, KLB 58, pp. 327–28.

91. Sworn Statement by Frank B. Farwell, December 9, 1899, in Reports File, OHS; James F. Randlett to CIA, March, 1900, KLB 83, pp. 333–34.

92. Acting CIA to Baldwin, October 1, 1895, Land LB 315, pp. 258–60, RG 75.

93. Baldwin to CIA, January 11, 1898, KLB 58, pp. 21–31.

94. Baldwin to CIA, January 8, 1898, KLB 58, p. 212.

95. Petition, January 10, 1898, OIA-LR, 1898, 1488; William D. Leonard, February 9, 1898, KLB 60, p. 223.

96. Council with CIA, March 17, 1898, OIA-LR, 1898, 12521½.

97. Council Proceedings, June 17, 1898, OIA-LR, 1898, 28646.

98. C. C. Duncan to Secretary of the Interior, June 24. 1896, OIA-LR, 1896, 26844.

99. CIA to Secretary of the Interior, September 3, 1898, Land LB 194, pp. 148–50, RG 75; E. L. Clark to Randlett, June 19, 1901, in Cattle Grazing File, OHS; CIA to Secretary of the Interior, January 22, 1902, Land LB 521, pp. 517–19, RG 75. The latter letter indicates that two of Conover's sons each received 320 acres.

100. Acting CIA to Secretary of the Interior, February 24, 1900, Land LB 216, pp. 134–38, RG 75.

101. CIA to Randlett, December 28, 1899, Land LB 123, pp. 158–59, RG 75.

102. CIA to Randlett, November 12, 1902, Cattle Grazing File, OHS.

103. "The Results of an Investigation Into the Affairs of the Kiowa Indian Agency" (ser. 4646, p. 12).

104. The Cache Register, October 12, 1905, 3.

To Shape a Western State:
Some Dimensions
of the Kansas Search for Capital,
1865-1893

Allan G. Bogue, University of Wisconsin

Addressing the Kansas legislature in early January, 1866, Governor Crawford maintained that the "days of trial have passed; freedom has triumphed; Kansas is free, and now offers the immigrant a home unsurpassed in richness, beauty and fertility. It is now for us to cultivate this magnificent garden, and make it blossom and bloom with beauty, and bear in rich exuberance the fruits of peace and plenty."[1] When the definitive history of the economic development of Kansas is written, it will picture the growth of the Kansas economy both in quantitative terms and in terms of the unique experience of the individual Kansan; it will describe the system of laws and institutions in which that growth occurred and will assess and explain the relation between the state's development and its legal and insti-

203

tutional framework. This is a large order, and many tasks still wait willing workmen. Moreover, the development of Kansas cannot be fully understood unless the processses of growth in this commonwealth are compared with those of neighboring states and, no less important, with those territories and states that were settled prior to that climactic date—1854. We must remember also that the land, transportation, military, and Indian policies of the federal government were of vital importance in determining the shape of things in the frontier territory and state. In this paper I wish to discuss some of the ways in which Kansans used their political and legal institutions to develop the Jayhawk state during the twenty-five years that followed Governor Crawford's message.

By the time that Governor Crawford rallied his constituents to the task of developing their "magnificent garden," they had prescribed certain of the ground rules of economic development in their constitution, and such provisions reflected, of course, both the era and the regional and political conditioning that the early Kansans had experienced before reaching Kansas. They began their task also at a time when the fundamental nature of the corporation and ideas as to its relation to the state were relatively well formed. Kansans would develop some rather definite ideas about corporations and their place in society, and that at no distant date, but there would be none of the groping to understand the basic concept of the corporation that Professor Oscar Handlin has described in the early national period in Massachusetts.[2] As Kansans turned their attention seriously to the conquest of the prairies, they gathered confidence from the fact that the major technological problems of railroading had been solved. There did exist the means to carry the products of any future Kansas settler to market.

In its simplest conceptualization the economic development of Kansas is to be seen as the application of people, technology, and capital to the natural resources of the state. In that task the state legislators could play an important role. In considering the activities of government, some historians have distinguished between promotional and regulative activity, which I assume to be much the same distinction that Oscar Handlin was making when he described commonwealth and police-state functions.[3] But the terms "promotional" and "regulative" require some additional elaboration. State action might involve promotional activity of a positive sort, as when lawmakers provided funds for a department of immigration, or instructed state officers to sell state lands and use the proceeds to support the construction of state buildings—in other words, when they intervened directly in the economy to stimulate the development of the state stock of manpower and capital. When the legislators passed a variety of laws authorizing counties, cities, and townships to float bond issues in support of railroad construction, the action was permissive only. But such action unleashed the most important of all government promotional activity in Kansas prior to 1900, if we use expenditures as a measure of importance.

By regulatory activity I mean the statement of the legal, political, social, and economic relations of Kansans, one to another —that is, the specification of behavioral patterns—and the provision of sanctions to insure that these were followed. Within the regulatory purview of the state, for instance, fell the choice of county boundaries, the general organization of county government, and prescription of the duties of the various county officers. At a different level, regulation involved establishing a penalty for stealing livestock or controlling the entrance of Texas cattle into the state. It takes little thought to understand that the regulative function might have important promotional implications. Although there are still unexplored opportunities in the study of positive and permissive promotion at both the state and local levels in Kansas, scholars have marked out a number of the trails.[4] I wish only, therefore, to block in some of the major patterns of government promotional activity for comparative purposes and to devote the remainder of this paper to a discussion of an important aspect of regulatory legislation—the credit laws, in so far as they applied to real estate security.

In what ways could the Founding Fathers of Kansas assist in providing the people necessary for economic development? They could, theoretically at least, lure settlers to the state, swell the ranks of its producers, and thereby build a massive home market. They could achieve these ends by advertising the resources of the state, by holding out inducements to immigrants, and by providing the kind of institutional environment that residents would find attractive.

The framers of the Wyandotte Constitution extended the suffrage to persons of foreign birth who had formally declared their intention to become citizens of the United States, after such individuals had fulfilled the residency requirements—six months residence in Kansas and thirty days of local residence prior to voting. Such immigrant voting rights have not yet received the attention that they deserve from historians, but there can be no question that such provisions enhanced the attractiveness of a state to the immigrant.[5]

The Kansas legislators had provided in 1865 that conscientious objectors might obtain exemption from military service by paying thirty dollars per annum to the public-school fund.[6] With Mennonite immigration in mind, Governor Osborne recommended in 1873 that the punitive aspect of this law be repealed; and the Kansas legislature followed his recommendation.[7] The governor's message was usually printed in German as well as English.[8] In 1867 the school laws were amended to allow the teaching of German in the public schools on the request of a requisite number of residents in a school district.[9] Minor bounties to assist in the development of a silk industry during the 1880s may be regarded in somewhat the same light, since it was French immigrants who were primarily interested in establishing that industry in Kansas.[10]

In other respects the lawmakers of the new state did considerably less to encourage immigration directly than successive governors believed to be appropriate.[11] Although they authorized the governor in 1864 to appoint unpaid commissioners to serve with him as the Bureau of Immigration, their successors were niggardly in supporting that body.[12] They did appropriate some funds to pay for the printing of pamphlets advertising Kansas and its resources, and they did authorize expenditures for the preparation and display of exhibits at a series of international and national exhibitions, including those in Paris in 1867 and London in 1887, as well as the Centennial and New Orleans exhibitions in this country.[13] Unquestionably these exhibits were supported mainly in the hope that they would attract settlers to Kansas. Kansas lawmakers, however, did not see fit to support a permanent immigration agent in New York or to send such individuals abroad for any length of time at state expense. Governors did confer the title "Commissioner of Immigration" on immigration agents employed by railroad companies that were interested in selling lands in Kansas and in developing the traffic potential of the regions that they served.[14] In part the appropriations of the State Board of Agriculture were justified in terms of its advertising functions, and the annual reports of that body were among the most impressive of their kind in this era.[15]

Still fresh in the minds of the Founding Fathers of Kansas when they wrote the state constitution were the problems which the efforts of Eastern and Midwestern states to subsidize internal improvement had caused.[16] As a result the Kansas Constitution contained both a provision limiting the amount of state debt to be incurred for the purpose of making "public improvements" to the amount of one million dollars and a specific caveat which ran as follows: "The State shall never be a party in carrying on any works of internal improvement."[17]

Restricted by constitutional limitations, the Kansas legislators could participate directly in the development of social overhead capital in only minor respects. They expended the million dollars of state debt authorized for public improvements in the construction of state buildings for the most part. They allocated to four railroads the income from the sale of the state's 500,000-acre grant, thereby overriding the wishes of those who had written the state constitution and had attempted to reserve the grant for educational purposes. The legislature also served as the intermediary custodian and supervisor of some federal land grants to railroads.[18] The latter authority was a restricted one, and in many cases in which the state legislators wished to influence the policy of railroad corporations they could resort only to heartfelt memorials to Congress, or, as in the case of the settlers on the Osage lands, they might provide relief legislation to aid the members of a group whom they believed to have been injured by federal railroad policy.[19]

In the field of education the direct role of the lawmakers was more significant. It was their task to provide for the administration of the common-school lands and the landed endowment of the institutions of higher learning as well as to provide other support for those schools.[20] But developmental strategies might on occasion conflict, one with the other. Were the common-school lands to be so managed as to deliver maximum revenue to the state school fund, or were they to be administered so as to assist local residents in obtaining cheap farms or speculative gains? This was the decision that the pioneer lawmakers had to make, and Kansas governors of the 1880s believed that the legislators had been too much concerned with fattening the pocketbooks of the settlers and too little with the long-run welfare of their children. Sale and appraisement procedures had cost the school fund dearly, argued Governor John A. Martin in 1885.[21] Under Article VI, Section 3, of the Constitution the school fund must be invested, and the Kansan lawmakers authorized the state auditor to purchase the bond issues of local school districts on terms difficult to duplicate in the open market. In so far as these issues were sound, and most of them apparently were, this was an ingenious and effective use of state resources.

But if Kansas was to grow, her citizens must provide the economic services that this generation of state-builders deemed essential for the task, and they must somehow provide any other services as well that the mores of the time held to be essential to social well-being. Eventually American state legislators were to develop various devices to circumvent constitutional limitations on state debt, but in Kansas the pressure to do so was apparently not great during this era. Rather, the state legislators adopted a strategy of permissive development, allowing municipal governments to bond themselves. The first territorial code gave no such general power to the counties, and as late as 1863 the Supreme Court of Kansas described that decision with some approval. In the opinion of that tribunal in the case of *Shawnee County* v. *Carter* (1863), involving the validity of bonds issued by Shawnee County's commissioners in payment of the construction costs of a courthouse when the law authorized only the use of county warrants and the current revenues for that purpose, State Supreme Court Justice Samuel A. Kingman held for the majority:

> They had no power to bind the county by bonds, and herein was the only safe-guard which the legislature had left the people against oppressive burthens which might in the end ruin them with excessive taxation. When there was no

money in the treasury to pay the warrants, if extravagant and speculative outlays for buildings were attempted, the measure would defeat itself because the warrants would be of so little value that cupidity itself would fail of a desirable object of investment in becoming the owner of such warrants. They would be so discredited as to become valueless in market, and the temptation to involve the county removed. The accumulation of debt would cease from the inability of the county officers to carry on projected improvements on a credit. Poor as was this barrier against extravagant or visionary contracts, it is one which would be likely in a new country to arrest the evil before it had reached the point of ruin, and the anxiety to advance . . . local interests at the general expense would receive a check for the want of means. If, however, the board could substitute for warrants, bonds bearing a high rate of interest, it would furnish an investment that might tempt men to take contracts for the erection of such buildings for the county as might suit the board, at ruinous prices, and rely upon making up for the present want of availability [of capital], by the high prices and high rate of interest obtained in the end.[22]

Was Justice Kingman's opinion in effect the dying gasp of a Jeffersonianism dedicated to simple and economical government? Hardly so—but the philosophy attributed to the legislators of 1855 does contrast strikingly with the actions of Kansas lawmakers a few years later. As Kansas entered its developmental era after the Civil War, the legislators approved general legislation, allowing the municipal governments to bond themselves for various purposes including the building of schools and county buildings and the encouragement of railroad construction by subscribing to the stock of railway companies or by giving other aid to such corporations. Various authors have told the story of municipal debt in Kansas prior to 1900 in varying degrees of detail.[23] The reports of the Kansas state auditor present a fairly good picture of the face value of municipal debt in Kansas from 1878 onward, but we know much too little of the workings of the municipal-bond market and the amounts realized on the securities by the municipalities and their beneficiaries, particularly the railroads. The bonds were seldom if ever sold at face value.

A period of rather generous bonding during the late 1860s and early 1870s was followed by a depression era in which the lawmakers increased restrictions on bonding somewhat and aided heavily burdened municipalities by authorizing local units of government to compromise their debts at lower figures and to refund them by issuing new bonds. Some of the details of this refunding appear in the records of court cases, and some indications of the amounts involved are found in the auditor's reports. But we need further research on the compromise movement. Despite the problems of the mid and late 1870s Kansas municipalities continued to bond themselves during the 1880s and found railroads and investors eager, or at least willing, to take their obligations. It is clear also that some of the county bonds of the late 1870s and 1880s represented floating indebtedness that had been accumulated in the day-to-day business of county affairs rather than investment in capital improvements. This was, however, a small part of county debt as was the fraudulent indebtedness which is often mentioned. There was some tendency also for municipal leaders to bond for objectives of a more highly promotional nature than for those purposes that we ordinarily consider to have been an investment in social overhead capital—to build factories and mills and to prospect for coal or salt deposits. Although the Kansas Supreme Court tried to distinguish between aid to enterprises of a public and a private nature, some activity of this sort marked both the 1870s and the 1880s.[24]

Kansas governors of the late 1870s and the 1880s regarded the load of municipal debt in Kansas with suspicion, and by the mid 1880s had become particularly critical of the debt developed in aid of railroads.[25] Indeed Governor Martin recommended in 1889 that the Legislature repeal "every law authorizing the creation of municipal debts for any purpose, whatever, except, perhaps, the building of . . . school-houses."[26] Historians have in general followed the governors' lead. We can now, however, bring a little additional perspective to the story by comparing in Table 1 the distribution of municipal debt in Kansas with the findings of Harry H. Pierce, reported in his study of government aid to railroads in New York between 1826 and 1875.[27]

Our comparison unfortunately cannot be an exact one, since Professor Pierce has provided us with an analysis of municipal debt in New York on January 1, 1875, in those units of local government that were aiding railroads at that time. The first comprehensive figures available concerning Kansas date from

Table 1
MUNICIPAL DEBT DISTRIBUTION
NEW YORK AND KANSAS

	Percentages				
	Jails & Public Offices	*Miscel- laneous*	*Railroads*	*War & Bounties*	*Bridges & Docks*
New York: (1875)	2.1	6.7	64.4	2.5	19.7
Kansas: (1878)	2.9	6.7	56.4	....	9.0
Kansas: (1890)	3.0	4.5	43.0	....	2.4

	Boulevards & Cemeteries	*Schools*	*Funding*
N.Y.: (1875)	2.8	1.7	....
Kansas: (1878)	1.3	16.5	11.
Kansas: (1890)	.6	15.8	20.6

	General Improvement	*Industrial Promotion*
N.Y.: (1875)	....	....
Kansas: (1878)	1.2	.6
Kansas: (1890)	9.2	.9

SOURCE: Pierce, *Railroads of New York*, Appendix, Chart 1; Kansas State Auditor, *First Biennial Report*, 1878, 274–305; Kansas State Auditor, *Seventh Biennial Report*, 1890, 416–98.

1878 and include all municipalities that had bonded themselves for any purpose whatsover. It was necessary also to include in the Kansas summary a "funding" category that included some debt for railroad aid, but probably not enough in 1878 to have raised the percentage of the total debt represented by railroad bonds to a significant degree. Despite such qualifications the comparison raises some important questions. Professor Pierce showed that 64.4 percent of the public debt in the New York municipalities was chargeable to railroad aid, and some three years later the Kansas figure was but 56.4 percent. Sixteen and one-half percent of the Kansas municipal debt represented school bond indebtedness at this time, and only 1.7 percent of the New York indebtedness was of this nature. The Kansans had apparently not allowed their desire for railroads to lead them to assume debts in support of railroad building that were wildly disproportionate to those assumed by the citizens of older states. And the prairie settlers were apparently allocating a relatively larger proportion of their public debt to the support of schools.

By 1890 the municipal debt in Kansas had risen from the $12,442,176 of 1878 to some $36,188,893, of which some $7.5 million, or 21 percent, represented refunding. Even if the funding category of 1890 had represented investment in railroads only—which it patently did not—the sum total of railroad bonds would still have been only 64 percent of the local government indebtedness in the state. School bonds represented 16 percent of the total debt in 1890. Such findings might appear in different light if related to the taxable resources of the state, but they seem to suggest that the effort of Kansas to develop railroads was not, in terms of the proportion of resources invested, so strikingly different from that in older regions. The amount of municipal indebtedness invested in new railroad mileage in the State of Kansas during the 1880s was slightly under $2,000 per mile—or less than one-sixteenth, probably, of the cost of construction.[28] Was this an unreasonable contribution for the local communities to make? Answering that question is of course a problem in itself. The proportion of the total indebtedness of municipalities, chargeable to schools, suggests a concern with the social environment that may have differed significantly from that on earlier frontiers and perhaps even from that in some older regions during the 1870s.

The investment of township, city, or county in railroad bonds or stocks typically met only a part of the cost of the construction of a railroad line to or through the municipality. The finished railroad line represented an amalgam of foreign capital and the pledge of local residents to pay the interest and principal of their municipal obligations. Municipal bonding in aid of railroads was a means, therefore, of attracting nonresident capital, and the generosity of local aid would presumably affect the success of municipal endeavors to bring railroads to aspiring, and sometimes conspiring, communities. It was the prerogative of the state legislators to prescribe the ground rules of such activity, and a veritable welter of legislation regulated municipal bonding in the period 1865–1890. Let us look briefly at two aspects of this legislation—those clauses governing the community decision to bond itself and the limitations placed on the amount of such aid.

During the legislative sessions of 1865 and 1866 the Kansas lawmakers passed general laws providing that county or city councils might place the question of a railroad bond issue before the voters of their community and prescribing that a simple majority of the votes cast was sufficient to approve a bond issue.[29] In 1870 the legislators extended the privilege of bonding for railroad aid to townships, provided that fifty qualified voters petitioned for an election and 60 per cent of the voters participating in the election approved the proposal.[30] Two years later the petitioning procedure of initiation was extended to cities and counties; now the required number of signatures on petitions in all types of municipalities was set at 20 percent of the voters, and a simple majority of the voters was needed for approval.[31]

With the depression of 1873 a different tone began to pervade the bonding legislation of the Jayhawk state. The legislators developed special and general legislation allowing municipal governments to compromise and refund their indebtedness. In 1876 they also recast the general law that governed municipal bonding.[32] Municipal authorities now might hold a railroad-bonding election only after two-fifths of the resident taxpayers had petitioned for it, and the proposal had to be approved by a two-thirds majority of the votes cast if bonds were to be issued. Nor could there be a second election on the same proposal unless one-half of the resident taxpayers petitioned for it. During the years of the great boom of the 1880s bonding went on merrily, nevertheless, and in 1887 the lawmakers once more "improved" the regulations governing local bond elections.[33] The election procedure in general was allowed to stay much the same, but a majority of the legal voters had to petition for a second election on a railroad-aid proposition. And in this law, moreover, appeared a provision requiring that the railroad company involved must deposit adequate funds to pay the cost of holding the election with the county commissioners before the election.

When the legislators of 1865 considered the question of how much railroad aid should be given by counties or cities, they provided merely that counties should not invest more than $300,000 in any one railroad and placed a comparable limitation of $250,000 on cities.[34] Their successors of 1866 closed the gate somewhat by deciding that no city was to assist railroads to an amount greater than $600,000 and that counties were to be limited to a figure of $1 million. When the lawmakers of 1870 permitted townships to join the game, they restricted the amount of their contribution for such purposes to an amount that would not require a tax levy for interest purposes equal to more than 1 percent of the township's taxable property. Two years later, legislators authorized municipal officers at county, city, or township level to issue bonds for public improvements, including railroad aid, to the extent of 10 percent of their taxable property. All counties could issue an additional $100,000 of bonds, and those with assets of $3 million could double this additional figure. If the assessed property in a township was less than $200,000 in value, its citizens might swell their contribution of 10 percent for railroad aid by an additional 10 per cent of a sum calculated by multiplying the proposed mileage of road in the township by 6,000. Bonds approved but not issued when the law was approved, or proposed in elections then pending, were not to be affected by the limitations of the law.

In 1876 the solons retrenched by restricting county aid to railroads to the amount of $100,000 plus 5 percent of the assessed valuation, while townships might raise $15,000 plus 5 percent of their assessment for the same purpose. Aid from all sources to any one corporation within a county was restricted by this law of 1876 to $4,000 per mile of track. The Act of 1887 lowered this maximum to $2,000 per mile.

So in both respects—that of railroad-bond voting procedures and that of the amounts of such aid—we find that initial generosity was tempered during the mid and late 1870s. The general-aid laws were allowed to stand largely untouched during the boom of the early and mid 1880s, but in 1887 the legislators placed additional restrictions upon the citizens of municipalities who wished to float bonds in aid of railroad construction. Special legislation, allowing deviations from the general laws in specific instances, seems to have followed the same pattern.

Described in such stark detail, these legislative patterns are less than colorful, but at the local level the bonding campaigns had their full share of dramatic incident. The citizens of early Leavenworth, city and county, cherished imperial designs, and by the mid 1870s had bonded themselves to a figure approximately twice the amount of the state debt allowed under the Kansas Constitution, to their own discomfort and the ultimate pain of investors who held Leavenworth bonds.[35] As elsewhere in the Middle West, railroad corporation contested with railroad corporation in Kansas in frenzied efforts to win the favor and bonds of township, city, and county. Local leaders orated at railroad-bond meetings to convince their fellow citizens that railroads would transform their locality into a wonderland of prosperous farms, bustling factories, and commercial enterprise, while other taxpayers opposed their efforts and subsequently challenged the legitimacy of bonding elections and the validity of local bond issues. As the members of the county board of commissioners of Jefferson County prepared to authorize a bond issue following an election on the question, its clerk defiantly locked the county seal in his office safe, pocketed the key, and thundered that he would not be a party to the fraud that they proposed to enact upon their constituents. He was removed from office by proceedings in quo warranto.[36]

The general bonding act of 1872 illustrates a number of interesting facets of the bonding movement. Legislators and the reporter of the Topeka *Commonwealth* considered this to be one of the most important bills of the session.[37] It's provisions required the state auditor to record municipal indebtedness and to register municipal bonds presented to him, certify to their genuineness, and thereafter instruct the appropriate county treasurer to levy a

tax sufficient for servicing such bonds. Then the local treasurers
were to forward such monies to the state treasurer, who in turn
paid the yearly interest to the bond holders. The author of *The
Financial History of Kansas* wrote of this legislation:

> There was a vague, general feeling over the state that new
> municipalities were getting heavily involved in their debts of
> different kinds, but there was as yet no social consciousness
> of the real magnitude of these obligations. It was deemed
> advisable, therefore, to provide by law for the registry of
> these bonds with the auditor of state, partly that the actual
> conditions might be known, and partly that the bonds might
> have a better standing with the money markets of the East.[38]

In this description he followed to a considerable extent the explanation given by Governor James M. Harvey when he recommended the law in his message to the legislature.[39] Letters from
the president of the Leavenworth, Lawrence and Galveston Railroad Company to the treasurer of the road, concerning this law
and the bonds of various Kansas counties held at that time by
their corporation, cast additional illumination upon this act. He
wrote, "Our act authorizing the registry of County Bonds has
passed the Kansas legislature and is a law. If it be as I suppose it
is . . . those bonds must now be about as good as State Bonds and
we ought to have no difficulty in selling them."[40] In a letter of a
week later, in which he enclosed a copy of the law, he wrote, "I
shall take steps to have the Bonds registered at once, when this
is done the securities are good and out of them we ought to raise
money without difficulty to meet our necessities."[41]

The successful development of Kansas, most of its leaders
agreed, would depend upon agriculture, at least in the immediate
future. If Kansans were indeed to transform 50 million acres of
land into prosperous farms and ranches, they required money
capital beyond their own resources. So entered the Eastern
moneylender, and I have told part of his story elsewhere.[42]
Lenders could not, of course, be expected to provide money capital under any and all circumstance, nor would the Kansas borrower wish to enter into transactions that did not seem beneficial
to him. That the state could specify some of the conditions under

which the borrower borrowed and the lender loaned, no one doubted.

Borrower and lender might, and usually did, have very different ideas of what appropriate agreements between them might involve. Let me briefly summarize those conditions which the lender and the borrower of the period, 1856–1896, would have probably considered most satisfactory from their very different perspectives. As we shall see, neither debtor nor creditor was to have his way completely. To the lender the most attractive market for funds was one in which he might set a rate of interest as high as he could find borrowers willing to pay, unrestricted by state or territorial legal maximums and unrestrained of course by penalties for the exaction of usury. If the lender was given his choice, the form of provisional transfer of security with which the borrower supported his note would be the deed of trust in which the property owner transferred the title of his real estate to a trustee, who was not a government officer, and who was authorized to advertise and sell the security in the interests of the creditor as rapidly as possible if the debtor defaulted on the interest or principal payments specified in his notes. If the deed of trust was not recognized in the laws of the state or territory, the lender hoped that he might protect or recapture his investment in case of default by invoking legal processes that were as simple, short-lived, and economical as possible.

The debtor, on the other hand, preferred a situation in which the maximum rate of interest chargeable had been set at a "reasonable" level by the state. He approved of stiff penalties for usury even to the extent perhaps of canceling the debt but certainly, at least, termination of the obligation to pay any interest on the principal. Should he lag in his interest payments, he did not wish to have the overdue interest compounded into the principal of his debt. The indenture should be, not a deed of trust, but a mortgage, enforceable in the courts. If so unfortunate as to face court action, the debtor did not desire the judgment rendered against him to be swelled by the addition of a large allowance to pay the fees of the creditor's attorney. If the creditor was to collect by court action, debtors preferred that a state appraisement law should require valuation of the property before the sheriff's sale and that it should not be struck down at a figure appreciably below the appraisement figure. If the appraisal was fair and the borrower had not exaggerated the worth of the security, such a provision would insure that the sale price would at least cover the amount of the debt and not leave a personal or deficiency judgment still hanging over the borrower's head after his real estate was surrendered.

If foreclosure did occur, the debtor's situation might be improved by a stay of execution, which would give him an opportunity to refinance his loan before the date of the foreclosure sale. The final act of mercy that the legal system could provide the delinquent borrower was a redemption law that would allow him to occupy his property for a period of time after the foreclosure sale and give him the opportunity to buy it back within the redemption period for the sum of the judgment and appropriate interest. Mortgagors believed also that notes and mortgages should be taxed as personal property and under some sort of arrangement that prevented the lender or mortgagee from passing the tax along to the borrower in the form of higher interest charges.

We can use the number of proposals to change the land credit laws introduced into the Kansas House of Representatives as a kind of rough measure of the amount of interest that such legislative concerns generated in the State. When this information was placed on a graph, it showed a major peak in 1861 (seventeen proposals), a trough in 1868 (one proposal), a minor peak in 1874 (seven proposals), a trough in 1879 (three proposals), and thereafter steadily increasing concern until no less than forty-five bills relating to the credit laws were introduced in 1891, falling off thereafter but continuing at a relatively high rate for the remainder of the decade. The depression following the crash of 1857, combined with the disastrous crop year of 1860, the hard times of the 1870s, and finally the price conditions and disastrous crop years that terminated the great settlement boom of the early and mid 1880s seem clearly reflected in this graph. Confidence in it is strengthened by comparison with one based on similar data derived from the proceedings of the Nebraska legislature, which shows an analogous pattern, although the peaks and troughs of the two do not coincide exactly.[43] The credit legislation that the Kansas lawmakers approved during this era shows some very definite trends, and these trends help to illuminate the nature of economic development in Kansas.

Territorial Kansas was an exciting place, but it was no debtor's heaven. One of the legislators who helped to produce the notorious laws of 1855 admitted that the interest law had given them some trouble, "but at last was settled by recognizing money as merchandise and let it bring what the demand would justify— in other words, we have no usury law."[44] In the very early years of the Territory's history the deed of trust was also a legal instrument, but of course we must remember that land became available for purchase only in late 1856 and that in limited quantities. The legislatures of 1857–1858 and 1859 hammered out the basic civil code of Kansas, and when their labors were complete, the creditor's position was still a very strong one.[45] Justice Kingman noted regretfully in handing down a decision relating to the interest law of 1859, "however obnoxious the interest law may be, and whatever may be its effects, it is clear, definite, and explicit, that any rate of interest, however extortionate . . . may be agreed upon by the parties in writing, and their contract has the sanction of law."[46] However, the legislators of 1859 did provide that "mortgages upon real estate, given to secure the payment of money, shall be foreclosed by petition in the district court of the county in which the real estate is situated" and that "all deeds of trust, given to secure the payment of money, shall be deemed mortgages . . . and shall be foreclosed in the same manner as mortgages on real estate are foreclosed."[47]

Indeed, according to Justice Robert Crozier, writing a decision of the Kansas Supreme Court in 1864, early Kansas mortgage law represented a clean break with English common law in which the mortgage was regarded as a definite transfer of title from borrower to lender. Under the common law, Crozier explained, the mortgage had been "a conveyance with a defeasance," under which the creditor or mortgagee might enjoy a right of possession even though the terms of the loan involved had not been broken. "If the condition was broken, the conveyance became absolute." But in Kansas, Crozier noted:

> The common law attributes of mortgages have been wholly set aside. . . . The statute gives the mortgagor the

right to the possession, even after the money is due, and confines the remedy of the mortgagee to an ordinary action and sale of the mortgaged premises; thus negativing any idea of title in the mortgagee. It is a mere security, although in the form of a conditional conveyance; creating a lien upon the property, but vesting no estate whatever, either before or after condition broken [*sic*].[48]

The lawmakers of 1859 placed an appraisal procedure in the foreclosure process. After the court had rendered judgment against a delinquent borrower, the sheriff was obligated to select "three disinterested freeholders" among the county residents, who appraised the true value of the security. The sheriff was then obligated to sell the security, after appropriate advertisement, at no less than two-thirds of the value estimated by the appraisers.[49] There was a strong chance, therefore, that the sale price would cancel out the judgment and that the debtor, although losing his real estate security, would not have to assume a personal judgment. But there was the danger that the appraisers might become disillusioned with the land values of their district in a time of depression and set the appraised value so low that a purchaser at the sheriff's sale might bid two-thirds of the appraisal and still leave a balance of the judgment unsatisfied, resulting in a deficiency judgment. On the other hand, oversanguine appraisers might set the value so high that a mortgagee must send good money after bad, in the absence of other bidders, in order to obtain possession of the property. The legislators of 1859 also approved a clause of the civil code which provided that courts were not to add more than two dollars to the amount of a judgment as fees with which the plaintiff might pay his counsel—a safeguard against the writing of inflated attorney's fees into the borrower's debt.[50]

The economic plight of the Kansas settlers during the late 1850s and the astronomic interest rates that they agreed to pay have been described elsewhere.[51] When the 1860 legislature met, Kansas had developed a hard-pressed and articulate debtor class, and Governor Medary recommended that its members be relieved. "Money loaners" and borrowers did not, he said, "meet on equal terms . . . the one is the master of his money, the other the slave of his necessities. . . . extremes should be avoided, and a law made, founded upon the experience of ages, fixing the standard of interest, with the proper punishment for usurious contracts."[52] The legislators responded with a law which set a legal maximum of 20 percent and provided penalties for usury, excess interest to be considered as payment on the principal and the usurer to forfeit all interest.[53] A writer in the Leavenworth *Herald* scoffed that the lawmakers "might as well have passed a law to limit the price of potatoes or eggs," and criticized them for failing to pass a redemption law and a bankruptcy statute.[54] The famine year that followed apparently convinced the representatives who met in the session of 1861 that more remained to be done. They passed a redemption law, allowing debtors to retain possession of their foreclosed property for two years, during which time they were allowed to pay off the judgment against them. During the redemption period the creditor was allowed to restrain his borrower from using the security in a way that would diminish its value.[55] Revision in 1862 was minor in nature, although by no means insignificant. A law of this year prescribed a fine of $100 to be assessed against the mortgagee who refused or neglected to file the release of a mortgage after having received full payment of the note that it supported.[56]

In 1863 the Kansas legislators approved another fundamental revision of the credit laws when they established 12 percent as the legal maximum rate of interest. Where 10 percent annually had been the rate of interest on debts when no interest rate was stipulated and on judgments, the lawmakers substituted 7 percent. Penalties for usury remained much as before.[57] The revision did not escape criticism, and the Topeka *Capital* printed a good example of the creditor and promotional point of view in the following comment:

> Capitalists will not bring their money into a country where the hazards of loss are a hundred fold increased over those of an old well-settled country where values are fixed and certain, to loan at a less rate of interest than can be realized in the latter. . . . The best regulator is the law of supply and demand. Give us good laws for the collection of debts, and for the protection of the creditor, and you will do

something that will cheapen money in Kansas, because it will bring more here for investment.[58]

With the revision of the interest law, interest in easing the money and credit laws of Kansas subsided; and in 1866 only two measures dealing with land credit originated in the lower house of the Kansas legislature.

For some years, beginning in 1867, the Kansas legislators revised the collection laws of the state to make them more attractive to moneylenders. These were years, you will remember, when the total number of measures concerning credit that were introduced into the Kansas House was small. The first, and a very important move in this direction, was an amendment to the redemption law of 1861, allowing mortgagors to waive their right of redemption.[59] During the next session the lawmakers decided that a mortgagee might pay the taxes on real estate security, when his mortgagor failed to do so, and that such tax payments were to be added to the judgment in case of foreclosure.[60]

The specific limitation on the amount of attorney fees allowed in judgments, set by earlier lawmakers at $2.00, seems to have been dropped when the solons approved the Kansas Code of 1868. Two years later the legislators specifically declared attorneys' fees to be a legitimate cost of foreclosure and left the amount to the discretion of the presiding judges. I believe that these were actions of some significance.[61] Eastern moneylenders dreaded a situation in which they must invest additional funds in order to obtain the security of defaulted loans. An attorney's fee of two dollars was unrealistic, and the law as it had stood therefore in effect forced the creditor to pay fees to his lawyer that could not be consolidated in the principal, interest, and costs represented in the judgment. It is true that the creditor who assumed title to the security might have to pay off his attorney out of pocket anyway, but the inclusion of attorney's fees in the judgment gave promise at least that he might not have to do so.

During the 1872 session the solons made two extremely important changes in the credit laws. They vitiated the appraisement law by allowing mortgagors to waive appraisement. This procedure could be eliminated provided "no order of sale or execution shall be issued upon . . . [a] judgment until the expiration of six months from the time of the rendition of said judgment."[62] Hereafter many Kansas mortgages would contain a clause specifying that the mortgagor waived all rights of appraisement and redemption. Although the judicial processes of foreclosure were lengthened by six months as a result of the change in the law, the mortgagor could now bid in the debtor's security at the sheriff's sale for a nominal sum, thus providing the opportunity of obtaining a personal judgment and removing the possibility that he might have to pay out additional funds to obtain the security. A writer in the *Kansas Daily Commonwealth* revealed the thinking underlying elimination of compulsory appraisement. Everyone who had studied the matter carefully, he assured his readers, was convinced that money was scarce because of the content of the statute books. Local appraisals, he suggested, were anything but true estimates of the value of foreclosed property. Instead the appraisers inflated them to help the judgment debtor sell out to his creditor as favorably as possible. "Make the security certain and beyond doubt," ran the article, "and rates will be low."[63] The legislators of 1872 also reconsidered the limitations on usury; they modified the penalty, providing that the usurer should lose only the amount of interest levied above the legal maximum. Such sums were to be regarded as payments on the principal.[64]

In 1873 the adjustment of the credit laws in behalf of the lender reached a bitter climax when the members of the legislature exempted from taxation all evidences of debt secured by mortgages on real estate.[65] The measure helped to crystallize latent opposition both to the trend in credit legislation and to the Kansas system of taxation. The editor of the *Kansas Farmer* termed it "one of the most iniquitous laws that ever disgraced the pages of our statute book" and snorted that the "plea urged by some, that this law will benefit the farmers by bringing more money into the State, and by reducing the rate of interest, is a specious one."[66] The law was an important cause that contributed to the calling of a farmers' convention in Topeka during the spring of 1873. Midwestern farm prices were softening, the tide of Grangerism was about to sweep across the Middle West, and John J. Ingalls, the brilliant young United States senator from Kansas, proclaimed that "a gigantic struggle is already inaugurated between the vast moneyed corporations of the East, and the toiling millions of the West; between the bank and the corn crib."[67] The legislators repealed the mortgage exemption law in 1874.

Through seven legislatures the developers had sought to revise the credit system of Kansas in order to attract capital.[68] Now as depression spread through the state and the cry of the debtor was heard once more, they must desist. Significantly, however, no other substantial changes in the credit laws were made in behalf of borrowers in the mid or late 1870s. During the late 1870s and early 1880s a veritable army of mortgage brokers and mortgage companies developed contacts with Eastern and foreign investors that allowed them to bring the mortgage money of nonresidents to Kansas farmers as never before. Their efforts fed the settlement boom of the early and mid 1880s. Although the lending rates on good farmland security had dropped considerably below the legal maximum by 1886 in most areas of Kansas, the very magnitude of the mortgage business, the recklessness of some brokers, the knowledge of earlier revisions in the statutes, and the fact that broker's commissions were calculated above the contract rate seem to have been responsible for some concern over the situation even before the great boom began to burst in 1887.

In their state convention of 1888, the Republicans declared themselves in favor of revising the interest law and of passing a redemption law.[69] And in the legislative session that followed, the lawmakers lowered the maximum rate of interest to 10 percent and set the statutory rate, chargeable against judgments or contracts in which no rate was specified, at 6 percent. The usurer was liable for double the excess interest written into a contract.[70]

The lawmakers of 1889 passed two additional measures related to mortgages. One was apparently a sop to the critics of the Kansas lending laws, while the other dealt with a problem faced by the mortgage companies. Mortgagees who refused to release paid-up mortgages within thirty days now became liable for a fine and the costs of the legal action involved.[71] This was aimed at the tardiness with which Eastern investors and Western mortgage brokers recorded mortgage releases at Western county seats. On the other hand, Chapter CLXXVII of the Laws of 1889 provided penalties for the removal of improvements from mortgaged property, a law of considerable value to mortgage brokers and mortgage companies that at this time faced the necessity of assuming title to the property of many defaulting debtors.[72]

Although interest in reforming the credit laws of the state was at high pitch in 1891, the fact that the People's party controlled the House and the Republicans ruled the Senate prevented any of the numerous bills from becoming law. But the judiciary committee of the House did introduce a comprehensive effort to revise the system, House Bill 540, accompanying it with a report, in which the committee members maintained:

> That the present system is absolutely bad in every part, does not admit of dispute. It turns men, women and children out of their homes, sometimes without even giving them a chance to harvest a crop. It deprives them of their property, frequently without even giving them a credit on the indebtedness it was pledged to secure; and, in addition to this, it imposes a class of utterly useless burdens upon both debtor and creditor.[73]

The committeemen, however, admitted that the mortgage companies of the state had also sunk into a hopeless mire of debt because of the default of mortgagors whose paper they had guaranteed to Eastern investors. The Committee maintained that there were three great evils in the credit system. In the first place the debtor had no right to occupy his real estate or to redeem it after the sheriff's sale. Secondly the costs of foreclosure were both high and unnecessary. Finally the plaintiff could buy his debtor's land at foreclosure sale for little above the mere costs of the case, leaving the debtor to face a judgment as large, in some cases, as the original debt and "a standing menace for the rest of his life."

The members of the judiciary committee of the House of Representatives proposed to do away with the expense of the foreclosure process on the one hand and to give the debtor two years of redemption on the other. Under the provisions of House Bill 540, borrowers might in the future assent to a clause in their mortgages, empowering sheriffs to sell out delinquent mortgagors with no further legal formality than advertisement of sale for thirty days. Total cost was to be a fee of ten dollars, payable to the sheriff. The delinquent mortgagor, however, was given two years in which to redeem his land after the date of sale and was allowed to retain possession during this period. Since the mortgagor could regain title to his land by paying the price of the sheriff's certificate of sale plus interest, there was little danger that creditors would not bid the full amount of their claim. The previous method of collecting debts secured by delinquent notes and mortgages was to remain on the statute books and could be used if debtor and creditor so agreed when the mortgage contract was drawn up. No doubt members of the Kansas legal fraternity breathed a sigh of relief when the judicial committee bill failed passage.

In 1893 the debtors of Kansas once more obtained the protection of a redemption law.[74] The lawmakers eliminated the practice of appraisement in foreclosure proceedings and gave debtors a redemption period of eighteen months. Waivers of redemption in mortgage contracts were to have no legal weight thereafter. Did the law apply to contracts negotiated prior to its passage? The Populists asserted that it did. A similar contention had been made concerning the law of 1861, but the Kansas Supreme Court had ruled otherwise.[75]

Mortgage brokers were convinced that history would repeat itself. When the Kansas Supreme Court considered the Populist contention in a case originating in Harper County, the attorney for the mortgage company involved, argued that it was

almost beyond controversy that a law which postpones the right of possession, which holds open the right of redemption for a period of 18 months longer than the terms of the contract provide, which gives the rents and profits to the owner of the title contrary to the terms of the contract, does impair the obligation of the contract within the meaning of the provisions of the constitution of the United States.[76]

The Court agreed, two to one, with the sole Populist member dissenting. As far as this jurist, Justice Stephen H. Allen, was concerned, the law did not impair the contract; it merely modified the remedy.[77]

Shortly after this decision was handed down, Chief Justice Albert H. Horton resigned and was replaced by Judge David Martin, an able railroad attorney who was regarded as appropriately "safe" by the leading Republicans of the state. To their consternation they soon observed that "the maggot of populism . . . appeared to have entered . . . [Martin's] brain."[78] Along with Justice Allen he agreed to a rehearing of one of the mortgage cases in which the retroactive validity of the Redemption Law was at issue, and the two justices then reversed the original decision of the Court by accepting the Populist argument.[79] At this there was much scurrying among the fraternity of mortgage men and their attorneys to take the case to the Supreme Court of the United States. They were relieved to discover, as they had hoped, that the maggot of Populism had not penetrated the minds of a majority of the members of that august body.[80]

Kansas lawmakers passed the last major credit legislation of the period when the combined Populist and Democratic majority approved a law in 1897 providing that a mortgagor could extinguish his debt by paying the mortgagee or the last assignee of record. If assignments were not recorded within ninety days, they would not be regarded as evidence in the state courts. This was in response to the efforts of Eastern mortgagees to collect payments of interest and principal from mortgagors that the latter claimed to have already paid to intermediary mortgage agents or companies, which had assigned ownership of the paper to the Easterners without either party recording that fact in the county records.[81]

The assignment problem reflected the practices of the highly competitive farm-mortgage business during the 1880s and early 1890s. Brokers and company officials became wary of recording mortgage papers that would reveal the names of Eastern clients lest competitors attempt to entice them away. And if Western borrowers did not know the names of those who held their mortgages, they would not be tempted to negotiate directly with them for renewals, thereby perhaps depriving the mortgage company or broker of commissions. When drought and low prices forced many Kansas farmers to default on their mortgages during the late 1880s and early 1890s, the majority of the companies went into bankruptcy. Undoubtedly in almost every bankruptcy the interest or principal payments of numbers of solvent farmers were caught in the receivership and never reached the holders of their mortgages. When Eastern mortgagees took over administration of their own mortgages, they attempted to obtain all back payments from the mortgagors and apparently sought to realize their claims through foreclosure in some cases. Some debtors in default found themselves accused of owing greater sums than they actually did. Nor can the possibility be eliminated that some dishonest brokers or company officials took advantage of the recording laws to appropriate some funds that should have been sent to Eastern investors.[82] The law of 1897, regarded as relatively harsh by some legal historians, was soon modified and the ninety-day penalty removed.

It is clear that the general pattern of legislative action concerning the relation between debtor and creditor was similar in some respects to legislative action related to local railroad-bond issues. The history of the general laws allowing municipal aid to railroads began, of course, after the Civil War, whereas the credit legislation actually was entering its second phase at that time. But both types of legislation reflected a generous attitude toward those who controlled out-of-state capital between 1865 and 1872. In each case the lawmakers tempered their position during the mid and late 1870s, although most markedly so in the case of community bonding. After a period of stability, if not relaxation, of the laws during the early and mid 1880s, Kansas lawmakers had become ready in both cases to impose further restrictions on the nonresident capitalist and the capital-mobilizing corporations. And we can, I suspect, fit other legislative activity into similar patterns. Note, for instance, the Kansas state auditor reporting in late 1878 and recommending changes in the tax-sale laws: "A few years ago, and at the time of the passage of the present tax law, money commanded from eighteen to twenty-four per cent. in ordinary business transactions. It required special inducements to cause men to invest in tax-sale certificates."[83] Much legislative activity, therefore, can be explained in terms of the search for capital to be used in conjunction with local resources in the task of building the state. This motivation underlay permissive promotional legislation at the state level and considerable promotional activity at the local levels of government. But at the state level, legislation that we usually regard as regulatory also reflected the search for capital; there was a promotional dimension to much regulatory legislation.

Leland Jenks once wrote, "railway building proceeded in an

undulating pattern, paralleling closely the general contours of major business cycles until the First World War."[84] So, too, apparently with capital-oriented legislation in frontier Kansas. But there was of course a difference. Railroad building, we have been accustomed to believe, lagged during times of depression because investors and the agencies of the money market in general lost confidence in the future or lacked the funds to continue investing in transportation enterprises. But we find also that the Kansas state legislators changed the rules of the game in good and bad times, forging a variety of weapons designed to "heat up" or to "cool down" the local economy.

Did the impulse for legislative change emanate from legislators representing the same groups in society through time, or did alternations of economic circumstance result in the wishes of different groups being reflected in legislation? Herbert Quick had Old Jake Vandemark recall of the westward-moving people on the Erie canal:

> I noticed . . . that class of men with whom we became so well acquainted later, the land speculators. These, and the bankers, many of whom seemed to have a good deal of business in the West, formed a class by themselves, and looked down from a far height on the working people, the farmers, and the masses generally, who voyaged on the same boats with them. They talked of development, and the growth of the country . . . while the rest of us thought about homes and places to make our living.[85]

Quick was in effect distinguishing between developers and producers, although it is obvious that no hard and fast line can be drawn between the two. And he was, of course, greatly oversimplifying, as the novelist must do. But the insight was a powerful one, and it is tempting to think that the patterns described in this paper may be explained in part by it. In times of relative prosperity or boom the developers had their way in the legislative halls, but as hard times and debt pressed upon the producing elements during periods of recession, the discontent of the producer was reflected in legislation designed to curb the developers to some degree.

These matters do, I believe, have some implications for our

understanding of Kansas Populism. Within our context this move-ment in Kansas ceases to be a unique manifestation of frontier discontent, although of course every situation is in a sense unique, but rather the third in a series of protests against the legal-institu-tional structure of Kansas, fed by recurrent depression and finan-cial stringency. Clearly the historian has explained Populism in the Plains States too largely in terms of *federal* monetary policy, *federal* land policy, and *federal* transportation policy, when not of course chasing the chimera of declining status, the mirage of the yeoman myth, or the will-of-the-wisp of anti-Semitic irrationality. There was a very important local institutional dimension in Kan-sas Populism. The "Agrarian Revolt" was not merely, figuratively speaking, a colonial uprising, but also, in part, a domestic insur-rection against the politicians who had allowed the Kansas statutes to be written too largely in the interests of the developers.

The history of credit legislation in Kansas rather uniquely reflects the frustrations of Populism at the state level. Bowing to the impending storm, Republican legislators lowered the legal interest rate but not to a level that interfered in most instances with the market price of money. Despite a veritable blizzard of proposals for reforming the credit system, the reformers settled for a redemption law, the same remedy as that prescribed in 1861. A punitive measure of 1897, designed to make the real owners of mortgages identify themselves in the county records, did not survive in its punitive form past the next legislature.

But Populism did mark the end of an era in the development of Kansas. Whatever the cost in human suffering, or in present and future interest and principal payments, Kansans for the most part now had their railroads, their schools, and their public build-ings—the social overhead capital that a developing state must have—and a foundation of improved farms and industry to sustain it. In its capital needs, Kansas would never be quite the same again.

I have not, in this paper, tried to present an elaborate tax-onomy of legislative categories. I have not discussed certain types of legislation, such as the use of bounties to achieve desired pur-poses. I have not described the precedents or models which Kansans may have found in other states for their legislation. I have not tried to relate the activity of pressure groups to specific legislation, although I have given an illustration of this type of relationship in discussing the bonding law of 1872. Nor have I endeavored to analyze the behavior of the Kansas legislators, as reflected in the roll-call records of the legislature. I have not tried to assess the impact of Kansas legislation on the actual behavior of the Kansas economy. These are all valid subjects for scrutiny, and I hope to treat them in the future. Here, I have been content to develop some of the major patterns of legislative activity that were, I believe, related to the developmental process and the efforts of Kansans to attract capital to their state. If I have shown that the subject is worthy of more attention, I have achieved my purpose.

Notes

1. *Kansas Senate Journal,* 1866, 18.

2. Oscar and Mary Flug Handlin, *Commonwealth: A Study of the Role of Government in the American Economy: Massachusetts, 1774–1861* (rev. ed., Cambridge, Mass., 1969), 106–33.

3. There is a slowly growing body of modern literature on the relation of state or local governments to economic growth in the United States. Mention of such authors as Louis Hartz, James Neal Primm, Milton Sydney Heath, and Carter Goodrich immediately brings to mind other contributors to the field. The reader will find most of the conceptual issues discussed or introduced in Oscar and Mary Flug Handlin, *Commonwealth;* Gerald D. Nash, *State Government and Economic Development: A History of Administrative Policies in California, 1849–1933* (Berkeley, Calif., 1964), 349–58; Harry N. Scheiber, *Ohio Canal Era: A Case Study of Government and the Economy, 1820–1861* (Athens, Ohio, 1969), 352–68.

4. James Ernest Boyle, *The Financial History of Kansas* (*Bulletin* of the University of Wisconsin, No. 247: Economics and Political Science Series, Vol. 5, No. 1, Madison, Wisc., 1908): William Frank Zornow, *Kansas: A History of the Jayhawk State* (Norman, Okla., 1957), 159–73; Glenn Harold Miller, "Financing the Boom in Kansas, 1879 to 1888, With Special Reference to Municipal Indebtedness and to Real Estate Mortgages" (M.A. thesis, University of Kansas, 1954).

5. *Kansas Constitution,* Art. V, Sec. 1. Chilton Williamson's brief treatment of alien suffrage in *American Suffrage: From Property to Democracy, 1760–1860* (Princeton, N.J., 1960), 277–78, does not explore the various interesting implications of these laws, although they may be viewed in one respect as evidence contrary to one of his major contentions.

6. *Kansas Laws,* 1865, Chap. XLIX, 116.

7. *Kansas Senate Journal,* 1874, 21. Cornelius J. Dyck, "Kansas Promotional Activities with Particular Reference to Mennonites" (M.A. thesis, University of Wichita, 1956), 94–111.

232 / *Allan G. Bogue*

8. See for example, *Kansas Laws*, 1864, Chap. III, 15; 1865, Chap. III, 25; 1866, Chap. VI, 32; 1883, Chap. XXIII, 36.

9. *Ibid.*, 1867, 210–11.

10. *Ibid.*, 1887, Chap. CCXXIII. 317–19.

11. *Kansas Senate Journal*, 1865, 22; 1866, 31–32; 1867, 41–43; 1869, 27; 1871, 32–33; 1877, 47; 1883, 34–35.

12. *Kansas Laws*, 1864, Chap. LXXV, 143–45; *Kansas Senate Journal*, 1868, 32.

13. *Ibid.*, 1867, 36; *Kansas Laws*, 1875, Chap. LXVIII, 99–100; 1881, Chap. XVIII, 40–43; 1885, Chap. XXII, 17–18; 1889, Chap. CVIII, 146–47.

14. Dyck, *Kansas Promotional Activities*, 107–10.

15. *Kansas Senate Journal*, 1872, 28; 1873, 25–26; 1881, 40; 1885, 122–23.

16. *Kansas Constitutional Convention: A Reprint of the Proceedings and Debates of the Convention Which Framed the Constitution of Kansas at Wyandotte in July, 1859* (Topeka, Kans., 1920), 328–29.

17. *Kansas Constitution*, Art. XI, Secs. 5 and 8.

18. *Kansas Laws*, 1874, Chap. XVIII, 13; 1877, Chap. CXLVI, 196–98.

19. Congress, however, never did approve the diversion of the internal improvement grant to educational purposes. See Thomas Le Duc, "State Administration of the Land Grant to Kansas for Internal Improvements," *Kansas Historical Quarterly*, XX (November, 1953), 545–52.

20. In his message of 1883 Governor G. W. Glick argued that Kansas was contributing "a greater sum *per capita* [for education] in proportion to population and wealth, than any other State in the Union," *Kansas Senate Journal*, 1883, 19.

21. *Ibid.*, 1885, 116.

22. *Board of County Commissioners of Shawnee County* v. *Luther M. Carter, Kansas Reports* (rev. ed.), 2, 123–24.

23. See note 4. Some general background is provided in A. M. Hillhouse, *Municipal Bonds: A Century of Experience* (New York, N.Y., 1936), 31–199. Railroad aid bonds are treated, pp. 143–99. Charles Fairman, *Mr. Justice Miller and the Supreme Court, 1862–1890* (Cambridge, Mass., 1939), 207–36, discusses some of the judicial issues involved in law cases relating to municipal bonding in this era. The judicial issues in Kansas were thoroughly discussed in *Commissioners of Leavenworth County* v. *Edward Miller, Kansas Reports* (rev. ed.), 7, 298–334, and *State ex rel. St. Joseph and Denver City Railway Company* v. *Commissioners of Nemaha County, ibid.*, 335–54.

24. *Commercial National Bank of Cleveland* v. *City of Iola, Kansas Reports* (rev. ed.), 9, 469–75.

25. *Kansas Senate Journal*, 1872, 15–16, 29–30; 1877, 31; 1885, 108–9; 1889, 27–29.

26. *Ibid.*, 1889, 28.

27. Harry H. Pierce, *Railroads of New York: A Study of Government Aid, 1826–1875* (Cambridge, Mass., 1953), Appendix, Chart 1.

28. Albert Fishlow cites the figures in *Poor's Manual for 1891* with
approval, and these showed a range in the total costs per mile of track in
eight regions of the United States, from $35,000 to $73,000 "with six of the
observations clustered from $35,000 to $45,000." Albert Fishlow, "Productivity and Technological Change in the Railroad Sector, 1840–1910," in
Output, Employment, and Productivity in the United States after 1800
(*Studies in Income and Wealth, Volume Thirty, by the Conference on Research in Income and Wealth,* National Bureau of Economic Research, New
York, N.Y., 1966), 595 and n. 24. Some historians believe that these values
were inflated in various ways, but of course the value of the local bonds fell
below the face value, since they usually sold in the open market at a discount.

29. *Kansas Laws,* 1865, Chap. XII, 41–42; *ibid.,* 1866, Chap. XXIV,
72–74.

30. *Ibid.,* 1870, Chap. XC, 189–92.

31. *Ibid.,* 1872, Chap. LXVIII, 110–19.

32. *Ibid.,* 1876, Chap. CVI, 212–17; Chap. CVII, 217–22.

33. *Ibid.,* 1887, Chap. CLXXXXIII, 275–76.

34. The laws cited in this paragraph are those referred to in the five
notes preceding.

35. Boyle, *Financial History of Kansas,* 59.

36. *State of Kansas ex rel. Henry Keeler* v. *Walter N. Allen, Kansas
Reports* (rev. ed.), 5, 124–31.

37. Topeka *Kansas Daily Commonwealth,* February 27, 1872.

38. Boyle, *Financial History of Kansas,* 59.

39. *Kansas Senate Journal,* 1872, 15–16.

40. J. M. Walker to R. S. Watson, March 7, 1872. J. M. Walker Letter
Press Copy Book No. 2, Burlington Archives, Newberry Library.

41. Walker to Watson, March 13, 1872. Walker Letter Press Copy
Book, No. 2.

42. Allan G. Bogue, *Money at Interest: The Farm Mortgage on the
Middle Border* (Ithaca, N.Y., 1955).

43. These data compiled from the *Kansas* and *Nebraska House Journals,*
1860–1900.

44. Atchison *Squatter Sovereign,* September 18, 1855.

45. See *Kansas Territory General Laws,* 1859, Chap. XXV, 82–184, for
the civil procedures of the late territorial period.

46. *Dudley* v. *Reynolds, Kansas Reports* (rev. ed.), 1, 274.

47. *Kansas Territory General Laws,* 1859, Chap. XCVII, 571.

48. *Chick et al.* v. *Willetts, Kansas Reports* (rev. ed.), 2, 385–86.

49. *Kansas Territory General Laws,* 1859, Chap. XXV, 152.

50. *Kansas Territory General Laws,* 1859, Chap. XCVII, Sec. 3, 571.
This became Chap. CXLIX, in *Compiled Laws,* 1862, 722.

51. Paul Wallace Gates, *Fifty Million Acres: Conflicts over Kansas Land
Policy, 1854–1890* (Ithaca, N.Y., 1954), 72–105.

52. *Kansas Territory House Journal,* 1860, 20–21.

53. *Kansas Laws,* 1860, Chap. LXXV, 129–30.

54. Leavenworth *Herald,* March 10, 1860.

55. *Kansas Laws,* 1861. Chap. LXV, 241–43.

56. *Kansas Compiled Laws,* 1862, Chap. CLI, 724.

57. *Kansas Laws,* 1863, Chap. XXXIII, 63–64.

58. Topeka *Capital,* January 20, 1863, quoted in Lawrence *Kansas State Journal,* January 29, 1863.

59. *Kansas Laws,* 1867, Chap. CX, 188–89.

60. *Kansas General Statutes,* 1868, Chap. 107, 1062.

61. See *ibid.,* Chap. LXXX, Sec. 399, 705, and secs. 589–91. *Kansas Laws,* 1870, Chap. LXXXVII, Sec. 13, 175.

62. *Ibid.,* 1872, Chap. LXVI, 105.

63. Topeka *Kansas Daily Commonwealth,* February 8, 1872.

64. *Kansas Laws,* 1872, Chap. CXXXIV, 284.

65. *Kansas Laws,* 1873, Chap. CXL, 264–65. This act was entitled "An Act to promote the improvement of real estate by exempting mortgages and other securities from taxation."

66. *Kansas Farmer,* April 1, 1873, 104.

67. *Kansas Farmer,* May 15, 1873, 152.

68. This was the contention of the editor of the *Kansas Farmer,* November 6, 1889, and the facts seem to support it.

69. Ottawa *Republican,* December 6, 1888.

70. *Kansas Laws,* 1889, Chap. CLXIV, 237–39.

71. *Kansas Laws,* 1889, Chap. CLXXV, 257–58.

72. *Kansas Laws,* 1889, Chap. CLXXVII, 259–60.

73. *Kansas House Journal,* 1891, 242–45. The quoted passage appears on p. 242.

74. *Kansas Laws,* 1893, Chap. CIX, 188–93.

75. *Bixby* v. *Bailey, Kansas Reports,* 11, 273–80.

76. *Watkins* v. *Glenn, Kansas Reports,* 55, 425.

77. *Ibid.,* 435–51.

78. "Editorial," Kansas City *Journal,* March 8, 1901; also "Obituary," *ibid.;* "Obituary," Topeka *State Journal,* March 4, 1901, all in *Kansas Scrap Book:* Biography, Vol. 4, Kansas State Historical Society, Topeka, Kansas.

79. *Beverly* v. *Barnitz, Kansas Reports,* 55, 451–65.

80. *Barnitz* v. *Beverly, United States Reports,* 163, 118–32.

81. *Kansas Laws,* 1897, Chap. CLX, 345–47.

82. My explanation of the background of this law is based on the research in *Money at Interest* and differs somewhat from that given by Charles M. Ward and John David Stewart, "Mortgage Assignments and the Payment Statutes," *Journal of the Bar Association of the State of Kansas,* 8 (May, 1940), 488–501.

83. Kansas State Auditor, *Report,* 1878, 201.

84. Leland H. Jenks, "Railroads as an Economic Force in American Development," *Journal of Economic History,* IV (May, 1944), 4.

85. Herbert Quick, *Vandemark's Folly,* (Indianapolis, Ind., 1922), 54–55.

9

The English and Kansas,
1865-1890

Oscar O. Winther, Indiana University

Englishmen were among the first pioneering whites to venture into Kansas—even before it was formally organized as a territory. One of the earliest of them, George Fervins, had left his wife and children on parish relief in Devonshire and was somewhere on Kansas soil as early as 1850. Having supposedly come to a land of plenty, Fervins had been asked by the Bishop of Devon to send for his family and to provide the necessary dollars for doing so. In reply, this harassed

The major portions of my research for this paper were done at the British Museum, the Kansas State Historical Society Library, and the Newberry Library. I wish to express my thanks and appreciation to these institutions for making their materials available and for the many courtesies extended to me.

Englishman wrote to one of the parish overseers in July, 1850, as follows: "Sir, what made me leave England was distress. I could not gain a living for myself, wife, and children. There was nothing more to look for but relief from the parish, if I had stayed in England. Sir, if you will send my wife Mary Fervins and children here I am ready to receive them and here I can maintain them if they were here." Fervins adamantly refused to send the necessary funds for transportation, and in January, 1851, he again wrote to the overseer: "I love my wife and children, but if you love to keep them and maintain them you can do so and be damned. . . . You can kiss my arse, I am living in the land of the free."[1]

Even though not many Englishmen had heard about Kansas in 1850 (for it was still Indian country), they were to do so after passage of the Kansas-Nebraska Act in 1854. Although the Civil War produced a blackout on English publicity respecting Kansas, cessation of hostilities brought about a renewal in England not only of published intelligence but of overt promotional activities leading to English migration to the land of the Kaw. There were two receptive audiences to be reached: one, the affluent and better educated English gentry who expressed interest in the American West as an area suitable for capital investment and for their younger and often wayward sons; the other, indigent farm laborers and urban unemployed who, caught in the vise of adverse economic circumstances, sought escape through emigration to such a place as Kansas where new and glowing opportunities supposedly awaited their arrival.

For all their reputed shortcomings, the English upper classes did read, and a surprising amount of what they read concerned Kansas as a place offering rich and exciting rewards alike to English visitors, sportsmen, settlers, and investors of British capital. Among the first of several English visitors to rush West immediately following Appomattox was a barrister and member of Parliament, Sir Morton Peto, who expressed special interest in the promotion of steam plowing on Western prairie lands. Judging from observations made, however, Sir Morton concluded that the steam plow would not be an adequate substitute for the sulky, so instead he looked upon an area such as the Kansas plains as one offering a potential market for an assortment of English-manufactured farm machinery.[2]

One travel account very widely read by educated Englishmen was William H. Dixon's *New America*, first published in London in 1867, which during the ensuing two years passed through numerous editions. Dixon's traveling companion was the distinguished Professor Charles W. Dilke, Trinity Hall, Cambridge, who in his book *Greater Britain* (London, 1869) also wrote about the American West. In his book Dixon devoted one entire chapter to a retrospective discussion of "Bleeding Kansas," and another to the "The Prairies," in which he singled out Kansas as "beyond dispute the region in which these plains display themselves on the largest scale, and with their points most perfect." He described the Kansas plains (and doubtless to an amazed audience believing Kansas to be a part of the "Great American Desert") as "green with trees, most of all along the lines of the Kansas River and its many creeks and inlets." Sunflowers thrive—"not the tawny gauds of our cottage gardens," but rather, "big and brazen bachelors, flourishing on a single stalk" with buttercuplike blossoms "numberless as the stars of heaven."[3] Dilke also had something to report on his personal observations of Kansas. Concerned as he was with social problems, Dilke noted that the Kansans were in the process of emancipating their women by granting female suffrage; that at the University of Kansas, for example, women were not only admitted for academic work but held professorships as well.

In their travels together Dixon and Dilke rode the Kansas Pacific Railroad Company (KP) trains and visited several towns along this route as far west as Manhattan—then the end of the line. At this place the two Englishmen continued their journey in "mule-drawn ambulance, which," Dilke wrote, "was to be at once our prison for six nights, and our fort upon wheels against the Indians." Passing through this open country, they had an opportunity to witness the settlement processes firsthand and to note some of the abuses of the Homestead Act, such as using miniature, hand-whittled houses to satisfy, fraudulently, entry requirements.[4]

Equally intrigued by the yet unsettled portions of western Kansas was Joseph Frith, who, like Dilke and Dixon, had traveled by means of covered wagon into the Indian and buffalo country beyond the line of settlement. Much to his amazement, Frith encountered there a countryman from Huddersfield. The man was long-haired, garbed in buckskin, and was living the savage life of a "mountain man." Frith was horror-struck by the whole-sale slaughter of buffalo. "My moral sense was wounded," he wrote, "at what seemed to me wanton cruelty to, and reckless slaughter of, a harmless animal, within its assigned and native domain."[5]

English visitors arriving after the completion or near comple-tion of major Kansas rail lines took full advantage of improved travel facilities, and most of them were impressed by, and re-ported to their countrymen, what they saw from their car win-dows. One such traveler, W. M. Stewart, found the scenery picturesque and the soil rich. "Kansas," he wrote, "offers great inducement to those of limited means."[6] Another, M. Davenport, related how the KP took him in hand and conveyed him into "the real wilderness and solitude of the west." Davenport was awe-struck at seeing from his car window a gigantic wheatfield com-prising, he was told, thirteen hundred acres, and at how with passing miles of travel the well-populated and cultivated portions of Kansas gave way to bleak, dangerous Indian country farther west. At Salina, Davenport was told how one of his countrymen recently had been captured by Indians, horribly tortured—"his finger and toe nails being drawn out, and his body then gashed all over with knives"—before finally being put out of his misery by means of tomahawk blows upon his skull.[7]

Not all Englishmen patronized the KP, for T. S. Hudson, another traveler, recounted how he rode through Kansas on the Atchison, Topeka and Santa Fe Railroad (ATSF) and how he was impressed by the countless numbers of cattle and sheep he saw grazing on the green range and by the fact—so he believed—that Kansas farmers had become rich in this "go-ahead" state. Hudson placed Kansas next to Massachusetts in "intellectual distinction" and noted that English enterprise abounded within its rectangular borders."[8]

Also extremely favorable to Kansas were Englishmen John G. Hyde and S. Nugent Townshend who, after extensive visits to the plains region, admonished their countrymen: Why consider various and sundry states as emigration sites "when the fertile fields of Kansas, Nebraska, and northern Texas are so much more suited to their acquirements, tastes, and constitutions." They declared Kansas to be their favorite state, but warned against settling there without some British pounds at their disposal.[9]

It was with such resources in mind (namely pounds sterling) that James MacDonald, a Scot, also addressed himself with special reference to Kansas. "Probably not one of the other 'young' states in the Union has a reputation in Great Britain equal to that of Kansas," he wrote in about 1877. MacDonald referred to the state's immense acreages of land, "situated so as to escape the pestilential climate of the South and the rigour of the North." It was a place with "general fitness for family"; in fact, he added, "Kansas is indeed an agricultural paradise" with lovely prairies and rich soil that was easy to farm. He underscored the need for capital for successful farming in Kansas and the need to produce blooded livestock there, and he urged more sons of English noblemen to follow the example of those who had succeeded in this prairie state.[10]

Taking cognizance of this steadily increasing interest in Kansas on the part of English upper and educated classes, the magazine *Field*, appropriately subcaptioned *The Country Gentleman's Newspaper*, decided in 1872 to send its roving correspondent to this promising scene of action. After spending time in Missouri and other parts of the West, *Field's* astute and scrutinizing columnist made a special tour of Kansas. In his writings that followed, this correspondent took the position that English brains and money, not brawn, were most needed in this state, and that of the two, "money for the direct use of the farmer . . . is almost omnipotent." It was in the special interest of the gentleman-farmer, he felt, to discourage emigration of English agricultural laborers, and he emphatically contended that the availability of cheap, fertile, easily cultivated land in Kansas was a "delusion and a snare."[11] This correspondent expressed praise for the state as cattle country; and as for its much publicized lawlessness, "Kansas," he wrote, "is now, on the whole, safer than England." And as for the aridity in the western portions, he was as convinced as were many Western farmers of that day, that humidity follows the plow. Farming, he wrote, increases instead of diminishes moisture; the farmer's plow "materially increases the capacity of the soil to soak up and retain for gradual evaporation, moisture which previously found its way more rapidly to the brooks, creeks, and rivers." So, concluded this correspondent, climate was changing Kansas for the better, and for this reason it was a promising area for the investment of English capital.[12]

Not all journals of opinion, however, shared the point of view of this *Field* correspondent. The *Agricultural Gazette,* which also enjoyed an upper-class following, took issue with American promotors who advocated general English emigration to the Great Plains region. In reply to particular pro-Kansas and pro-Nebraska articles that had appeared in the English *Country Gentleman,* the *Gazette* described this Midwest region as "a country ravaged with insect pests." It urged its readers to take particular heed of the grasshopper plagues then (in 1875) besetting Kansas and Nebraska and of wheat crop failures that had occurred there during the years 1871–1873. Anyway, argued this conservative newspaper, "There is no reason for wholesale emigration from England."[13]

Not all of the upper-class Englishmen who were interested in Kansas were concerned with such materialistic aspects. Sportsmen were among those who viewed this plains state from a purely adventurous standpoint. English hunters were much intrigued by the North American buffalo or, as they preferred to call them, bison. To hunt and to shoot this mighty game in its natural habitat, centered on the grasslands of western Kansas, marked for the sportsmen not only the epitome of hunting success, but an event worth recounting in widely read publications of their time. One such sportsman was the English lord Grantley F. Berkeley, whose account of his Kansas big-game hunt, published in 1861, set a pattern for others that followed in later years.

Lord Berkeley approached his prey well armed and with more than minimal equipment. He arrived with an arsenal of guns and ammunition at Kansas City, Missouri, by means of public transport. While there, he procured a two-mule spring ambulance wagon in which to sleep and to haul his light baggage; a second and much larger wagon to be pulled by a four-mule team, for hauling heavier luggage such as tents and supplies for a period of six weeks; a third, light one-horse vehicle for hauling the gentleman's hounds; and one fast-riding saddle pony to be used in the chase. Hired to manage this caravan were eight men, plus a guide.

Then on one bracing September morning in 1859, Berkeley

and party made what Berkeley called their "jump into the desert." After ten days of rough, trudging travel they reached Fort Riley, where Berkeley was courteously received. Two other hunters assigned to the fort joined the English party, which during the following day or two saw buffalo—a sight, wrote Berkeley, "more magnificent than my fondest imagination could have depicted." After having killed perhaps as many as twenty buffalo (all but two of which were bulls) and having removed their tongues for eating and a tail and beard as souvenirs to be displayed in his trophy room back home, a happy condescending English lord returned to compose his recollections.[14]

Other accounts of exciting buffalo hunts followed. Englishman William A. Bell, a Fellow of the Royal Geographical and Ethnological Society who served as a photographer for the KP's 1867–1868 survey expedition, likewise related exhilarating experiences hunting buffalo in Kansas.[15] So, too, did John S. Campion, who during the mid 1870s still alluded to the Kansas prairies west of Fort Riley as the great buffalo country of the American West. Taking off from this fort, the Campion party moved on to the Republican River, at which place they first heard "the tramp of thousands of feet, the splash of water . . . blended into one mighty tumult"—the prey they had come to slaughter.[16]

Not only did sportsmen write about the abundance of wild game in Kansas—an ideal place for getting "the mixed bag" ranging from buffalo to grouse, but they, perhaps more so than other English visitors, were moved to comment ecstatically upon the beauty of the Kansas countryside. Campion, for example, wrote about the rolling prairie with its "ever-moving sea of waving grass," a horizon like that of the ocean, and "a balmy, invigorating, almost intoxicating air . . . untainted and unpoisoned by the breaths, smells, and smoke of cities."[17] Also scattered throughout this sporting literature were at least covert bids to the English gentry to consider Kansas as a suitable place for emigration and investment. The response to these and other more direct overtures became increasingly pronounced during the decades of the 1870s and 1880s.

In contrast to this highly literate and somewhat sophisticated introduction of Kansas to English upper-class strata, the larger, more general English public was exposed to more deliberately contrived and astutely executed techniques of various and sundry promotional concerns. Most active among the promotional agencies were railroad companies with more than eight million acres of lands to sell within the state. Under terms of a succession of federal land-grant acts, specifically designated chartered railroad companies were awarded lands from the public domain as one of the inducements for constructing rail lines into or across the state. The chief recipient of such a grant—one made in 1863—was the Union Pacific, Eastern Division, which name, incidentally, was changed six years later to Kansas Pacific Railroad Company. Under terms of this particular grant the KP constructed 394 miles of railroad within the borders of the state and in turn received from the federal government 3,925,791 acres of land.[18] In turn the ATSF, chartered in 1859, constructed 497 miles of track within the state by 1873, receiving as its reward 2,944,788 acres of public land. Smaller awards were made to other railroad companies operating within the borders of Kansas, making the grand total of federal land grants to railroads in Kansas 8,346,603 acres. Second only to railroad-land-sales promotions were those of the Kansas State Bureau of Immigration. Although the bureau was set up as a state agency, it is clearly evident that its promotional activities respecting England were closely interlocked not only with the Kansas State Board of Agriculture but with land-grant railroad companies and some of their private, or independently operated, land companies as well.[19]

Here, then, existed an enormous equity in land that needed unloading, and among several areas selected for promotional exploitation was England. English immigrants were deemed to be highly desirable, and steps were deliberately taken to tap this particular segment of Europe's population reservoir. Several avenues for promotion were deemed effective, and one of these was the English press. In addition to rather skimpy general news coverage,[20] English newspapers did, however, give considerable space to planted news releases, while paid advertisements pertaining to Kansas land sales appeared frequently and boldly in the classified sections of the press. Among the English newspapers most intrigued by Kansas emigration prospects were the Manchester *Labourers' Union Chronicle*, London *Labour News*, Liverpool *Weekly Courier*, Liverpool *American Herald*, Manchester

American News, London *Times,* and (almost exclusively concerned with English emigration to the American West) the
London *American Settler.* Reflecting as it did the policies and
aims of Joseph Arch, leader of the English agricultural labor
movement, the Manchester *Labourers' Union Chronicle* advised
emigration as a solution to farm-laborers' problems. Even though
Arch preferred Canada over the United States as a haven for his
distressed followers, the *Chronicle* nevertheless stated: "We per-
ceive there is a fine opening for farmers in America!" and also
expressed the opinion that "labour in Kansas has high value." It
pointed in particular to western Kansas, where an English workingmen's colony was being founded.[21]

The Liverpool *Weekly Courier* also favored the exodus of
Englishmen either to the United States or to Canada. The business interests of Liverpool tended to look upon emigration—the
sheer movement of people out of England—as an integral part of
trade, and for this reason, if for no other, endorsed the *Courier's*
position that the more embarcations at their city's busy Mersey
docks, the better.

Throughout the 1870s the London *Times* continued, as it had
done in the past, to report upon the United States. It took frequent note of the cattle boom on the Great Plains that involved
Kansas in particular, and it reported as well upon English colony-
founding activities then occurring in this state. The *Times,* however, was neither a staunch advocate of English emigration as a
cure-all for England's economic ills nor in any sense an apologist
for Kansas. For example, it did not hesitate to publicize this state's
tragic struggles with grasshoppers and with drought. During
January, 1875, the *Times* reported that the grasshopper plague
had left twenty thousand people destitute in western Kansas and
that assistance from Great Britain in the form of food, clothing,
and seed was desperately needed.[22]

London's *American Settler* was, unlike the English press as a
whole, largely concerned with English emigration to the United
States, and, in particular, to the American West. The *American
Settler* was established in January, 1872, as a separate publication
by the London *Anglo-American Times* and was intended to serve,
as it states in its initial announcement to its readers, as "A Guide
to British Emigration to the United States." Its aim was to bring

about what it referred to as "an intelligent emigration, not an emigration of clods alike ignorant and hungry." Perhaps more than any other single English publication, the *American Settler* was to serve well the interests of the promotional agencies of Kansas. The state was given extensive coverage, and interested readers were kept informed of lands available under terms of the Homestead and Preemption acts, the KP, and the ATSF—all done in fairly glowing terms. "The Kansas Pacific, running up the Valley of Kansas," was, the newspaper stated in 1872, receiving "the strongest tide of settlement" anywhere in the United States. "At every junction of a branch a town has sprung up, and some of them now number thousands of inhabitants."[23] During the same year this newspaper also commented upon the profitable cattle-fattening (feeding-yard) industry around Abilene and Ellsworth. And that year, too, it quoted extensively from a handbook explaining why emigration to Kansas was important then, not later, and informed its readers on how best to reach this promising settler-hungry state.[24] General human-interest accounts were also run in the *American Settler,* and one of these published in 1872 was a description by Samuel Bowles of the Kansas buffalo country as viewed from aboard a KP railroad train. Bowles had written that "for nearly half a day we rode through open and rich pastures, meeting vast herds of grazing buffalo and numerous companies of dainty antelope." Bowles pointed out that the areas through which the KP passed were "favourite pasture grounds."[25]

The *American Settler* also had much to say in behalf of Kansas soil and climate—the kinds, it contended, Englishmen like. It admitted of some uncomfortable vicissitudes of Kansas weather, but reported: "He who seeks a paradise on earth, who expects to find a land perfect in every respect, will spend his life in a vain quest and go to his grave a disappointed man."[26] Also during 1872 a Scottish settler in Kansas addressed himself to the readers of this newspaper with these added words of advice: "I should select Kansas as the most suitable field for emigration, both for the capitalist and the working man." He declared the climate to be suitable, and he asserted that if groups of about six prospective emigrant families could arrive in Kansas with about three hundred pounds in cash on hand, they could manage nicely: buy needed horses, a cow, and other livestock, some implements, and, in short, get started with a new life on the plains.[27]

In addition to surfeiting its readers with material of general interest on Kansas, the *American Settler* published information and advice on land procurement by means of homesteading, preemption, and outright purchase from railroad and other private concerns with land to sell. The overall tone of this literature was, however, promotional in character. Both land companies and railroad companies (the first often subsidiaries of the other) tended to portray Kansas in glowing colors, an impression strongly reenforced by prominently placed paid company advertisements. The ATSF, for example, declared its land to be a "garden," "a large portion of which is similar in almost every characteristic to the famous 'Bluegrass Region of Kentucky.'"[28]

The role of the Kansas State Bureau of Immigration consisted for the most part in the preparation of special publications specifically designed to inform prospective emigrants on definite settlement opportunities in Kansas and on the advantages that would accrue from such settlement. By 1880 functions of the bureau were absorbed by the State Board of Agriculture, which was then designated the sole agency of immigration into Kansas. By 1883 the board managed to obtain legislation providing both authorization and funds for the preparation, publication, and distribution of an official pamphlet designed not only to encourage foreign immigration but to provide essential practical information for all prospective immigrants. Immigrants from northern Europe were looked upon with special favor over those from other parts of the outside world, and provision was made for the distribution of twenty thousand copies of this pamphlet in England and smaller numbers of copies in Germany and the Scandinavian countries.[29]

Promotional work thus undertaken by the state was further augmented by the land-grant railroads. In order to promote its land sales both at home and abroad, the KP, for example, had from the outset of its corporate existence maintained close working arrangements with separately organized land companies. One of these, the National Land Company, was founded in 1868. Not only did this concern represent KP railroad interests but it secured as well the official blessings of state agencies seeking to promote immigration into Kansas. Even though the National

Land Company sold KP land to all customers, regardless of national origin, it, too, made a special effort to push sales in England. In London it established and was represented by an agency known as the Kansas Land and Emigration Company. John Miller was chosen to manage this London office, and it was with Miller that an agreement for the first of the English colonizing schemes concerning Kansas—the Wakefield Colony in Clay County—was negotiated during the year 1869.[30]

In support of its overseas sales operations the KP not only advertised its lands in English newspapers but issued an emigrants' guide, which stated on its title page that not four but six million acres of company lands were for sale in Kansas. This guide addressed itself especially to young people, but it also stressed that all prospective emigrants, regardless of age, should have some capital at their command before undertaking settlement in Kansas.[31] Stated land prices and terms, however, were moderate: two to six dollars per acre, one-fourth off for cash payment, or eleven years credit at 7 percent interest per annum.

Much less is known about promotions and sales in England of ATSF lands. That this company did seek English immigrants is, however, indicated by the fact that ATSF maintained an office in Liverpool jointly with the Southern Pacific Railroad Company[32] and advertised its lands for sale in English newspapers.[33]

Information intended to induce settlement and the sale of land in Kansas did not, as has already been indicated, emanate solely from the land-grant railroads. Through various and sundry publications, would-be English emigrants were also made fully aware of opportunities provided by the Homestead, Preemption, and other related federal land acts. At the beginning of the 1870s there were approximately forty million acres of public land within the borders of Kansas, and most of it was open for entry.[34] Moreover, many emigrants preferred, or for lack of capital were obliged, to file for homesteads; but Englishmen with adequate financial resources appear to have preferred the fairly generous terms offered by the railroad companies which, subject to mortgage conditions, provided for immediate and outright ownership of lands being purchased.[35] Land procurements by the English were not limited, however, either to railroad land or to land that was a part of the government domain. As elsewhere in the West, there were land companies that operated independently of both the rail lines and the state and federal governments. One of these was the Kansas Land Company, formed in 1871. It parceled out its land sales in sixty- to one hundred-acre lots and offered to build a dwelling on each. Upon down-payment of eighty dollars, the purchaser would receive a ticket entitling him to transportation from England to the States with the White Star Line and rail passage to "his own door, with a farm ready to be tilled."[36]

The complete list of individual promoters is as varied as it is long. Free-lance writers appear to have had their connections with land companies (doubtless for considerations), and their writings contributed greatly toward broadcasting throughout England the virtues of Kansas, especially of the lands of this state. Religious leaders made land deals with railroad companies and then in turn pushed land sales with their parishioners. Newspaper publishers were also deeply involved in promotional schemes and backed many of them editorially. So, throughout the period 1865 to 1890 the publication market appears to have been surfeited with promotional literature that included books, guides, gazetteers, pamphlets, directories, and newspapers—much of it specially intended for diverse segments of the English public that included religious elements, upper-class groups, utopian societies, agricultural workers, and industrial laborers.[37]

Nor was this the extent of English public awareness of Kansas. In addition to publishing paid advertisements and promotional releases, English newspapers—surprisingly interested in and fascinated with the American West in general—printed an impressive number of random letters and statements submitted to the respective newspaper editors for publication. Not all such communications concerned with Kansas were favorable to it, but regardless of the position taken, the feelings expressed were usually quite pronounced. Many such items were published in the *American Settler*, but they appeared as well in the London *Times* and in the English provincial press. Some of them carried the names of contributors, but others indicated authorship by initials and pseudonyms. Those who might have questioned the printed word (and wisely so in many instances) could and sometimes did make official inquiries concerning Kansas. One such cautious but inquiring Englishman was Captain Bertie Cator, who addressed himself to, and received the following reply from, the American legation in London concerning prospects in Kansas: "I am quite convinced that any respectable, industrious, young man with small capital would do well in Kansas or Nebraska; but life in a new country is always uphill work. Still, patience and a few years' toil are always certain to be rewarded with success." Another communication took the form of this question: "Will you give me space for this in your next issue [?] I should select Kansas as the most suitable field for emigration, both for the capitalist and working man." The writer acclaimed Kansas climate, and in general lauded this state as a land of opportunity, providing the arriving immigrant possessed at least a few pounds sterling.

Not all communications were favorable to Kansas, and W. Frank Lynn, member of the Royal Colonial Institute, who published letters in both the London *Times* and the *American Settler*, denounced both the private land speculators and the railroad companies for their gross misrepresentations. In a letter addressed to the editor of the *Times*, March 9, 1872, Lynn stated that inasmuch as "hundreds of people will probably leave England in the Spring," with a view to settling in the Kansas, Nebraska, and Colorado area, he felt obligated to inform such prospective migrants in advance that winters in this region were of a severity "rarely equaled in Canada." He urged emigrants going there to arrive with "the warmest clothing" because many families there "have been frozen to death." About three weeks later, Lynn wrote a second letter to the *Times* in which he stated that in addition to warm clothing prospective settlers should come provided with such essentials as ploughs, horses, implements, seed, cattle, housing materials, and fencing (presumably purchased at a place such as Kansas City, not brought from overseas). Moreover, Lynn warned Englishmen against going to the outer fringes of settlement without first gaining some experience in the settled portion of the state.[38]

In spite of an occasional sour note, letters of the type alluded to tended to be increasingly favorable to eastern Kansas as a place for settlement. Writing from Newton, Kansas, one Charles Bingham of Derbyshire addressed himself in an open letter to Charles H. Branscombe, English land agent for the ATSF. Bingham appears to have been overwhelmed by his observations of and experiences in eastern Kansas. "The transformation of these prairies into beautiful farms in about five years' time, ornamented also with a variety of trees, and splendid orchards . . . is what no Englishman can possibly realize who has not seen it with his own eyes." Bingham indicated that he planned to buy from the ATSF two hundred and forty acres of land located in the vicinity of Atchison.[39]

Most of those who published their observations on Kansas wrote as Bingham had, about the more humid eastern portion of Kansas, and not about the semiarid pariries of the western part of the state. But an exception was one using the nom de plume "F.A.G." who in 1884 commented critically upon this western region. "We could not," he wrote, "help being struck with the oddities of Kansas, especially the Western part—the great timberless prairies." F.A.G., ignorant of conditions on the plains, attributed the prevalence of dugouts and soddies in this region to the danger of cyclonic activity. The aridity of western Kansas was further emphasized in reference to one scientist's opinion that it was doubtful that western Kansas, "lying outside the immediate track of vapor-laden winds, could ever have a rainfall adequate to maintain successful agriculture." Finally, in 1886, the editor of the *American Settler* concluded that local Kansas newspapers had in fact been overrating this western region, and he declared editorially that the "line of demarcation between the farming country and the arid land is no fanciful or imaginary line."[40]

While no precise cause and effect relationship can be established between this on-the-whole favorable Kansas image within England and emigration, it is a fact that English people were attracted to this state and that many of them emigrated to it during the first two decades following the Civil War. In 1860 there were approximately 1,400 persons of English (including Welsh) birth in Kansas; in 1870 there were 7,147; and in 1880 the number had swelled to 14,748.[41]

Unlike the distribution pattern of Russians, Germans, and Scandinavians in Kansas, the pattern of English settlement reveals an absence of concentration in given areas. But even though the English tended to spread themselves more widely than other immigrant groups, figures indicate that by 1880 sixteen counties reported no Englishmen, whereas one county, namely Osage, contained 1,239 of them. By 1890 there were Englishmen in all Kansas counties, with a low of 4 in Scott County and a high of 1,025 in Shawnee County (the number in Osage County having by then dropped to 905). Not only did the English spread, but they tended to pursue all avenues of economic opportunities open to the people of Kansas.[42]

The reasons for this relatively wide dispersal are apparent. Unlike other ethnic groups, the English experienced no serious communication problems. In spite of a desire on the part of railroad companies to sell large tracts of land to individual immigrant groups, the English demonstrated no strong desire to form cooperative colonies that normally called for closely integrated living.[43]

Once decisions to emigrate to Kansas had been reached by the English, the trans-Atlantic crossings and transits overland to intended locations within the state followed a generally familiar pattern. In most instances emigrating parties converged with their personal belongings upon Liverpool, at which port they boarded vessels of varying types and seaworthiness that belonged for the most part to British lines. The more affluent Englishmen purchased first-class accommodations, but those of modest means were obliged to travel steerage.[44] The main port of disembarkation was New York City, where rail connections to Kansas City, Missouri, and points beyond were obtained. Some Kansas-bound emigrants landed at New Orleans, where upriver steamboat services to Kansas City awaited them. Distances traveled to, and places reached within, Kansas kept pace with rail-line construction, while destinations beyond the "end-of-the-track" could usually be reached by commercial stagecoach services offered by the prominent Kansas Stage Company or its competitors.[45] At some of their stations, railroad companies maintained hospitality houses for emigrant customers, a service which freed heads of households from routine family cares long enough to make necessary purchases or to transfer from freight cars such items as horses or oxen, wagons, a few farm implements, household goods, and miscellaneous supplies needed to begin immigrant life on a Kansas farm or ranch. Once at the site of their acreage (or homestead), all able-bodied hands shared in the construction of a soddie or dugout, broke sod for seeding or planting, and in other ways got on with the hard work of pioneer living.[46]

One of the most revealing and delightful of the available accounts—the author of which lived his youth in Kansas and then returned to "merrie England"—was by Percy G. Ebbutt. In a fascinating book entitled *Emigrant Life in Kansas,* Ebbutt related that in 1870 he (then a youngster) with his father, brother, and three other men left their native town of Blanxton, in the south of England, and set out for Junction City, Kansas. They took with them, he wrote, enough luggage to stock a colony. Included in this luggage were guns of various kinds, a grain grinder containing a large flywheel, a huge jackknife, and of course clothing and tea. None had previously engaged in farming, and yet their reason for emigrating to Kansas was to engage in ranching.

Junction City at the time was a small but growing western town with a population of 2,778. Upon arrival, Ebbutt and party stayed at the town's Empire Hotel and remained there for six weeks before moving on to Parkertown (a place with nineteen houses in it), twenty-five miles distant. After two weeks of living at a boardinghouse, the Ebbutt party moved onto land acquired in this particular vicinity. Ebbutt relates the move to this land:

> On the 18th of February, 1871, having hired a couple of waggons, we moved up on the prairie with all our luggage, and boards to build our house with. On arriving at our destination, seven miles from town, the large boxes were piled up, and the boards laid slanting from the top to the ground for a roof, and thus we made a very comfortable shanty. . . . We were very well off for provisions, having a good supply of bacon, biscuits, eggs, cheese, coffee, sugar, flour, rice, etc.
>
> The cook, Harry Parker, made his first attempt at bread-making . . . but not over successful. The bread was baked in a great iron pan, and was as hard as a well-done brick, and about as digestible. The outside could not be cut with a knife, we were obliged to use a hatchet to make any impression.[47]

Finally horses and oxen and ploughs were procured, the breaking of prairie sod and seeding of crops were undertaken, and a routine lonely life on the prairies was at last under way. Gradually neighbors (the first one was another Englishman) moved in. Occasionally Indians came to beg for food, freezing winters were endured but not without loss of livestock, a new house was built, a cattle herd was acquired and with it the dreary monotony of herding, and then one day there was the report that they were about to be visited by a grasshopper plague.

About a fortnight before they arrived with us we heard they were at Junction City, so it took them fourteen days to travel about thirty-five miles.

It was the beginning of August, and the small grains, such as wheat, etc., were carried and stacked, so that these were secure. The maize, however, . . . was destroyed with the other, after the beastly things arrived. They came on gradually like a fall of snow. We first saw a glittering cloud high in the sky, and all sparkling in the sun. . . . they alighted on houses, people, animals, fences, crops, covering everything, while the ground was strewn several inches thick, so that it was impossible to walk about without killing dozens at each step. . . .

All the trees in the woods were divested of their leaves, and the whole place looked as though there had been a fire raging in every part. . . .

After the grasshoppers had finished every green thing, including chewing the tobacco, they began to seek "fresh fields and pastures new."[48]

Time passed and Kansas life for young Ebbutt was such that he decided to return to England. In the conclusion to his interesting book he offered this advice to prospective emigrants: "Make up your mind to rough it. . . . be prepared to cook your own dinner . . . wash and mend your own clothes . . . handle an axe well. . . . Show yourself willing to be taught. . . . Take due precautions against prairie fires. . . . You must leave all idea of luxuries behind." And then by way of consolation he concluded: "If you are not happy in the old country . . . you might do worse than go west."[49]

Throughout the decades of the 1870s and 1880s Englishmen's observations on living in Kansas and its surrounding plains country continued. As settlement extended rapidly westward during these years, so too did the focus of attention move westward, away from small grain-farming operations in the lower reaches of the Kansas Valley, and out onto the semiarid cattle- and sheep-ranching areas in western Kansas, where life was more rugged and prospects less certain. Out there on the western prairies prospects indeed looked grim, but in spite of this, one English traveler was able to write in the late 1870s that he had witnessed a "continuous line of emigrants travelling in wagons across the prairies of Kansas, many of them from the old country. . . . These emigrants, both young and old, are huddled together in these wagons, and all looking as dirty and miserable as it is possible for poor creatures to look."[50]

One unidentified author, for example, described life on a prairie sheep ranch in anything but glowing terms. Basing his comments upon firsthand experience as a sheepherder, he described his experience as "a severe trial of endurance," a denial of comforts and conveniences that in England would have been considered absolutely necessary. "But the crowning touch of all, to my mind," he wrote, "was a Colt's revolver, strapped around the waist." He related the necessity for this by quoting the words of an old frontiersman: " 'You may carry a six-shooter twenty years and never use it once, except fur skunks, and at the end of that twenty years you might want it so almighty bad, that you'd wish you'd packed it all the time.' " The unfriendly climate and conditions of range living—heat, cold, thirst, hunger—were as nothing compared to "the complete isolation, the almost maddening monotony of the life."[51]

The English were not only heavy investors in the range-cattle business but they also participated actively in the range life on the prairies. Major W. Shepherd, who traveled widely throughout the West during the early 1880s, had words of caution for his countrymen who may have considered heedless plunges into Western cattle business. He advised not to listen to stories of 30 percent annual profit at cattle-ranching and "to be on the safe side, if you have capital, leave it at home; learn the business you wish to follow by working at it with your own hands, pay no premiums, but hire yourself out, if active and willing, you are well worth your keep . . . the tenderfoot who takes his dollars in his trouser-pockets is a lost man." He reminded his English readers that would-be stock raisers would have to go farther west than the farm area, but that homestead and preemption opportunities were still available.[52]

Representing but a relatively minor segment of the involvements of the English in Kansas were their attempts at colony-founding. Nevertheless, the dramatic, even flamboyant character of English colonizing efforts has attracted considerable attention —more, perhaps, than is merited. During the period under review at least five attempts were made by the English at group colonization within the state. One of these colonies was at best feeble and scarcely merits consideration in comparison with the others. It concerns a group of Englishmen and Scots who in 1870 formed in England what became known as the First Excelsior Colony. The initial contingent of this colony consisted of eight men, one woman, and a six-weeks-old baby. The party settled on Rose Creek, Liberty Township, in Republic County. Junction City was its nearest land office and source of supplies. Two of the men involved had been stonecutters in London before emigrating, and none knew how to harness and hitch up a team of horses, let alone how to cultivate the Kansas prairie. But they nevertheless managed to build a common dugout and to persevere. The men were all avowed atheists and experienced no religious deprivations, but the woman, who embraced the faith of the Church of England, was deprived of religious services for a period of fourteen years. Not much is known about this tiny colony except that—like many of their fellow countrymen in Kansas—they eventually moved to other, but unknown, locations.[53]

A much more ambitious and formidable but no more successful attempt at founding an English community in Kansas was Wakefield Colony. Established in Clay County in 1869, this colony was founded by the Reverend Richard Wake, an English Methodist who at the time was a resident of Wilmington, Illinois. Wake had emigrated from England in 1854 to Illinois, where in addition to performing pastoral duties he had contributed articles to the English religious press, such as the *London Christian World,* staunchly advocating English emigration to the American West as a way of relieving the motherland of her excess population. Wake's special appeal was to English agricultural laborers. In 1866 he had returned to England where he personally organized a group of 115 men, women, and children who left England to establish, in this same year, the Palmyra Colony in Otoe County, Nebraska.[54]

In an account published a quarter-century later, Wake recounted how he came by his interest in founding a colony in Kansas. It appears that while on his 1866 trip to England, he encountered in Yorkshire R. H. Drew, a London land agent, and John Wornald of Wakefield, who were both seeking to found a colony in Missouri but who in the course of subsequent developments made inquiries about settlement possibilities in Kansas. A collaboration ensued. Drew and Wornald had in mind the founding of a cooperative colony, but Wake—with on-scene experiences in the American West—favored what he called an "associated immigration plan" which provided for individual ownership of land and produce, but called for lump purchase of a large tract of land that could in turn be resold to individual colony members at a small profit to the founders. Wake, as indicated, returned to the states, and nothing much happened until one day in June, 1869, when he received a cablegram from London reading: "Select 100,000 acres in Kansas for colony." Wake subsequently related that he first went to Topeka to investigate Santa Fe lands, but he found them too high-priced. He then went to Junction City where he approached agents of the National Land Company (connected with the KP) and purchased from them 32,000 acres of land located on the Republican River sixteen miles northwest of Junction City and in Clay County. The sale price was fixed at $102,000 and called for 20 percent down-payment.[55]

Out of this transaction there emerged during the following August the Kansas Land and Emigration Company in which Wornald became the heaviest investor and of which Wake was chosen president. The experienced Wake lost no time in platting the company's baronial acres and in laying out a town to be named Wakefield. On September 30 he wrote his London office: "Send out as many hardworking people as you can; they need not want of employment here, men and women, if they can work. . . . If any servant girls wish to come by all means send a few."[56] In addition, Wake prepared copy for a guide for English consumption in which he declared that Kansas crops were surprisingly excellent. Corn (Indian corn), he wrote, grew twelve to fourteen feet high there, so high, in fact, that the ears could not be reached with umbrella tips. Wakefield, he added, was for the "common folks" of England truly a "Land of Promise."[57] Circulars were also prepared, and these were addressed mainly to, and circulated widely among, poor English tradesmen. The promotions produced results. The first contingent of seventy-seven colonists left Liverpool during mid September, 1869, and arrived at Wakefield on October 6. These first arrivals were in turn followed by others during the spring of 1870, and still more during 1871.[58]

Unfortunately there was to be little resemblance between the glowing prospects portrayed by the Kansas Land and Emigration Company and the actual experiences of those who emigrated to Wakefield. Not only did the colonists come devoid of capital, but they also came unskilled in the art of farming—either in England or on the American prairies. They also encountered all the devastations that nature occasionally bestows upon Kansas: grasshoppers, a summer drought, "fitful and violent changes in temperatures," and a tornado. But in spite of these adversities the struggling neophytes made a desperate effort to survive and, if possible, to make their colony succeed. Funds for their support were raised in England, and the townsite was developed to include a town hall, store, postoffice, blacksmith shop, meat market, hotel, company office, Methodist church, and private dwellings.[59] Except for the few who became involved mainly with town affairs, there is every indication that most of the Wakefield families settled upon nearby quarter sections (or less) which they attempted to develop into productive and, hopefully, prosperous farms.

But for most of the colonizers it appears that such goals were to be denied. Wrote a second-generation member of this colony:

> The glowing accounts issued by immigration companies and the sharp practice often connected with real-estate deals were among the grievances of the colonists. . . . The greatest drawback to the colony was found in the general economic conditions. The country had not recovered from the civil war. . . . There was no local demand for agricultural products and the Kansas City market was easily glutted.[60]

By the mid 1870s, at a time of heavy locust infestation, the Wakefield Colony for all intents and purposes ceased to exist as

an integrated English community. The Reverend Wake moved
to Topeka, and other leaders also moved on—to such widely scattered parts of the Union as Washington, Virginia, and Texas, as
well as back to the mother country.[61]

Founded one year after Wakefield, in 1870, was Nemaha, or
what was at times also called the "Old English Colony." Located
in Nemaha County next to the Kansas-Nebraska boundary, this
colony too had its identification with the KP. The distinctive
feature of Nemaha Colony was its Utopian character. John W.
Fuller, one of the original members, recalled for newsmen many
years later the circumstances surrounding its founding. Fuller
related that a meeting of workmen took place at 18 Denmark
Street in London's gay Soho district where workers customarily
congregated and discussed their problems. At this particular
meeting in 1870 someone proposed forming a cooperative colony
in Kansas, and a company known as the Mutual Land, Emigration, and Cooperative Colonization Company was founded. One
of the group, Edward G. Smith, was chosen to be superintendent,
and in due course about fifty English families (all very poor)
migrated to Nemaha County where a 720-acre piece of land had
been acquired from the KP (or what was then the Union Pacific,
Eastern Division) as the place for their cooperative enterprise.[62]

The Nemaha Colony scheme called for allocation of ten to
forty acres of land to each member and for the construction of an
eight-room house of large dimensions that would serve as a com-
mons. When built, this particular structure came to be known in
the county as the "Llewellyn Castle." Individual colonists built
soddies or dugouts on their acreages, which were to serve them as
family dwellings.

Unfortunately, Nemaha Colony also suffered from the rav-
ages of nature: droughts, grasshoppers, blizzards, and prairie fires,
and, in addition, internal dissensions. By 1874 the cooperative
character of this enterprise had ceased to exist. As with Wakefield,
individual colonists tended to drift elsewhere, although a few
families remained in Nemaha County where in time they became
prosperous farmers and craftsmen.[63]

By far the most publicized and most widely known English
(more properly British) settlement enterprise in Kansas was Victoria Colony in Ellis County. The founder of this colony was

George Grant, a native of Scotland. Moreover, the early life of the enterprising Grant—first in Scotland and then in London—had an important relationship to what might well be called a bizarre venture into the game of colony-founding on the Kansas frontier.

George Grant was born in Banffshire in north Scotland in 1822, the son of a poor crofter. As a boy, George was apprenticed to a Banff draper and merchant, and out of this association and training Grant was eventually to emerge as one of London's most prominent silk merchants—a partner of the widely known and respected firm of Gask and Grant, Oxford Street, London.

Grant was attractive in appearance—tall, of good proportions, and in possession of an affable and generally attractive personality. He was an interesting conversationalist and was well informed. Not only did Grant do well in the normal course of his business life, but his remarkable astuteness as a merchant enabled him on occasion to reap extraordinary returns from his London enterprise. For example, in 1861, Grant, on the occasion of the fatal illness of Prince Albert, the royal consort, anticipated the prince's passing. He proceeded to corner the market on black crepe in London and to sell it to the mourning English public at a huge profit. And again it was the sharp merchant Grant who at the 1867 Paris Exposition managed to outdo all rivals in the exhibition of silk, with a resultant rush of profitable business at the London store of Gask and Grant.[64]

Successful though he was as a merchant, it was apparently a combination of health problems and a desire for adventure, at a profit, that caused Grant in 1871 to become interested in the American West and subsequently to establish an English-Scottish colony in Ellis County, Kansas. There is evidence that as a prominent London merchant, Grant had established many business as well as cultural and artistic connections with Americans, and perhaps not unrelated to this fact, he became interested in lands offered for sale by the KP. Among other things Grant had been attracted by this company's advertisements on its land sales. During 1871, accompanied by KP land-office agents, he personally examined the real estate offerings within Ellis County. Then after having considered other moves in the United States, he accepted the KP offer the following year. This transaction was the largest of its kind made by the KP land office. The land lay south of the KP tracks, 287 miles west of Kansas City and 11 miles east of Hays. It consisted of seventy sections interspersed with alternating sections retained by the government for homesteading, so that Grant's holdings were actually contained within an area that extended thirteen sections to the south of the KP track and nineteen sections parallel with the track in an east-west direction. For this land Grant paid prices ranging from forty cents to eighty cents per acre and he apparently made a down payment of $10,000.[65]

In making a purchase of this magnitude it is clear that Grant had in mind the resale of much of his land—hopefully, but by no means exclusively—to upper-class Britishers of means, thus establishing a colony for Englishmen and Scots. It is likewise apparent that he planned to carry on under his own management large-scale ranching, featuring blooded stock. In order to do these things he chose to completely sever his London business connections and to henceforth live a new and more exciting, more health-giving life on the Kansas prairies. As a special consideration in behalf of the purchaser the KP offered its good offices in helping to promote British settlement for Grant's colony-founding schemes, and it also proposed to erect a railroad station at the site of Grant's holdings and to give it the same name Grant adopted for his projected colony: Victoria.[66]

Once transactions had been officially completed, Grant set out for Kansas on what for him was to be a new and an exciting adventure. He set sail from Glasgow on the steamer *Alabama* on April 1, 1873. In his party was the first contingent of prospective Victoria settlers and Grant employees. And aboard, too, were draft horses and blooded livestock that included black hornless Aberdeen Angus and shorthorn bulls and long-wooled sheep. The *Alabama* was destined for New Orleans, at which port transfer was to be made to the packet *Great Republic* for the upriver run to St. Louis, whence the remainder of the journey would be covered by rail transportation. Some difficulties were encountered when the *Alabama* stranded at the mouth of the Mississippi River. During this delay the Grant party suffered from intense heat, humidity, and mosquitos, and concern was felt for the safety of the precious livestock. But finally both men and beasts arrived safely at their destination on May 17, 1873.

At first, developments moved ahead as planned. The KP more than kept its part of the bargain by building not just another standard-type railroad station on the prairies but a formidable two-storied, thirteen-room stone station-hotel containing a common kitchen for use by newcomers. The structure was designed in the proper Victorian style of architecture and in keeping with plans was given the name of Britain's illustrious reigning queen.

Plans also called for the laying-out of a new city surrounding the station. It was to be a highly moral city—free of saloons, gambling dens, and dancing casinos. Steps taken to realize this dream were, however, slow and minuscule. After the first five years of development, Victoria was at best a struggling village containing a few residences, a grocery store, meat market, blacksmith shop, school, and the foundation for a church. As yet there was no grain elevator in Victoria, although such was planned for and sorely needed.[67]

While Grant lost no time in pushing his colonizing or landsales plan, he at the same time proceeded to provide for his personal living and to develop his own large-scale ranching operations. He selected as a site for his "villa" an attractive spot five miles south of Victoria station near Victoria Creek. There, on a rise that offered a commanding view of his broad acres, Grant erected a substantial house of English design. When completed, it was two-stories high, constructed mainly of stone, and had four gables and a veranda which extended around the house on three of its sides. On the lower floor to the right of the main entrance was a spacious parlor, and on the left a dining room. There were altogether ten "elegantly furnished" rooms. The house was enclosed by willow growth that was trimmed in Russian style by Russian workers who had meanwhile settled in the vicinity of Victoria. In addition, plans were laid for the planting of ornamental and fruit trees within a fenced-in area surrounding the house. Wrote one who later visited Grant after his place was fully developed: "It is a house that kings might covet, and we would too were it not for the commandment."[68]

Grant had, however, not come to Kansas simply to live an indulgent life in a big house on the open prairies. He had come to Victoria in order to engage in large-scale ranching and to develop a colony, and he proceeded at once to realize his objectives. He designated certain portions of his land for personal use, the remainder to be laid out in assorted sizes and placed on sale to prospective settlers. The interspersed government lands were, of course, out of Grant's control, but it was hoped that these too would be occupied under terms of existing homestead and pre-emption laws.[69]

In the development of his own ranch Grant planned to do two important things new to the Great Plains: raise blooded stock and introduce large-scale scientific farming by use of pure seed, proper cultivation, and employment of equipment driven by steam power. To implement this program he engaged the services of S. Douglas Smith, one of England's noted agronomists and an authority on the use of steam plowing. In keeping with these objectives Grant broke about eight hundred acres of this prairie land on which he successfully raised wheat, oats, rye, corn, and millet.[70]

Fluctuations in the amount of annual rainfall in western Kansas offered no assurance of bumper crops. For this reason Grant's stock-raising program, which was dependent in large measure upon utilization of the natural grasses not only on his own estate but on railroad and government lands as well, proved to be the most successful aspect of his Victoria operations. When James MacDonald, another distinguished British agronomist, visited Victoria in 1877, he had this to say about Grant's ranching operations:

> Exclusive of calves, Mr. Grant owns over 800 cattle, about an equal number of cows, two-year-olds, and yearlings. The cows are a selection of Missouri grades and improved Cherokees and Texans; and, for crossing with these, really good shorthorn and polled [Aberdeen Angus] bulls were imported—the former from England, and the latter from the herd of the late Mr. George Brown, Westertown, Fochabers, Scotland. . . . I had heard and read very favourable accounts of this herd, and, after a careful inspection, I cannot say I was disappointed.[71]

MacDonald added that while many of the cattle were "unshapely, big-boned, and of inferior quality" (judged by English standards), they were, nevertheless, better than any "native stock I have seen elsewhere in the Far West or South." He pointed out that Grant supplemented grazing by feeding grain to stock slated for market.[72] His introduction of blooded stock to the range country to be crossbred with longhorns at a time when little effort was being made to improve the quality of livestock remains an important contribution to the economic well-being of Kansas. Grant's own financial reward for having improved his stock through crossbreeding (such cattle were known to the range country as "black daddies") was a better-than-average market price for his commodity. Moreover, he kept the breeds of some of his cattle pure, and for this he is credited by the American Aberdeen Angus Breeders' Association with being the first to import Angus cattle into the United States.[73] MacDonald also had praise for Grant's sheep-raising accomplishments. He indicated that Grant had imported Southdown, Cotswold, Lincoln, and Leicester breeds, and that by 1877 his flocks numbered about eleven thousand sheep.[74]

Important as farming was to Grant's scheme of things at Victoria, it did not necessarily take precedence over his colony-founding and land-sales efforts. What may have been rather nebulous plans initially, soon sharpened and expanded. Once the purchase had been formally transacted and announced, Grant, businessman that he was, quickly recognized the need to establish land-sales offices. He did this in the two cities from which he expected to receive his clientele, namely, Edinburgh and London. His Scottish agents were Curror and Cowper, located in India House, Edinburgh; and the English Agency was that of R. W. Edis, 14 Fitzroy Place, London. Actually, Grant also established a New York City agency, namely, the firm of Cobbe and Fowler, 52 Wall Street.[75]

It was through the work and publicity of these agencies that Grant's scheme for Victoria colony became internationally publicized. Pamphlets, news releases, and sponsored visitations by distinguished people all gave zest and notoriety to these promotional activities. Brochures contained the standard exaggerations of the day. Even the publication issued by conservative D. Curror, head of the Edinburgh firm of Curror and Cowper, for example, was entitled *Mr. Grant's Great Property: Victoria, in Kansas.* It describes the region in which the land was located as a "Second Eden." In no place in his publication did Curror resort to so-called British understatements. This pamphlet continued: "Those green prairies, rolling like gentle swells of the ocean, starred and gemmed with flowers, and threaded with dark belts of timber which mark the windings of the streams are a joy forever."[76]

The pamphlet issued by the London office was entitled *New and Attractive Field for Emigrants . . . Victoria;* and this one noted that "for richness of soil, purity and abundance of water, and supply of building material, this tract has been pronounced by highest authority to be of the best in the State of Kansas." It credited Ellis County with "champagne air" which "not only stimulates nerve centres, irrigating the body, but it has also an invigorating effect upon the mind." Thereupon this English document drew upon Albert D. Richardson's *Beyond the Mississippi* for support, quoting him as follows: "I wonder if the Almighty ever made a more beautiful country than Kansas."[77]

As previously stated, Grant hoped to interest the so-called better-class Englishmen in settling Victoria and to encourage the development of a moral community. But judging from his land sale prices, it would appear that financial liquidity as well as utopian goals dominated his thinking. By the summer of 1873 his lands were widely advertised not only to his own British agents but also by the KP's London and Liverpool offices headed by A. MacDonald. His terms were these: £1 to £3.10.0 per acre, 20 percent down and the balance to be paid within four years. The interest rate was set at 6 percent. Town-lot options were obtainable at £1.0.0, or $5.00.[78] Special low railroad fares were offered by the KP as part of the bargain.

Interestingly enough, Grant appears to have been more interested in the dollar and the pound than in the achievement of his declared objectives. As it turned out, one of his first major sales was not aimed, as Grant had repeatedly stated, to provide a haven for British gentry but for humble workingmen of England. The purchaser was J. Bates of London, who bought from Grant roughly seven sections of land which Bates planned to resell in small allotments to indigent English workingmen and farm laborers. Farming caused a small flurry in English labor circles, but as it turned out, the plan did not materialize. The Manchester *Labourer's Union Chronicle*, did, however, declare Victoria to be "a fine opening for the farmer." This newspaper went on to say that for the person in possession of one to two thousand pounds of capital, Victoria offered "not simply a vast field for healthy homes and farming enterprise, but the potentiality of vast fortunes. . . . Away to Victoria, Kansas, and speed the plow there."[79]

In keeping with his desire to gain publicity and in that way catch the attention of upper-class Britishers, Grant's agents, in cooperation with KP officials, sponsored a special visitation to Victoria. Among those invited to make this tour under the joint sponsorship of Grant and KP were R. Scott Skirving, former president of Scotland's Chamber of Commerce; H. Bethune, a Scottish deputy lieutenant; R. W. Edis, Grant's London agent; and W. Wester, general agent for the KP. That this visitation achieved its purpose is indicated in the press. "When men of such high standing append their names . . . it should give confidence," said one Kansas newspaper.[80] Among those who greeted these distinguished visitors at Victoria were the first settlers who had made the crossing on the *Alabama*, namely, Grant and his nephew Alexander, George Staples, George Philip, and George MacDonald—all Scots; also James Hider with wife and child, Frank Mason, J. Douglas Smith, A. A. Smith—all English. Altogether thirty persons had made up this first contingent. The resultant publicity from this visit and the work of agents at home and abroad (combined with highly satisfactory crops during 1873 and 1874) produced modest, and for a time satisfactory, results.

Available estimates on the number who actually settled at Victoria vary. Indications are that successes at recruitment were correlated with the successes and failures of crops during the decade of the 1870s. Grasshoppers during 1874 and severe blizzards during the ensuing winter caused some settlers to leave Victoria, but the return of good crops brought new arrivals during the period 1876 to 1878. One estimate credits Victoria and environs with about three hundred English at what could have been an all-time high in 1876. In any event, the 1880 census count on English in Ellis County (and nearly all the English there were located at Victoria and its immediate environs) was 128. In a letter addressed to *The Scotsman* James MacDonald commented

upon what was happening. He pointed out that the British had
found Victoria "much as nature and the buffalo had left it"; then
drought, grasshoppers, wolves, and stormy weather devoured
many of their crops and played havoc with their stock. Many
settlers lost all, and left; those with larger pocketbooks remained.[81]

Grant, who had spearheaded the colony, died suddenly on
April 26, 1878, and this proved a discouragement to many. For
this and for other reasons (among them the encroachments of
more eager and energetic Russian settlers from their adjoining
colony named Herzog) more Englishmen departed during the
1880s than arrived. By 1890 census takers counted only 107
English in Ellis County, and at the close of the century this
number had further declined to 63.[82]

The importance to Kansas of Grant's British colony of Victoria cannot, however, be measured in terms of numbers. Grant
and his Victoria received international notoriety and so contributed much to outside interest in western Kansas—a region that
prior to Grant's arrival there was known simply as a sportsman's
hunting ground and as part of the Great American Desert. But if
Grant's reputation as an English colonizer has become tarnished,
the fact that he was the man who introduced purebred Aberdeen
Angus cattle into the United States gives him a lasting place
among those who made important contributions to Kansas and to
the development of the American West.

One other attempt at founding an English colony in Kansas
transpired. This one was in Harper County, and the time was the
early 1890s. The name of it, Runnymede, was unmistakably
English and so, too, were many of its characteristics. First steps
taken to found this colony were in the early 1880s when Edward
Turnley, an Irishman by birth, arrived in Kansas from England
and purchased 17,000 acres of land at $1.50 per acre. The land
was located on the bank of the Chikaskia River, nine miles northeast of Harper and forty miles southwest of Wichita. The colony
of Runnymede, however, was not formally founded until 1889, at
which time its plan was first publicized in England.

Turnley's proposal was to settle in his colony untitled English
gentlemen (in short, remittance men) who would possess some
capital and who might wish to combine pleasures and adventures
with making a living in the American West. Runnymede was

idyllic in concept—"a Western paradise where golden birds sing in the trees and silver rivers run tinkling to the sea . . . [where] corn grows as high as an elephant's eye, and the climate is so healthy it puts to shame any reference to Elysian Fields."[83]

Those who chose to join this colony were required to pay a five-hundred-dollar membership fee which entitled each holder to a pony and saddle and the privilege of buying land. They might either build a home on their land or, not wishing to do this, live in barracks called Chikaskia House, which Turnley had constructed for residence and club purposes.

The first group of settlers, consisting of sixteen men and women, departed from England for Kansas aboard the steamer *Britannic* on May 29, 1889, and it in turn was followed by others until the number reached approximately one hundred. A small village emerged, boasting a three-storied hotel, some stores, stagecoach facilities, and several homes.[84]

Runnymede did not escape the country-club atmosphere intended for it by its founder. It contained a track on which carriage races took place. Polo was played, fox hunts were held, and bootleg liquor was copiously consumed. But farming was slighted —tried, in fact, by few, and successfully by none.

As it finally turned out, Kansas and the Runnymede colony proved incompatible. A cyclone hit the area in 1890, the Panic in 1893, and crop failure in 1895. Some of the colonists returned to England, others left to go elsewhere. One woman colonist became a drug addict, and Richard Whetmough, Runnymede's best-liked citizen, burned to death when his barn caught on fire following a convivial party. The colony had hoped for railroad connections, but when these failed, Runnymede withered on the vine. In later years, one of its members reminisced: "Runnymede, you must know, was a combination of British inexperience, credulity, some money, considerable cockneyism"—a romantic idea of getting-rich-quick on "champagne and venison."[85]

In addition to being for the English a sportsman's paradise, a place to see, and a suitable location for settlement for emigrating Englishmen, Kansas is known to have attracted some English investments during the post–Civil War years. One sizable and long-lived English concern founded to do business in this state was the Kansas and New Mexico Cattle Company, Ltd. This company was founded in 1883, with its head office in Manchester, and was capitalized at £ 150,000. The stated purpose of this company was to acquire cattle ranches in the United States, in particular one owned by Harold and Edmund S. Carlisle, located in Sedgwick County, Kansas. The purchase was consummated. Harold Carlisle, who accepted a sizable block of shares as part payment, became manager, and his brother Edmund for a similar reason became secretary. The company continued in operation (subsequently changing its name to Kansas and New Mexico Land and Cattle Company, Ltd.) until the close of the century.[86]

A comparable concern was the British Land and Mortgage Company of America, Ltd., incorporated also in 1883 and capitalized at £ 1 million with headquarters in London. The purpose of this concern was to buy and hold land and securities in various parts of the United States, but it is significant to note that one of the three largest shareholders in this concern was James S. Worden, a Frankfort, Kansas, banker.[87] Worden served as the company's American agent for a short time following the inception of the company, then during the late summer of 1883 this position was filled by E. B. Percell at Manhattan. But American connections do not end here. Sir Stuart James Hogg, of London, the company's president, spent considerable time in Frankfort and Manhattan during 1883 in behalf of the company's interests. Subsequently, Sir Stuart's son came to Kansas, where he attended briefly the Kansas State Agricultural College. He later returned to England, where he married an English girl whom he brought as a bride to Manhattan. There the couple lived for several years, and there, in 1890, Stuart, Junior, assumed the managership of the company's Kansas operations.[88] These developments created a stir in the Kansas press, as well they might, but in 1903 the British Land and Mortgage Company of America, Ltd., was officially dissolved.[89]

Such phasing out of English investment companies was not unique at the end of the century, which marks a turning point—an actual termination in many instances—of active English participations in the affairs of Kansas. The role of the English in the development of this state during the period 1865–1900 was, however, as significant as it was diversified; and while the aggregate number of English immigrants to Kansas was relatively modest in comparison with other ethnic groups, the overall impact, first of the land of the Kaw upon the English consciousness and then, in turn, of the English upon Kansas was profound.

Notes

1. Letters, George Fervins to Overseers of Cheriton Bishopric, Devon, July 21, 1850; January [?], 1851, Emigrant Letters File, London School of Economics Library, England. This correspondence does not reveal where in "Kansas" this Englishman was residing during the years indicated.

2. Sir S. Morton Peto, *The Resources and Prospects of America* (London, 1866), 107–10.

3. William H. Dixon, *New America* (London, 1867), 36–37. See "Note to New [1869] Edition" for author's statement on the remarkable sales success of this book.

4. Charles W. Dilke, *Greater Britain* (London, 1869), 58, 63, 69, 106, 173.

5. Joseph Frith, *Far and Wide: A Diary of Long and Distant Travel* (London, 1869), 444–47, 456.

6. W. M. Stewart, *Eleven Years' Experience in the Western States of America* (London, 1870), 21–22.

7. Montague Davenport, *Under the Gridiron: A Summer in the United States and the Far West* (London, 1876), 55–56.

8. T. S. Hudson, *A Scamper Through America* (London, 1882), 203–4. Another Englishman, scampering in Kansas about this same time, was J. B. Loudon, who like Hudson traveled through south-central Kansas. Loudon observed what he described as a "continuous line of emigrants traveling in wagons across the prairies of Kansas, many of them from the old country." See J. B. Loudon, *A Tour Through Canada and the United States* (Coventry, 1879), 100.

9. John G. Hyde and S. Nugent Townshend, *Our Indian Summer in the Far West* (London, 1880), 4, 14, 21.

10. James MacDonald, *Food from the Far West* (London and Edinburgh, 1878), 70, 72, 76, 88. Reenforcing MacDonald's upper-class approach to English migration and investment in such a state as Kansas was the magazine article "Gentlemen Emigrants," *Macmillan's Magazine*, LVIII (January, 1888), 30–36.

11. *The Field* (London), March 15, 1873, p. 244; June 28, 1873, p. 634.

12. *Ibid.*, April 19, 1873, p. 371.

13. London *Agricultural Gazette*, April 18, 1874; June 19, 1895.

14. Grantley F. Berkeley, *The English Sportsman in the Western Prairies* (London, 1861), 115–16, 170, 230–46, and passim. See also by same author, *My Life and Recollections* (2 vols., London, 1865), II, 282.

15. William A. Bell, *New Tracks in North America* (2 vols., London, 1869), I, ch. 3.

16. John S. Campion, *On the Frontier: Reminiscences of Wild Sports . . .* (London, 1878), 25–27.

17. *Ibid.*, 8–9.

18. Paul W. Gates, *Fifty Million Acres: Conflicts over Kansas Land Policy, 1854–1890* (Ithaca, N.Y., 1954), 251.

19. Thelma J. Curl, "Promotional Efforts of the Kansas Pacific and Santa Fe to Settle Kansas," M.A. thesis, University of Kansas, Lawrence, 1960, pp. 41–49.

20. English newspapers gave considerable space to the post-Civil-War West in their general news coverage, but only rarely to Kansas as a state within this area. See, for example, *The Official Index to the Times* (London, 1865 and after).

21. Manchester *Labourers' Union Chronicle*, October 25, 1873; December 20, 1873. This article does not identify the particular colony referred to, but in all probability it was the Nemaha or Old English Colony which will be discussed in this paper.

22. London *Times*, January 20, 1870, alluded, for example, to an English colony in Kansas to be known as Wakefield. See also *ibid.*, January 5, June 9, 1875.

23. *American Settler*, January, 1872.

24. *Ibid.*, February, 1872. Beginning March, 1872, the day of the month is also given.

25. *Ibid.*, February, 1872.

26. *Ibid.*, March and April, 1872.

27. *Ibid.*, May 1, 1872.

28. For its account of the Homestead Act, see *American Settler*, June 1, 1872. One land company, the Kansas Land Company, with an office at 42 Fleet Street, London, is described in *ibid.*, August 11, 1872. For an account of ATSF railroad lands, addressed to English readers, see *ibid.*, August 1, 1873.

29. Curl, "Promotional Efforts," 18–24.

30. Curl, "Promotional Efforts," 44–51. Replacing this English-formed Kansas Land and Emigration Company during the 1870s was a concern called the London and Kansas Lands and Colonization Association, Limited, which, like its predecessor, served the KP as its land-sales agent in the United Kingdom.

31. [Kansas Pacific Railroad Company], *Emigrants' Guide to the Kansas Pacific Railway Lands . . .* (Lawrence, Kans., 1871), title page, 23. See also advertisement, *American Settler*, October 1, 1873; July 10, 1880.

32. This office was managed by Charles H. Branscombe and was located at 1 India Buildings, Water Street, Liverpool. Branscombe was officially listed in *Gore's Directory of Liverpool . . . 1882* (Liverpool, [1882]), 86, as "manager of the Atchison, Topeka and Santa Fe and Southern Pacific Railway and agent for Kansas immigration." It is of interest to note that the

ATSF can locate no records in any of its offices regarding Land Office activities or the existence of branch offices in England. C. R. Lake, Secretary and Treasurer, ATSF, to author in personal conference and by letter May 28, 1969.

33. See, for example, *American Settler,* October 1, 1873. The particular advertisement stated that information regarding its lands could be obtained at the office of the London *Field,* 346 Strand. See also London *Commonwealth,* July 23, 1881.

34. The *American Settler,* June 1, 1872, noted, for example, in a feature article taken from the New York *Times* entitled "Homesteads," that public lands in Kansas then totaled 39 million acres, and that United States government land offices were located at Topeka, Salina, Independence, Wichita, and Concordia. This article pointed out that the best government lands were to be found in the valleys of the Arkansas, Smoky Hill, Solomon, and Grand Salina rivers; also "along the line of the Kansas Pacific Railroad." Books, guides, directories, and other English publications frequently contained information concerning Kansas lands and land-disposal policies. See, for example, [Edward Marston], *Frank's Ranche* (London, 1886), 206–13, which contained all pertinent information for interested persons.

35. See, for example, [Kansas Pacific Railroad], *Emigrants' Guide to the Kansas Pacific Railway Lands . . . 6,000,000 Acres for Sale* (Lawrence, Kans., 1871).

36. *American Settler,* August 1, 1872. Information regarding procurement opportunities in general within Kansas was obtained by prospective English emigrants in the form of independently published guides. One that at least in part addressed itself to European peoples was Wayne Griswold, *Kansas: Her Resources and Development . . .* (Cincinnati, Ohio, 1871).

37. Curl, "Promotional Efforts," 26, 29. Guidebooks, of which there were many, included such assorted ones as J. A. Bent, *Handbook of Kansas* (Chicago, Ill., 1869); [Kansas Publishing Company], *Kansas as She Is* (Lawrence, Kans., 1870); Geo. W. Hamblin, *The Kansas Guide* (Ottawa, Kans., 1871). Many of these indicated the audiences toward which their literature was especially directed.

38. London *Times,* March 9, 29, 1872; *American Settler,* May 1, September 2, 1872.

39. *American Settler,* April 23, 1881. See footnote 32 for explanatory statement about Branscombe.

40. *Ibid.,* June 14, 1884; February 14, 1885; August 14, 1886.

41. These figures were compiled by Wallace E. Miller, *The Peopling of Kansas* (Columbus, Ohio, 1906), 96 (explanatory note), 100–101.

42. *Ibid.,* 65, 100–101. The pattern of English settlement in Kansas is similar to that in Nebraska, namely, wide dispersal throughout the state. See Oscar O. Winther, "The English in Nebraska, 1857–1880," *Nebraska History,* XLVIII (Autumn, 1967), 217.

43. Curl, "Promotional Efforts," 29; Miller, *Peopling of Kansas,* 65. There were minor exceptions as will be indicated in the text that follows.

44. Winther, "English Migration to the American West, 1865-1900," *The Huntington Library Quarterly*, XXVII (February, 1964), 170-71.

45. Griswold, *Kansas: Her Resources and Development.*

46. See, for example, Percy G. Ebbutt, *Emigrant Life in Kansas* (London, 1886).

47. *Ibid.*, 17-18.

48. *Ibid.*, Ch. 3, and 127-30.

49. *Ibid.*, 229-33. Even though Ebbutt's book was published sixteen years after the experiences described, it attracted considerable attention from English reviewers. The *American Settler,* for example, devoted a full page review to it. This review contains a lengthy summary of the book and in conclusion urges "intending settlers" who wish to know about Kansas to read Ebbutt's book and thereby obtain "a clear, homely, every-day view of the work before them." See *American Settler,* June 12, 1886.

50. London, *A Tour*, 100.

51. [   ], *Macmillan's Magazine*, XLVIII (August, 1883), 293, 296, 298.

52. Major W. Shepherd, *Prairie Experiences in Handling Cattle and Sheep* (London, 1884), 3, 5, 17.

53. Ida Lucretia Smith, "A History of National Group Settlements in Republic County," M.A. thesis, Kansas State College, Fort Hays, n.d., 28-38.

54. Winther, "The English in Nebraska," 211; Nell Blythe Waldron, "Colonization in Kansas from 1861 to 1890," Ph.D. dissertation, Northwestern University, Evanston, Ill., 1923, p. 54.

55. William J. Chapman, "The Wakefield Colony," *Kansas State Historical Collections* (Topeka, 1907-1908), X, 488-89. Wake's quotation from Wakefield *Advertiser,* November 8, 1892, appears in *ibid.*, 489.

56. Quoted in Waldron, "Colonization in Kansas from 1861 to 1890," p. 55.

57. [R. H. Drew, publ.], *Emigration to Kansas, the Glory of the West* (London, [1869]), 2, 5-6. The London *Times* took a jaundiced view of the Wakefield scheme, stating if Englishmen must emigrate, they should be encouraged to go to "their own colonies," not to Wakefield. See London *Times,* January 20, 1870.

58. Chapman, "The Wakefield Colony," 491-93. See also Angie Debo, "An English View of the Wild West," *Panhandle Plains Historical Review,* VI (1933), 25.

59. Chapman, "The Wakefield Colony," 493, 495. See also [William Weston], *Weston's Guide to the Kansas Pacific Railway,* (n.p., 1872), 51-52.

60. Chapman, "The Wakefield Colony," 517.

61. *Ibid.*, 519.

62. Ralph Ternal, *History of Nemaha County* (Lawrence, Kans., 1916), 85; Topeka *Daily Capital,* November 15, 1931, clipping, Kansas State Historical Society Library (KSHS). This contains a reminiscent account by John T. Bristow.

63. *Ibid.;* Waldron, "Colonization in Kansas," 53.

64. "George Grant, Esq.," in *United States Biographical Dictionary: Kansas* (Chicago, Ill., 1879), 733. See also D. Curror, Clippings in KSHS copy of *Mr. Grant's Great Property: Victoria, in Kansas* (Edinburgh, 1873).

65. [   ], *New and Attractive Field for Emigrants . . . Victoria* ([London, ca. 1873]); *Report of the United States Commissioner of Agriculture for the Year 1873* (Washington, D.C., 1874), 286 (hereafter cited as *Commissioner Report*). According to *American Settler,* January 24, 1874, Grant subsequently enlarged the size of his original purchase.

66. *Commissioner Report . . . 1873,* p. 286.

67. *American Settler,* December 2, 1872, March 1, 1873; Waldron, "Colonization in Kansas," 60–62; [Gaff], *Rambles,* 16. See also Marjorie G. Raish, "Victoria: The Story of a Western Kansas Town," *Fort Hays Kansas State College Studies,* No. 3 (Topeka, Kans., 1947), 56.

68. [Gaff], *Rambles,* 4–5, 8–10.

69. *American Settler,* December 2, 1872.

70. Clippings from the British Press in KSHS copy of Curror, *Mr. Grant's Great Property;* MacDonald, *Food from the Far West,* 85. Little specific information is available on use or non-use of steam-powered equipment.

71. *Ibid.,* 85–86.

72. *Ibid.*

73. I. D. Graham, "George Grant, First Importer of Aberdeen Angus Cattle in the United States," *Thirty-Second Biennial Report of the Kansas State Board of Agriculture, 1939–40* (Topeka, Kans., 1941), 204.

74. MacDonald, *Food from the Far West,* 87. See also [Gaff], *Rambles,* 11.

75. These agencies are listed in the brochure *New and Attractive Field for Emigrants . . . Victoria,* 8.

76. Curror, *Mr. Grant's Great Property,* 5, 9.

77. *Ibid.,* 5–8.

78. *Ibid.;* Raish, "Victoria," 13–14.

79. Manchester *Labourers' Union Chronicle,* December 20, 1873. See also *Commissioner Report . . . 1873,* p. 286; Curror, *Mr. Grant's Great Property,* 15; *American Settler,* September 1, 1873; January 24, 1874. The London *Labour News,* April 4, 1874, pointed out that Victoria was not for the laboring man, and that the land had already been taken up in one- to four-section tracts by "gentleman farmers."

80. Leavenworth *Daily Commercial,* September 26, 1873, clipping.

81. Quoted in William Saunders, *Through the Light Continent: or The United States in 1877–8* (London, 1879), 134–35. See also Raish, "Victoria," 18; Miller, *Peopling of Kansas,* 101; Charles M. Correll, "Other Immigrant Elements," *Kansas,* ed. by John D. Bright (New York, 1956), I, 357.

82. "George Grant, Esq.," 734.

83. Virginia S. Hooper, *They Had a Good Time While It Lasted: Runnymede, 1889–1894* ([Santa Clara, Calif., 1968]), mimeographed, 2.

84. *Ibid.,* 68–69.

85. Charles Seton, "Reminiscences of Runnymede," *Collections of the Kansas State Historical Society,* XII (Topeka, Kans., 1912), 467.

86. Microfilmed records at the Registrar of Companies Office, Bush House, London, of British companies in western North America. Microfilms in possession of Bancroft Library, University of California, Berkeley, No. 18075.

87. In 1883, Worden held 25,804 shares of 100,000 issued. See *ibid.,* No. 17965.

88. Louise Barry, ed., "A British Bride in Manhattan, 1890–1891: The Journal of Mrs. Stuart James Hogg," *The Kansas Historical Quarterly,* XIX (August, 1951), 270.

89. Microfilm, Bancroft Library, No. 17965.

10

Banks, Mails, and Rails, 1880-1915

George L. Anderson, University of Kansas

To some the title of this paper may seem to be only a feeble attempt to strike an alliterative note. Actually it is an effort to capsulize a series of relationships which were basic to the economic development not only of the Trans-Mississippi West, but to that of the entire nation. The underlying premise of this study is that no transaction above the level of simple barter was complete until a number of pieces of paper had been exchanged by the persons concerned. Whether the products involved came from the farm, the ranch, the mine, the forest, or the sea, they could not become part of the stream of commerce until someone, someplace, sometime, was willing to assume responsibility for conducting them through a maze of local markets, processing plants, commission or wholesale houses, and, finally, to a retail merchant who endeavored to supply the wants of his customers. And it was not circulating currency whether gold, silver, banknotes, or greenbacks that was needed unless one really wanted to hand-carry the amounts required or to pay express charges. What was needed was some form of credit that was readily available, reasonably acceptable in all parts of the nation, and thoroughly negotiable. By June 30, 1881, the percentage of daily receipts of banks accounted for by instruments of credit reached 95.1 percent and remained well above 90 percent until 1909. By 1915 the use of drafts and checks in the conduct of the nation's financial and commercial affairs accounted for 95 percent of the total.[1]

In the period 1880–1915 the kinds of paper that were used to complete transactions included checks, drafts, bills of exchange, acceptances, bills of lading, warehouse receipts, promissory notes, and perhaps chattel mortgages. Even express-company and postal money orders were used much to the bitter dismay and open hostility of the bankers. When the student of history contemplates the magnitude, complexity, and increasing use of instruments of credit, he may wonder why many of his colleagues continue to focus their attention on, and devote their energies almost exclusively to, the volume of circulating currency, and why they accept the contemporary premise of Western agrarian leaders that the per capita amount of circulating media was declining in the face of expanding trade. Because the Pendletons, Weavers, Harveys, Blands, and Bryans acted upon their knowledge and not ours, they can be excused for looking backward to Andrew Jackson and demanding that the national banking system be abolished, although they seem to have overlooked the utter chaos that his policy produced, instead of looking forward to something like the Federal Reserve system. But the same consideration cannot be extended to historians who refuse to recognize that deep and fundamental changes were taking place in the financial structure of the West and of the nation. On the issue of silver or government notes versus the bank check the Populists among others were backward-looking folk clinging to an outmoded treatment of financial abuses and not well-informed, forward-looking statesmen attempting to secure improved procedures for conducting business in the industrial-financial world of their day.

But historians have been equally short-sighted in recognizing what really made possible the transition from currency to instruments of credit. A few members of the profession have recognized the fundamental importance of the communications revolution, but detailed attention has not been given to the Post Office Department. Obsessed with the notion that it was merely the patronage agency of the political party in power, historical scholars have made scarcely any studies of its actual working bureaus and divisions.[2] One of the neglected organizations has been the Railway Mail Service, whose recent demise has produced a crisis in the distribution of the nation's mail. Additionally, they have ignored the nationalizing impact of a federal service that reached people even in the remote areas of the nation and touched their lives more intimately and more frequently than did any other federal agency. For many the United States Post Office was their only tie with relatives and civilization. If historians have neglected this aspect of the Post Office Department, its officials did not. In 1880 Thomas J. Brady, Second Assistant Postmaster-General, remarked: "A peculiarity of the mail service is its more intimate relation to the daily life of the individual citizen than is sustained by the operations of any other branch of the government. This is particularly true of the sparsely settled and newly developed regions of the West, where the comparative scarcity and expensiveness of telegraph communication renders business correspondence entirely dependent upon the mails for transmission."[3] Almost a decade was to pass before Postmaster-General John Wanamaker echoed and elaborated this theme. After asserting that the Post Office Department maintained communication between the near and the remote places of the country with "frequency, celerity, and security," he declared, "The post office is the visible form of the Federal Government to every community and to every citizen. Its hand is the only one that touches the local life, the social interests, and business concern of every neighborhood. It brings the Government to every door in the land and makes it the ready and faithful servitor of every interest of commerce and society."[4]

Historians have been guilty on another count. Together with many popular writers they have been content to focus their attention on the Pony Express and Overland Mail companies. It is true that these operations served their day and deserve careful analysis and attractive presentation, but there is in history a quality called perspective. If these rudimentary agencies counted their pieces of mail in dozens or perhaps some in hundreds and their periods of service in months and years, the Railway Mail Service counted the pieces carried in a year in millions or even billions and its period of service in decades. The writer has not estimated the number of horses it would have taken to carry the open pouches, the locked pouches, the registered boxes, and the other kinds of matter carried in one railway post-office car, but the number would be substantial.

Historians and writers generally can be forgiven for seeing something dramatic in the small figure of a man or boy astride a fleet horse, riding across prairie, desert, and mountain into the teeth of a storm or out of the reach of hostile Indians. But there is something equally dramatic in a highly trained postal clerk standing deep-knee in bags, pouches, and boxes; distributing mail at a higher level of accuracy than any of us could hope to attain in our profession; sorting mail in the face of fire, flood, and wreck; throwing out the pouches at his point of delivery; catching other pouches on the run at the risk of being pulled out of his car; and, finally, reaching the terminal with all mail distributed and ready for immediate delivery to banks, offices, and homes.[5] Actually the task of the railway postal clerks was more dangerous than any branch of the federal service other than the armed forces. It is little wonder that they developed an esprit de corps that matched that of the U.S. Marines.

Although there is only one comprehensive history of the Railway Mail Service in print, this is not the time or place to attempt to produce another one. Suffice it to say that the link between the past and the present in the Trans-Mississippi West was forged on the old Hannibal and St. Joseph line. The close connection between the arrival of the train from the East and the departure of the Pony Express did not permit the sorting of the mail in the St. Joseph post office in time to be carried westward. It occurred to George B. Armstrong that if the mail could be sorted en route in the mail car, all that would be necessary would be the few minutes required to transfer the proper bags.[6] Herein was the germ of the idea that grew by careful study and refinement until the sorting and distributing of mail by carrier routes, substations, and individual addresses for cities like New York, Chicago, and Boston was completed before the trains reached their destinations.[7]

The Post Office Department officials tried to save time on city and suburban as well as intercity deliveries in many other ways. Automobiles and airplanes were scarcely in effective operation before the postal service was experimenting with them. European experience with pneumatic tubes was emulated in the major cities. Post-office buildings were built above, below, or beside depots. The Railway Mail Service placed postal cars on streetcar lines and on electric interurban lines as well. Railway post-office cars were subjected to constant study and redesign until every square inch was utilized. Anything to save a few minutes seemed to be the rule as the post-office people sought to handle an increasing volume of mail.[8]

At their level of administration the superintendents of the Railway Mail Service literally fought to reduce time in transit. At first, time that was saved was expressed in terms of days, then of hours, and then of minutes. A few minutes saved in Chicago, St. Louis, or Kansas City might enable the westbound mail from the East to connect with a train for the Pacific Coast and thus save a full business day in San Francisco, Seattle, or Los Angeles. And saving a full business day was dear to the heart of the bankers, although so far as the writer knows, none of them took the trouble to recognize the assistance of the Railway Mail Service. Cash items like checks and drafts that are in transit do not contribute to the profits made by bankers, so just as the Railway Mail Service fought to save hours and minutes, the bankers struggled to reduce transit or "float" time.[9]

In either case the pressure was placed upon the agency that actually pulled the railway postal cars with their bags and pouches full of checks, drafts, notes, and acceptances. This, of course, was the railroad network of the nation. Time will not permit a road-by-road analysis of this network, even if the writer could do it. Judging by the number of contracts made, one could conclude that every railroad, whether trunk line or countryside jerkwater branch, carried the mail. It may be safe to suggest that no one has plumbed the depth and variety of American railroads until he has scanned the printed lists of contracts to carry the mail.

Around 1880 some of the trains crept along at an average of ten, twelve, or fifteen miles per hour. By the end of the century, average speeds were generally in the twenty- to twenty-five-miles-per-hour bracket. By 1915 some lines attained averages between thirty and thirty-five miles per hour. Of course the fast mail trains moved at a much higher level of speed. Between 1884 and 1905 the time between New York and Chicago was reduced from twenty-seven hours and thirty minutes to eighteen hours. Just as significantly the time between New York and San Francisco was reduced from one hundred and eight hours and forty-five minutes in 1889 to eighty-two hours in 1906, a time that is slow by jet standards, but fantastically fast to a generation conditioned to dealing with much slower speeds.[10]

In railroad history as in other areas, historians have been much too myopic. They have been too much concerned with matters of financing construction and operation, with land grants and construction companies, and with fraud and subsidies. It may well be that the most important subsidy conferred by the federal government upon the railroads, upon the business community, and upon the American people generally was in the form of mail contracts. But on some occasions the railroads paid a high price for those contracts. They were under constant pressure from the Railway Mail Service to place the post-office cars on their fastest trains, to adjust schedules, to discard obsolescent cars and build new ones, in short, to give preferred treatment to the Railway Mail Service even at the cost of better and more remunerative freight and passenger service. The fast mail trains presented a particular problem. Anyone who has seen a train composed exclusively of mail cars moving majestically on the main line while even the best passenger trains took to the sidings knows that the mails took precedence over persons and products.[11]

Some historians feel that railroads have been overemphasized as a factor in the growth of the American economy, but given the services that the railroads contributed and the procedures and practices of American business, it is difficult to imagine alternative forms of transportation in the period under consideration. Certainly the telegraph and the telephone were significant developments, but as long as banking officials and, indeed, courts of law demanded actual signatures on the right documents, by the right persons, at the right time, all that bankers could do by wire was to make sure that their customer or their correspondent had adequate funds on hand to complete a transaction. Curiously enough, the writer has encountered only two contemporary discussions of the interrelationship between banks, mails, and rails. Under the title "Banks and Railroads" Charles W. Stevenson discussed the question in the September, 1909, issue of the *Banker's Magazine.* In part he said:

> The reciprocal relations of the bank and the railroad are not so direct as they are important and fundamental. The bank furnishes the sinews of trade in that it furnishes the credit on which the buying and selling is done. . . . Again, if there were no railroads, and the surplus of the soil must lie rotting in the fields, there would be less need for the banks, and less capital or stored up labor on which they might build their foundations. Together the two institutions work in unison for the benefit of all the people. . . . they are the servants of the same constituency . . . . And the bank, outside of the mail service of the road, may have little to transport, yet it furnishes the means whereby the merchant buys his goods and the farmer feeds his cattle.
>
> . . . .
>
> Just in the matter of the mail service the bank is hardly prepared to appreciate the benefit of the railroad. The latter hurries the check and draft to its destination and in such a way as to make the momentum of trade much greater than it otherwise could be. And the bank that cannot profit by swift railroad service has a great handicap on it, and cannot perform the full functioning of the institution.[12]

Four years later in a perceptive address to the Baltimore chapter of the American Institute of Banking, J. M. Fitzgerald, president of the Western Maryland Railroad, discussed "The Banks and the Railroads." Without glossing over the evils and abuses that accompanied the development of banking and railway transportation, Fitzgerald devoted the greater part of his address to a comparative analysis of the evolution of state and federal regulation, but the following sentences indicate that he understood the fundamental relationships:

> The banks by the discount of notes and the payment of checks, facilitate the transfer of commodities and merchandise from seller to purchaser. That development which has made commerce not only nation-wide, but world-wide, would not be possible without the service of transportation in actual physical distribution. That development which has made commerce not only nation-wide, but world-wide, would have been impossible without the service of the modern banking system.
>
> Therefore one analogy between the railroad business and the banking business is that everyone of the rank and file in either vocation takes part in performing a service that is not only essential to the prosperity of the nation, but under the conditions of our present civilization, is vital to the very existence of the nation.[13]

The purpose of the preceding paragraphs has been to portray in a general way the relationships between the banks, the postal services, and the railroads. The more detailed analysis which follows is concerned with two of the three agencies, the banks and the mails. Three primary areas of interaction and competition will be considered. In order of emphasis and detail of treatment these are the problem of the country check, the development of the postal savings system, and the use of the postal money order. The last two subjects obviously represent areas of competition and are more familiar to students of history. The problem of the country check, on the other hand, is less well known, more significant in the development of banking, and accordingly will receive the greater amount of attention.

In a sense the postal savings system was an importation from abroad. Its establishment testifies to the magnitude and the importance of the immigration from Europe into the United States during the latter part of the nineteenth and early years of the twentieth century. Accustomed to governmental savings institutions in the countries from which they came and fearful for the safety of their savings, especially after the bank failures in the

1890s and in 1907, the immigrants hoarded their funds or sent them back by way of postal money orders to the old country.

It may seem curious to some that two of the most ardent advocates of the postal savings system were John Wanamaker, Postmaster-General under President Benjamin Harrison, and Frank H. Hitchcock, who held the same position for a time under William Howard Taft. In between these two men William McKinley's Postmaster-General favored the system, but those who served in this capacity under Grover Cleveland and Theodore Roosevelt were either silent on the issue or actively opposed to it.[14]

For practical purposes Wanamaker's 1889 *Report* set the stage. Indulging himself in a bit of purple prose, he said:

> To connect more intimately countless numbers of citizens with this country is a patriotic service. It would tend to weaken incipient disturbances; it would aid in breaking down sectional feelings. The State and private savings banks in many of the states where small deposits can be made are few in number. In some parts of the country there are no such opportunities offered. The chimney corner, the trunk, the closet, and the old stocking hide another surplus, not unlike that heaped up in the Treasury, and practically it is as much withdrawn from circulation.[15]

Wanamaker thought that in order to reduce competition with banks, deposits might be limited to $150 per person per year, and the Secretary of the Treasury might be directed to redeposit the money in banks located in the states where the deposits originated. The banks would be required to deposit United States bonds to assure the safety of the funds.[16]

The recommendation was repeated by Wanamaker in 1890 and 1891, and by James A. Gary in 1897. The arguments were essentially the same: encouragement of thrift, restoration of hoarded funds to the channels of commerce, and development of a higher level of citizenship, especially among newly arrived groups of immigrants, by providing a stake in maintaining the government's credit. Attention was called to the support of the large city banks, of the newspapers, and of labor and agricultural associations. The opposition of rural banks and private savings banks was noted. A decade was to elapse before the subject was raised again, but little was added to the earlier arsenal of arguments.[17] Some of these arguments were based upon detailed analyses. Foreign postal savings banks were advertising for American funds. As a result in the four-year period from 1906 to 1909, more than $300 million in international money orders payable in Austria-Hungary, Great Britain, Italy, Norway, and Russia had been sold. The total amount of money in the United States was estimated at $3 billion, nearly 65 percent of which was in the pockets of the people or was being hoarded. If only one dollar per capita per year could be called into circulation, it would add $90 million to the circulating medium each year. In effect the sixty thousand post offices would become the agencies for mobilizing funds that would enter the stream of commerce by being redeposited in the national banks.[18]

In spite of the vision of a flood of funds described by Postmaster-General Frank H. Hitchcock, the American Banker's Association remained adamant in its opposition.[19] Its Committee on Postal Savings thought that 98 percent of the bankers opposed the idea. The major premise of its argument was that it is "as improper for the Government to extend its paternalism and enter the banking business as it would be to enter the grocery or any other business." At various times the committee, of which E. F. Swinney of Kansas City was a member, asserted that the Postmaster-General was using inaccurate statistics and that more stringent immigration laws instead of a postal savings system would solve the problem of the immigrant worker. But in spite of its most strenuous efforts, the committee had to confess defeat. Yielding to pressure from the executive branch, the Congress passed the postal savings law on June 25, 1910.[20] Within five years, partly due to the outbreak of war in Europe, there were more than half a million depositors taking advantage of the system. More than 58 percent of these were foreign-born, and their deposits totaled more than $65 million.[21]

The relevance of the foregoing account of the postal savings system to the history of the Trans-Mississippi West may seem to be a bit strained, but there are two areas of impact. The first of these involves the intransigent opposition of Western bankers who regarded the far more numerous post offices as their competitors and who derived no benefit from the redeposit feature of the system. The second is the possibility that the postal savings banks were in part the response of the federal government to the state deposit-guaranty laws that had been enacted in such Western states as Oklahoma, Kansas, Nebraska, and the Dakotas. In an indirect way the federal government had a deposit-guarantee mechanism in operation more than two decades prior to the establishment of the Federal Deposit Insurance Corporation. At least it was alleged that the depositors in the post offices felt that their funds were entirely safe. Even the redeposit of funds in national banks did not limit this assurance, because in the event of failure, the federal government would be a preferred creditor and it required special security for its funds.[22]

If the reaction of bankers in general to the postal savings system was somewhat ambivalent, no ambiguity characterized their feelings toward money orders, whether sold by express companies or by post offices. They were opposed to all money orders unless sold by banks or under the auspices of a state or national banker's association.[23] Given the nature of banking in the period under consideration, it is not difficult to understand the position of the bankers. For many years prior to 1880 two of the principal sources of banking profits were the sale of exchange and the collection of checks and drafts. For purposes of discussion, exchange will be defined simply as a charge made for the transfer of funds, whether specie, currency, or credit. Originally the amount charged bore a definite relationship to the cost of shipping actual specie or currency. Later it was more a question of supply and demand.[24] For various reasons, exchange on New York set the pattern and the price on exchange at the lesser financial and commercial centers. A simple illustration or two from the period before checks and money orders achieved great popularity will indicate how the system brought business and profit to the Western banker. A merchant in a Western town would buy a stock of goods from a New York wholesale firm. In due course he received an invoice and the bill which had to be paid. He went to his bank and bought a cashier's draft or a bank draft. This was a simple operation if his bank kept a deposit in some New York bank. But it cost the banker something to keep his New York account replenished, so he felt justified in charging the going rate for selling a portion of his credit to the merchant. In an earlier day the banker might have had on hand some bills against New York business firms that were buying Western products. Several of these might be put together to equal the amount of the local merchant's bill. These the banker would sell to the merchant at a profitable margin. In any case the banker charged his customers for making it possible for them to pay their Eastern creditors.[25]

Included in this operation in some instances were the charges made by the bankers for collecting bills of Eastern creditors against Western debtors. Again it was a simple matter of transferring cash or credit, but the customer, whether an Eastern firm or a Western merchant, was charged for the service. Even after bank checks entered the scene the Western banker characteristically made a charge for cashing them. Altogether the exchange operation could be made into an extremely fruitful source of profits.

But it was quite otherwise when money orders, whether express-company or post-office, increased in popularity. The former could be bought and cashed at an express-company office; the latter could be bought and cashed at post offices. Not only could the bankers be by-passed, but they could be compelled to contribute to the operation at substantial cost to themselves. Local offices of express companies might have inadequate funds to pay express orders, because they were required to transmit their funds to a central or regional office. In such instances the local manager would advise holders of express-company money orders to go to a bank to get cash or currency for their orders. If perchance the bank ran low on its reserves of cash or currency, it would have to pay the express company the regular price on shipments of currency from a city correspondent. In a sense post-office money orders posed the same problem. If a bank was under pressure from its customers to cash money orders beyond the amount of cash on hand, it might be forced to have currency sent in by registered mail.[26] Thus the banks lost the profits from selling exchange and might be required to pay a price for the privilege of cashing their competitor's money orders. In any case the whole matter of money orders aroused a considerable volume of opposition in banking circles, mixed with the expressed praise of a few who admired the successful working of the money-order system.

Measured in terms of dollar amounts of postal money orders issued, the system was a success. Beginning with a few more than $1.3 million issued in 1865, the volume rose to over $122 million in 1884 and to more than $600 million in 1913.[27] The rapid growth in the early years of operation was attributed to large-scale immigration from Europe and to the rapid settlement of the Western states and territories.[28] Other factors were at work as well. The expansion of the mail-order business, especially after Montgomery Ward and Co. and Sears, Roebuck and Co. entered the field, the establishment of rural free delivery and the authorization to the carriers to sell money orders on their routes, and the simple convenience of the system, all contributed to the popularity of the post-office money order.[29]

Two additional factors intimately related to the banking function were at work. Long before the postal savings banks were authorized, the postal money order was being used as a safety device.[30] This was made possible when a general order from the Postmaster-General authorized payment to the purchaser at the office of issue.[31] Thus a depositor in a savings bank who was more concerned with safety than with interest could buy money orders payable to himself at some future date. The other factor did not necessarily increase the volume of postal-money-order business, but it did indicate that an arm of the federal government, in this case the Post Office Department, was reacting more rapidly and more effectively to changed conditions than the private sector whose domain was being invaded. Hindsight aided by a generous volume of contemporary evidence enables the historian to see that improved transportation and communication facilities, including the more rapid transmission of the mails, required a truly national system of banking, even, perchance, a central bank with branches throughout the United States. This the postal-money-order system provided. A money order issued in Lick Skillet, Texas, was as good as one issued in Washington, D.C. This uniformity of value was achieved by a system of regional depositories capped by a central depository in the New York post office. For example, in postal-money-order matters the postmaster at Ft. Laramie forwarded his receipts to Cheyenne. From Cheyenne the sequence was to Denver, to the Chicago postmaster, who deposited with the Assistant Treasurer in Chicago, who in turn deposited with the Assistant Treasurer in New York to the account of the postmaster there, who functioned as the banker for the entire system.[32] This role was even clearer because it included a reverse flow of funds as well. If the postmaster in a busy commercial or financial center did not have sufficient funds either from the sale of money orders or by transfer from his general account, he could draw on the New York postmaster for additional funds. The transfer was generally made by a national bank draft which could be cashed easily and quickly. The system worked well partly because every time a postmaster sold a money order he had to send a card of "advice" to the paying office so that the postmaster at that point would be prepared to pay on presentation. Some local post offices, including the one at Topeka, Kansas, had an established line of credit with the postmaster in New York and had on hand a limited number of drafts that permitted him to draw against postal funds even more rapidly.[33] It should be added that the postmasters at San Francisco and Portland were empowered to play the part of banker to offices in the western part of the nation.[34] In 1897 the Postmaster-General could say in summarizing the way the system worked, "In this manner $147,879,391.86 were remitted last year."[35]

The express companies followed a similar pattern of having local offices forward receipts to a regional office which in turn forwarded them to a central office.[36] The return flow was not quite so well organized, partly because customers with express-company money orders to cash were urged to take them to a bank if they were presented for payment at times when the local agent had closed his accounts or found himself short of funds.

The significant implications of this centralized system, particularly the handling of postal money orders, should not escape the attention of the reader. The effective system of handling the mail devised by the Post Office Department, made possible by the particularly efficient Railway Mail Service, was the key to the whole operation. Additionally, it is possible to detect some characteristics of the Federal Reserve system in the postal operation. The pattern of flow from local to regional to national office is one of these. Another is the return flow of funds in response to local needs from the top down to the local office. A third feature is not quite so clear. It is suggested in the following statement of the

First Assistant Postmaster-General in 1902, "The system [of postal money orders] is unique among the substantial financial factors of the world. Its business is of enormous extent, yet is conducted without a dollar of capital of its own! It has the confidence of the world, yet is without a dollar of surplus; if all of its obligations were paid, nothing would remain. It is maintained solely through the temporary use of the amount of its unclaimed orders."[37] Here is an idea to conjure with, especially when translated into banking and monetary terms. If a collateral source of funds is available, tax money for example, or in private terms, warehouse receipts or short-term business paper, a system of temporary currency could be maintained partly because all of it would not be presented for payment at one time. Moreover, when it had passed its stage of usefulness, it might be completely withdrawn.

For obvious reasons members of the banking profession disliked a competitor that paid no taxes, kept no capital or reserve fund, and maintained no separate offices.[38] When that competitor took a substantial slice of the fees paid by the American people for transferring funds and when that competitor made little use of banks, the opposition of some bankers should not occasion any surprise. But curiously the severest criticism of the system came from within the Postmaster-General's administrative staff. Henry M. Castle, of Minnesota, was Chief of the Auditing Bureau in 1899 and for several years thereafter. Obviously distressed by the necessity of handling each one of sixty million money orders five different times during the auditing process and after referring to it as "the nation's colossal money order system," he said:

> The issue and payment of money orders is not in any strictly legitimate sense a governmental function. It is a feature of banking business pure and simple, and is regarded by many thoughtful men as a dangerous development of state socialism. It is a wonderfully convenient thing for great masses of the people, hence it is universally popular. It is carried on with such enlightened skill, such diligent enterprise, and such marvelous success by the Department officials who superintend its operations and by the local postmasters and clerks who directly conduct them that one who looks

only on the surface sees everything to praise and nothing to condemn.

Only the auditing bureau work can disclose the dangerous possibilities that lie in the general principle involved.[39]

In 1899 Castle speculated that the success of the postal-money-order system would lead to demands that the federal government should own and operate the railroads and the telephone and telegraph systems.[40] In 1900 he returned to the attack, added the parcel-post idea to his *argumentum ad horrendum,* and asserted that "no banking business is or can be carried on successfully in this [the] loose manner" of the postal-money-order system.[41] This reference to looseness was occasioned by the fact that auditing took place months after the orders were issued. As an alternative, Castle proposed that Congress authorize a series of postal notes and checks to replace money orders. These would have the same design as government notes and "actually circulate from hand to hand as such currency, until by writing the name of the payee on the blank line provided, a note is transferred into a personal check of the United States government, and made as safe for transmittal by mail as a money order now is."[42] It is difficult to believe that Castle was entirely serious in making this proposal. It would have implemented the most extreme solution of the problem of an inelastic currency, except that the Post Office Department and not the Treasury Department would have been the channel for the issuing of fiat currency.[43] Irrespective of Castle's criticisms and proposed alternatives, the sale of postal money orders expanded until the $600 million level was reached in 1914.

If the administrators of the postal- and express-money-order systems were willing to take advantage of an increasingly efficient system of communication and thereby enter the twentieth century, a good many members of the banking gild, particularly those in the rural areas of the West, were not. Still captive to pre–Civil War procedures and principles, they opposed any form of centralization, whether of reserves, of note issues, or of redemption. They remained adamant in their opposition to branch banking, persisted in making exorbitant charges for exchange and collections, and sought refuge in quasi-isolation.

Students of banking history know of the chaos and confusion

at all levels of business activity that plagued the country for thirty years after the destruction of the Second United States bank. By 1860 fifteen hundred state banks were issuing bank-note currency in many denominations. If fifteen hundred banks issuing circulating notes in several different denominations produced chaos and confusion, it is instructive to consider what happened when hundreds of thousands of depositors began to write personal checks on thousands of banks. A cardinal rule of banking in handling checks is to require identification. Perhaps one could add the footnote that if the person who cashes a check cannot know the drawer, he should know the bank that it is drawn on. But how could any cashier or paying teller know all of these persons or institutions? This device for transferring funds, the check, became popular after 1880, but the mechanism for handling it was not developed at the national level for three decades and more. In the meantime, country banks continued to charge for making collections and for what continued to be called exchange. When new techniques appear, but people associated with them are committed to an outmoded system, a performance gap is almost certain to appear with all of its penalties and losses.

Prior to 1913 there was no really national system of banking, to say nothing of a central bank with branches or twelve regional bankers' banks. Then, too, it is possible that many banks did not have correspondent banks in regional centers or in New York. Additionally, the New York banks were afraid of losing business if they received country checks for collection only, thus denying their customers the use of the funds until the check had been collected. The effect of this would have been that business houses would have refused checks that could not be treated as cash items. This drastic remedy would have placed responsibility right where it belonged, on the drawer of the check and on the bank that permitted him to write it. Finally, these same country banks that refused to maintain adequate correspondent relationships also charged handsome fees for making collections.[44] These charges fell upon precisely the wrong party, namely upon the last endorser. It cost him money for postage, stationery, envelopes, and clerical time to send the check to a bank that he thought might pay it. If in addition he had to pay a fee, that was too much. Again, there were at least two other negative characteristics of the no-system method of collecting country items. A good deal of time in transit or "float-time" was involved. To the banker, the time between crediting his depositor with a cash deposit, which reduced his own capacity to loan to other customers, and receiving a return on the item was dead-time or sterile time.

Looking at the transaction from the other side, one sees that the drawer of the check was compelling some unknown city bank to make him an interest-free loan for the amount of the check and for the duration of the transit time.[45] Indeed, the drawer might be counting on the float-time to write several checks against the same sum on deposit, hoping to replenish his account before all of the checks came in. An interesting example of this occurred in connection with a western-Kansas cattle buyer during the past year. On Friday afternoon he bought several thousand dollars' worth of cattle and gave his check in payment, knowing that his deposit account was inadequate, but expecting to have the weekend to mobilize his resources and make it good before the check cleared and was returned. But the banks in that area, after the demise of the Railway Mail Service, had subscribed to a form of banker's dispatch by which checks and other items are carried by automobile to a regional clearing center.[46] The auction firm had taken the buyer's check to the bank in time for the late afternoon pickup. It was taken to the regional clearing center, where a force of employees working all night with the benefit of advanced machines processed all of Friday's business. By Saturday morning the driver on the return trip started his deliveries, which included the buyer's check, and before noon the cattle buyer had a call from his bank to come in and make his account good.

Beyond its local and contemporary implication, the illustration indicates the importance of an effective clearing-house system. Float-time can be reduced to a matter of hours or a day or two instead of many days, perhaps weeks. But except for a very few financial centers like Boston, Atlanta, and Kansas City the bankers themselves were not willing to devise regional clearing houses, not to mention a national one like the Post Office Department operated in New York. Instead they resorted to devious and circuitous methods of escaping collection charges. The most extreme example of this system that has come to the attention of the writer was described by a Southern banker who stated in all seriousness that a check for thirty-seven cents had passed through fourteen banks and still had not been paid. In order to escape a collection charge on such an insignificant item each bank had mailed it to another bank. Fourteen two-cent stamps, fourteen envelopes, fourteen pieces of stationery, fourteen segments of a clerk's time, and still the check was afloat.[47] For some reason direct mailing to the bank upon which the check was drawn was prohibited either by law or by regulation. Thus the case of the peripatetic check developed. But it was not an isolated case.[48] Other equally extreme examples of circuitous routing to avoid paying exorbitant collection charges could be given, but enough have been described to illustrate the costs and penalties of perpetuating outworn and outmoded practices.

In a fundamental way the similarity of the three early twentieth-century developments—the postal savings system, the money-order mechanism, and the development of an agency to handle country-bank checks—comes into clearer focus in the discussion of the direct inclusion of the country banks in the clearing-house process. All three were dependent upon a network of railroads and an efficient mail service. All three were instrumental either in mobilizing small amounts of funds or in multiplying the impact of money in circulation, including instruments of credit. All three encountered the opposition of many bankers because they required changes in time-honored modes of banking procedures. And all three foreshadowed to some degree certain aspects of the Federal Reserve system.

Fortunately for this study the bankers in Kansas City, Missouri, led by their clearing-house manager, Jerome C. Thralls, were among those who chose to enter the twentieth century. The tributary area of the banks of Kansas City included a large segment of the Trans-Mississippi West. The system devised by Thralls was in its technical details rather complicated; but viewed generally and in historical perspective, it was fairly simple and so significant that Thralls deserves mention as one of the men who made Kansas City the financial center of the Tenth District of the Federal Reserve system.

The reasonably simple solution proposed by Thralls to the country-check problem was to establish the Kansas City Country Clearing House division of the Kansas City Clearing House. Like this solution, the origin of the clearing house was quite simple and entirely accidental, occurring in a London coffeehouse sometime in the early 1670s. It came to New York in 1853 and to Kansas City in 1875. In its simplest terms the country clearing house merely substituted the mail service for hand carriage of the items, and it invoked the representative principle by using the city correspondents of the country banks as an essential feature of the clearing mechanism. Thus the country-bank checks were included in the charging and crediting process. The Kansas City Country Clearing House division was established in 1905. It is probable that the idea was derived from the Boston Clearing House, whose country section had been established earlier and was modeled upon the Suffolk system for the redemption of country-bank notes which was put in operation in 1824.[49]

When the Kansas City Country Clearing House was established in 1905, it was limited to three hundred banks in Oklahoma and Indian territories. Included among them were banks that were charging particularly exorbitant collection rates and were especially slow in making returns. The rates varied from twenty-five to thirty cents per hundred. One immediate result of concerted action was the reduction of rates by half and of the time by an even greater proportion. Most of the skeptics among the Kansas City bankers were convinced of the effectiveness of the system and consented to its extension to include the banks in Kansas, Missouri, and southern Nebraska on a mandatory basis, and those in northern Nebraska, Colorado, New Mexico, and Texas on an optional basis. Some notion of the magnitude of the system is conveyed by the fact that at least 5,600 banks in several thousand towns were involved. In his description of the system Thralls noted that 1,600 to 2,500 banks received daily letters. There is scarcely need for further demonstration of the significance of the mail and rail services to the entire operation. Clearly they were in the indispensable category.

Postal costs can be approached somewhat differently. If ten Kansas City banks had items on a particular town in Kansas it would have required from two to four cents postage on each letter. By consolidating the items in one letter, the estimated saving was from sixteen to eighteen cents in postage or from thirty-two to thirty-six dollars per day when all the banks in all of the towns were included. Equally important savings were made on clerk-hire, envelopes, and stationery. A great deal of time was made available for interest-producing investments, and, curiously enough, as the country bankers came to understand the system, their deposits with their Kansas City correspondents increased by as much as 56 percent. Even after a set of rules and regulations was adopted, the Kansas City banks could deal directly with their country correspondents provided their rates coincided with those charged by the clearing house. Conversely the banks could levy any charge they wished in making collections for Kansas City banks, but the latter agreed to charge the recalcitrant banks at the same rate for making city collections. Thus the basic and simple premise for most of the banks was that of reciprocity. Stated simply, whatever the country banks decided to charge was charged against them. No longer could country banks take advantage of city-bank competition for their deposits. When the Kansas City plan reached its full maturity, all country checks coming in to the banks that were members of the Kansas City Clearing House were forwarded to the Country Bank section. Here they were sorted, recorded on duplicate forms with the use of modified Burroughs machines, and credited to or charged against the members. The settlement slips allowed three or four days of transit time to (and from) the country banks. The completed collections went directly to the clearing house, but all protested, refused, or slow items went back through the country-bank section for investigation and appropriate action. Clearly it was an ingenious system which influenced the economic development of a large section of the Trans-Missouri West. It was based on complete information with respect to each bank, its officers, its Kansas City as well as other city correspondents, and its current condition. The officials in charge of the Country Clearing House even knew the times of departure and arrival of the Kansas City mails.[50]

The Kansas City plan was at the center of debate on the country-check problem, which was one of the hottest issues in banking circles in the period between 1905 and 1913.[51] In vain did its advocates try to get the plan adopted more generally. In vain did lecturers point out that unless bankers put their own house in order, the federal government would put it in order for them. In addition to the handling of country checks the central issues in discussions of banking problems revolved about the inelasticity of the currency, the reserve requirements of the national banking system, and inadequate provision for rural credits. Seemingly the fact that perhaps as much as 95 percent of the nation's business was being done by check, draft, or other credit instruments failed to impress some of the powerful bankers in Chicago and New York who thought that the only answer to the country-check problem was to eliminate them or sharply limit their use.[52]

Meanwhile the so-called banker's panic of 1907 occurred; the National Monetary Commission was established to study the issues in 1909, and stimulated four years of debate and discussion; and the Federal Reserve Act was passed on December 23, 1913.[53] The prediction of federal action unless the banking profession initiated its own reforms was fulfilled.[54] Only the selection of Kansas City, Missouri, as the site of the Tenth District Federal Reserve Bank will be considered here.

Perhaps it would be sufficient to assert that the men who presented the case for Kansas City before the location committee were a remarkably able group, but they also had a full arsenal of persuasive arguments to present. Although only eighteenth in population, Kansas City was seventh in total bank clearings in 1913.[55] Nearly five and one-half billion dollars' worth of business passed through the clearing-house banks of Kansas City. In that year total clearings amounted to nearly three billion dollars compared with less than a billion for Omaha and less than half a billion for Denver. Clearly Kansas City was dominant in this respect in the region west of St. Louis. The impressive showing on clearings was reenforced by the fact that the Kansas City banks had an effective mechanism for collecting country-bank checks. In all likelihood it was not a matter of political pressure or accident that the three cities with such mechanisms, Boston, Atlanta, and Kansas City, each received a Federal Reserve Bank.[56] Perhaps it was partly due to country-bank collections that Kansas City's clearings increased 165 percent in the ten years from 1903 to 1913. Between 1906 and 1913 the increase for Kansas City was 113 percent, whereas in the same period New York's clearings declined 9 percent, Chicago's increased only 50 percent, and the clearings of the St. Louis banks increased only 30 percent. In

1913 the Kansas City Country Clearing House section handled $107,522,900 dollars arising out of relationships with 3,300 country banks.[57]

These figures have added significance when placed in the context of statements made by H. Parker Willis, one of the architects of the Federal Reserve system. In an extemporaneous and unofficial talk before the clearing-house section of the Richmond Meeting of the American Banker's Association in 1914, Willis compared the problem of the bank check with that of the nineteenth-century bank note, asserted the need for "a more uniform system of domestic exchange in the United States," identified the essential prerequisites of the check as recognizability and uniformity, and concluded that "the idea in mind in drafting the Federal Reserve Act [was] to attain that degree of uniformity."[58] On his part O. Howard Wolfe, secretary of the clearing-house section of the American Banker's Association, in a 1915 address agreed with *The New York Times* that exchange charges were a "common nuisance," emphasized the need for concentration and redemption of bank checks at par throughout the country, summarized Section 13 of the Federal Reserve Act, which required the Federal Reserve Banks to act as clearing houses for member banks within their districts, and criticized the bankers who opposed the proposed changes in the system, especially the city bankers who thought that they would lose the deposits of country banks and the country bankers who thought that they would lose the profits on making charges for collections. Before concluding his address, Wolfe quoted at length from a letter that a Kansas City banker had written to him. The relevant paragraph follows in its entirety:

There are many bankers, both city and country, who are anxious to have the reserve banks begin clearing operations because it will give them a service in return for the balances which they are now carrying with their reserve banks. The conviction is growing that the check collection functions of the reserve system can be made the most used and the most valuable of all the facilities provided by the regional banks. The most distressing feature of the panic of 1907, which was notably a currency panic, was the breaking down of our check collection machinery. The result was that we could not use the very instrument that our business habits had taught us to look to for relief. Exception must be mentioned with respect to those sections where country checks were provided with facilities of collection through the clearing house as in Boston and Kansas City. The prediction may be made that a free and general system of check clearing will be found to be as important a factor in the solution of our currency problems as the issues of Federal Reserve notes. On the basis of present statistics the one affects 95 per cent. of our medium of exchange, bank checks, and the other is concerned with the remaining 5 per cent.[59]

Obviously the experience of the Kansas City Country Clearing House had a direct bearing not only upon the location of the Federal Reserve Bank in Kansas City, but also upon some features of the Federal Reserve system.[60] But the significance of two essential prerequisites of the Kansas City system did not escape the attention of those who presented the city's case to the location committee. They pointed with pride to the sixteen railroad trunk lines and the thirty-two subordinate roads that served the Kansas City area; to the 260 passenger trains that came into the city every day; and to the Union Depot in process of construction. Some of the railroad lines reached as far as the Pacific Coast, notably the Santa Fe and the Union Pacific; some as far south as the Gulf cities; and some extended the city's transportation network far to the north and west. The rails were clearly a significant aspect of the city's case.[61]

Similarly the mails received a great deal of attention from Kansas City's advocates. The city had a total of 126 dispatches daily—24 to the west, 15 to the south, 21 to the north, 18 to the southwest, 11 to the southeast, 13 to the northeast, and 6 to the northwest. It has been said that more railway post offices came into Kansas City than into any other city in the country, including Chicago and New York. While the brief submitted by the city did not include this statement, it did include the allegation that more pieces of baggage were handled at the Kansas City Union Depot than at any other station in the world and the assertion that "Montgomery Ward & Co. and Sears, Roebuck & Co., two of the largest mail-order houses in the world, selected Kansas City as the proper place in which to locate the largest mail-order houses west of the Mississippi River. Their reasons for selecting Kansas City were that this city offers better railroad and mail facilities than does any other city in the entire west and southwestern territory."[62]

Thus the case for Kansas City was brought to a close. The bankers of the city had not chosen to spend all of their time and energies bewailing the competition provided by postal savings and postal money orders. Instead they had chosen to make the bank check an inexpensive and effective instrument for the transfer of funds by devising the necessary mechanism. Rail lines had elected to make Kansas City the center of a magnificent network of lines reaching in every direction to almost every town and hamlet, whether on plain, or mountain, or desert. The United States Post Office Department by means of its most efficient arm, the Railway Mail Service, had chosen to capitalize on the presence of the rail lines and had given to Kansas City the best service that was possible in 1913. Banks, rails, and mails had combined to make Kansas City the dominant financial center in this region and to give to Kansas City a prominent place in the formulation and functioning of the Federal Reserve system.

Notes

1. *Report of the Comptroller of the Currency for 1915*, 2, Table 30, 38; and *Journal of the American Banker's Association*, 7 (January, 1915), 450. Hereafter cited as *Jour. of the A.B.A.*

2. An important exception to this general statement is Wayne E. Fuller, *RFD: The Changing Face of Rural America* (Bloomington, Ind., 1964).

3. Pm.-G., *Report for 1880*, 75-76 (1958). This is the form that will be used to cite the annual reports of the Postmaster-General. (The figures in parentheses are the Serial Set Numbers). No effort will be made to identify the reports of heads of divisions and bureaus except in very special cases.

4. *Ibid., for 1889*, 3 (2723).

5. As early as 1885 the author of the "History of the Railway Mail Service" called attention to the fact that "every new convenience added to the facilities of communication for the public makes a large increase in the amount of mail to be handled. Thus the money-order system, the registration system, the introduction of postal cards, and more recently of postal notes, the conveyance in the mails of samples, merchandise, not to speak of the

influence of a material reduction in the rates of postage, all tend not only to swell the mails with new correspondence, but with articles involved in the correspondence." *House Ex. Doc.*, 48 Cong., 2 Sess., no. 40, 73 (2261). John Jameson as general superintendent of the Railway Mail Service was in charge of the preparation of the *History.* Frank Hatton was Postmaster-General.

6. Railroad companies in Canada provided traveling post offices as early as 1859. *Ibid., for 1859,* 1403 (1025); *ibid.,* p. 60. William A. Davis did the first sorting of mail in transit. Bryant Allen Long and William Jefferson Dennis, *Mail by Rail: The Story of the Postal Transportation Service* (New York, N.Y., 1951), pp. 106–7.

7. Pm-G., *Report for 1883,* 344 (2189); *ibid., for 1889,* 474–75 (2723); *ibid., for 1895,* 397–98 (3380). George Buchanan Armstrong, who early in life was a postal clerk and later assistant postmaster in Chicago, has been labeled "the father of the Railway Mail Service." The service was formally organized on July 1, 1869. Long and Dennis, *Mail by Rail,* 112.

8. The earliest reference in the *Reports* to the use of "horseless wagons" occurred in the *Report for 1896,* 211 (3487). By 1899 the department was experimenting with automobiles in Chicago, and by 1906 they were in use in such cities as Detroit, Baltimore, Buffalo, and Milwaukee. *Ibid., for 1899,* 266 (3913); *ibid., for 1906,* 138 (5116); *ibid., for 1907,* 113 and 151 (5293). Aerial mail service was first tried in September, 1911. Later that year an appropriation of $50,000 was requested for experimental purposes. By 1913 temporary routes had been authorized. *Ibid., for 1911,* 145 (6217); *ibid., for 1913,* 13 and 141 (6403). There is a good deal of information on the use of pneumatic tubes. An example can be found in Pm.-G., *for 1897,* 173 ff. (3639). By 1894 extensive use was being made of electric lines. Pm.-G., *for 1894,* 21 (3304); *ibid., for 1895,* 165 (3380); *ibid., for 1896,* 218–19 (3487).

9. As early as 1834 Postmaster-General W. T. Barry recognized the importance of utilizing new forms of transportation in carrying the mail. In part he said, "The celerity of the mail service should always be equal to the most rapid transition of the traveler; and that which shortens the time of communication, and facilitates the intercourse between distant places is like bringing them nearer together." *Annual Report for 1834,* quoted in Pm.-G., *Report for 1882,* 226 (2098). A writer in *Banker's Magazine,* 89 (November, 1914), 519, made the following comment, "Business men depend on their letters arriving on time. Banks depend upon the mail in calculating interest, exchange charges, and in permitting checks to be drawn against deposits." One of the best appraisals of the significance of saving time was written not by a banker, but by a general superintendent of the Railway Mail Service who in commenting on the effects of obstructing mail trains, observed that the patrons of the Post Office Department were deeply interested "because it interrupts and embarrasses them in their business transactions and . . . does . . . impose upon them . . . absolute financial losses. When such interruptions occur, moneys due and forwarded in time to meet obligations

fail to arrive as expected, notes and drafts are protested, mortgages foreclosed, sales negotiated are not consummated, and the financial standing of individuals and firms are more or less jeopardized." Pm.-G., *Report for 1896*, 486 (3487). Essentially this same statement, somewhat longer and with obvious relationship to the strikes then in progress, had been made in 1893. *Ibid., for 1893*, 424-25 (3208).

10. These estimates have been made on the basis of tables that appeared regularly in the *Reports* of the Postmaster-General. It was the Department's practice to review rates paid to railroads for carrying the mails every four years. In this connection data relating to speeds and number of deliveries per week, as well as to many other aspects of the mail service, were published. Examples of speed on Western railroads may be found in the *Report for 1888*, 356 and passim (2635); *ibid., for 1898*, 556 and passim (3755); and *ibid., for 1906*, 212 and passim (5116). In 1905 Postmaster-General George B. Cortelyou was aware of the fact that commercial paper leaving New York in the afternoon and arriving in Chicago in time to pass through the clearing house the next day meant a gain of a full business day. *Ibid., for 1905*, 58 (4957).

11. Pm.-G., *Report for 1905*, 196 (4957). By 1904 fast mail trains were in service on every trunk line in the country. *Ibid., for 1904*, 428 (4796). As early as 1891 there were 145 mail trains arriving in Chicago and 144 departing ones. *Ibid., for 1891*, 65 (2932). The fast mail trains received regular attention in the *Annual Reports of the Postmaster-General*. For examples see Pm.-G., *Report for 1881*, 37 (2016); *ibid., for 1884*, 25 and 289 (2285); *ibid., for 1888*, 342-43 (2635); *ibid., for 1905*, 58 (4957); and *ibid., for 1909*, 168-69 (5739).

12. 79 (September, 1909), 341-42.

13. *Jour. of the A.B.A.*, 6 (December, 1913), 458.

14. President Woodrow Wilson's Postmaster-General agreed with Wanamaker on many points including government ownership and operation of the telegraph lines. Pm.-G., *Report for 1913*, 15. This recommendation was repeated in 1914. *Ibid., for 1914*, 15.

15. Pm.-G., *Report for 1889*, 30 (2723).

16. *Ibid., for 1889*, 30-31 (2723).

17. *Ibid., for 1890*, 11-13 (2839); *ibid., for 1891*, 90-91 (2932); *ibid., for 1897*, 24-32 (3639).

18. *Ibid., for 1909*, 17-21 (5739). See also *Ibid., for 1907*, 6-7 (5293).

19. Some bankers in order to offset the convenience of postal savings accounts advocated banking by mail. An especially persuasive argument on this point was prepared by the National Bank of Commerce of St. Louis. The statement read in part, "Banking by mail is simply the application to the use of individual depositors of the system in vogue among banks. It is perfectly safe. In the enormous daily exchange between banks of different cities, amounting to millions of dollars, there is never a dollar lost. This method of banking is convenient, private, and time saving." *Banker's Magazine*, 78 (February, 1909), 297. Several illustrations of banking by mail had appeared

in *ibid.*, 76 (February, 1908), 241–42, and a specific suggestion that banking by mail might offset the advantages claimed for postal savings had been published in *ibid.*, 77 (December, 1908), 868–69. In addition the breakdown of the inhibitions that restricted advertising by banks seems to have stemmed from the same source.

20. U.S., *Statutes at Large*, 36, 814–19. *Proceedings, 1909*, 35, 248–49; *ibid., 1910*, 36, 46–47. *Jour. of A.B.A.*, 2 (January, 1910), 264–67; *ibid.*, 3 (July, 1910), 192–93. *Proceedings of the Annual Conventions of the American Banker's Association* will be cited simply as *Proceedings*, plus year, volume, and page.

21. Pm.-G., *Report for 1915*, 30 and 248.

22. The use of national banks as depositories was a regular although small feature of the system. *Ibid., for 1903*, 526 (4643).

23. The bank money-order system devised by the Minnesota Banker's Association was described by Joseph Chapman, Jr., secretary of the association, in an address to the New York Banker's Association. He stressed the importance of centralized control, recognizability, and simplicity. He asserted that both postal money orders and express-company money orders had the active support of newspapers, magazines, and mail-order houses and that the Minnesota requisitions were distributed to newspapers and jobbing seed firms in Wisconsin, Iowa, North and South Dakota, and Montana. *Banker's Magazine*, 67 (October, 1903), 548–50. By 1904 bank money-order systems were in effect in Minnesota, New York, and Texas and were either in effect or being considered in Kansas, California, Washington, and the Indian Territory. *Ibid.*, 66 (June, 1903), 861; 67 (August, 1903), 233; 69 (August, 1904), 218–19. On the national level, the discussion by the American Banker's Association about devising a bank money-order system continued through 1909, when the first orders were issued. The principal issues were presented and attention was called to the fact that express companies were receiving deposits and really acting like a "vast branch banking operation" without supervision, without reserves, and without paying the taxes usually imposed on banks. *Ibid.*, 55 (September, 1897), 468–70; 67 (November and December, 1903), 758–61 and 916–20; 78 (May, 1909), 839; and 84 (April, 1912), 550–57. A full summary of the work of this committee can be found in *Proceedings*, 1912, 38, 175–82.

24. A good discussion of the problem of "Exchange" was presented to the Dallas chapter of The American Institute of Banking by H. P. May, cashier of the City National Bank of Dallas. *Jour. of the A.B.A.*, 5 (July, 1912), 49 ff. Bankers regarded the supplying of exchange as one of the particular functions of banks. *Banker's Magazine*, 74 (June, 1907), 871–72. There was some sentiment in banking circles in favor of recovering the $700 million yearly business that was done by the government and express companies simply by offering "a better and a cheaper service." *Ibid.*, 81 (July, 1910), 8. Additional discussions can be found in the *Jour. of the A.B.A.*, 6 (February, 1914), 613–14, and the *Proceedings, 1910*, 36, 206–8.

25. Under the title "Modern Banking Methods" the system of collecting

notes, time drafts, and sight drafts was discussed in *Banker's Magazine*, 60 (May, 1900), 690–97. The explanation, including the use of the telephone, was continued in *ibid.*, 61 (July, 1900), 30–35.

26. *Proceedings*, 1908, 34, 180–81. A banker from Tacoma, Washington, had emphasized this point several years earlier. *Banker's Magazine*, 63 (November, 1901), 781.

27. Pm.-G., *Report for 1913*, 29–30. A table exhibiting the growth of the system is contained in *ibid.*, 1910, 298 (5971).

28. Pm.-G., *Report for 1881*, 10 (2016). Included in the explicit recommendations were provision for money orders for less than five dollars. *Ibid., for 1889*, 20–21 (3913).

29. The mail-order houses also competed for banking business, offering 6 percent interest on deposits by prospective customers and permitting them to draw against these deposits in payment for orders. *Banker's Magazine*, 73 (September, 1906), 376.

30. Pm.-G., *Report for 1907*, 326–27 (5293); *ibid., for 1908*, 293 (5447).

31. Postal money orders made payable at office of issue were authorized in 1899. The Postmaster-General was well aware of the fact that he was establishing a postal-savings-bank system. Pm.-G., *Report for 1899*, 20, 175 (3913).

32. Pm.-G., *Report for 1897*, 142 (3639).

33. Pm.-G., *Report for 1890*, 967–68 (2839); *ibid., for 1900*, 177; *ibid., for 1901*, 143 (4288).

34. Postal-money-order payments through the San Francisco post office assumed particular importance in 1906 because of the San Francisco earthquake. Pm.-G., *Report for 1906*, 285 (5116).

35. Pm.-G., *Report for 1897*, 142 (3639). The next year an even larger sum was remitted, but because the practice of using coin or currency for the transfer of funds occasioned too much trouble and loss, the post office shifted to the use of drafts and checks on national banks and to "indirect membership" in clearing-house associations.

36. The parallel between the express companies and a central bank with branches was drawn by a writer in *Banker's Magazine*, 58 (June, 1899), 814. Express companies were also accused of accepting deposits and drawing sight drafts. *Ibid.*, 61 (October, 1900), 565. The competition in making remittances was emphasized the following year. *Ibid.*, 63 (December, 1901), 939–40. A simple solution was proposed, namely, making a charge for cashing express money orders.

37. Pm.-G., *Report for 1902*, 153 (4456).

38. The American Banker's Association carried its opposition to express companies to the extent of providing a special committee on the matter, which lodged a formal complaint with the Interstate Commerce Commission. Thornton Cooke of Kansas City was a member of the committee. *Jour. of the A.B.A.*, 2 (May, 1910), 458–62. A writer in *Banker's Magazine*, 59 (August, 1899), 161–63, proposed the simplest and most effective solution to the

problem, namely, for the New York Clearing House to force country banks to make checks on them payable at par in New York. This in effect would have implemented an important feature of the Federal Reserve system.

39. Pm.-G., *Report for 1899*, 873 (3913) . The reference to five handlings is contained in *ibid., for 1903*, 658 (4643).

40. Pm.-G., *Report for 1899*, 873 (3913).

41. Pm.-G., *Report for 1900*, 854, 856, and 857–58 (4099). In his 1902 *Report*, Castle asserted that if all of the relevant costs were taken into account, the money-order bureau actually lost $500,000 in 1899, and that the loss was greater in 1902. *Ibid., for 1902*, 676–77 (4456); *ibid., for 1900*, 860–61 (4099).

42. Pm.-G., *Report for 1900*, 860–61 (4099).

43. The authorization of postal checks limited to five dollars in any amount, payable to the bearer or order had been recommended in 1898. Pm.-G., *Report for 1898*, 185 (3755). In this way depositor's could have monetized their deposits.

44. A St. Louis banker whose institution handled 800 to 1200 country checks a day objected to paying a Texas bank twenty-five cents as a collection charge and then waiting for the return. *Banker's Magazine*, 50 (March, 1895), 549. A woman bank official from Lexington, Texas, described the collection problem from the point of view of a country bank. She concluded that there was less profit in it than in any other phase of banking. *Ibid.*, 84 (February, 1812), 144–45.

45. All of these shortcomings of the country-bank checks were discussed by John C. Russell, of St. Louis, in addresses to the Missouri Bankers' Association at Sedalia, on June 9 and 10, 1892. At various points he said, "Some of our correspondents wish to send us all the trash they can work off on us and have it put to their credit. . . . They wish to get as much interest on such balances as they can. . . . This class of out-of-town business is the kind that causes as much criticism of the banking business as it is causing many collections to be sent in roundabout ways in order to have them collected at par." Russell thought regional clearing houses and not a national one was the answer. *Banker's Magazine*, 47 (July, 1892), 30–31. The first editorial discussion of the country-bank-check problem appeared in the *Banker's Magazine*, 53 (November, 1896), 502–4. John Cofer Shirley, in an article "The Principles and Practices of Country Clearings," *ibid.*, 85 (August, 1912), 135–37, described the current 1912 practice as "antiquated, slow and insufferable," and asserted that the "floating" of checks to distant points or "hawking" them back and forth across the country really converted demand paper into time paper.

46. Many private letter-carrying companies had been organized as early as 1884, which indicated to the Postmaster-General that the free-delivery system had not "progressed so far as to meet all the wants of energetic business life in large commercial cities." Pm.-G., *Report for 1884*, 13 (2285).

47. *Banker's Magazine*, 47 (August, 1892), 136. An Ohio banker de-

scribed the collection of country-bank checks as a "burlesque." *Ibid.*, 53 (November, 1896), 566.

48. See *ibid.*, 57 (July, 1898), 69, for a summary of the itinerary of a small check that originated just six miles from the bank upon which it was drawn, traveled one thousand miles, and went through the same city as many as four times before it was paid. In 1898 *Banker's Magazine* printed a detailed analysis of cost and time of collecting country-bank checks. The average time was about five days and average cost 4 percent. *Ibid.*, 56 (February, 1898), 221–31.

49. The Boston country-bank-check collection system was described in *Banker's Magazine*, 63 (October, 1901), 626–29. Some idea of the volume of business that banks handled by mail may be derived from the experience of the National Shawmut Bank of Boston, the largest bank in New England. It required a staff of fourteen men working from 8 P.M. to 4 A.M. and eight additional men from midnight until 8 A.M. just to handle the night mail received by this one bank. Some nights checks amounting to $15 million were received. The mail deliveries were made every half-hour until 6:30 A.M., when the New York mail came in. All items had to be prepared for the clearing house by 10 A.M. *Ibid.*, 84 (March, 1912), 397. In a proposal to establish a country-bank clearing-house system in Connecticut, the following phrase appeared, *ibid.*, 60 (February, 1900), 257–58: "The mails have to be substituted for the messengers of the local banks." The close parallel between the substitution of national bank notes and greenbacks for the irredeemable bank notes, the collection of country-bank checks through some kind of a national mechanism, the similarity of the Suffolk system to the Boston country-check clearing system, the role of the federal government in bringing about the homogeneity of the bank note, and the creation of a central bank were discussed in *ibid.*, 684–86.

50. The preceding summary of the Kansas City country clearing-house system as devised by Jerome C. Thralls has been derived from three principal sources. The longest account and a record of the discussion which followed is in the *Proceedings*, 1912, 38, 508–24. *Ibid.*, 1910, 36, 731–32, and *Jour. of the A.B.A.*, 5 (September, 1912), 200–203.

51. An example of considerable attention to the Kansas City system can be found in the full report of the debate between the Cincinnati and Pittsburgh chapters of the American Institute of Banking on the subject of transits in the *Jour. of the A.B.A.*, 4 (May, 1912), 702–7. For a more general discussion of transit problems see *ibid.*, 5 (January, 1913), 467–69.

52. *Banker's Magazine* consistently favored the use of the check, criticized the bankers who wished to curtail its use, and supported the clearing-house system under the auspices of the banks. Central in its argument were the importance of deposits and the expanded use of the check as the answer to an inelastic currency. The effect of the check in monetizing deposits was emphasized. In this connection the role of deposits was put briefly by S. R. Flynn, a banker from Chicago. His formulation stated: "When in actual circulation a dollar is but a dollar. When in actual concealment it might as

well not exist. The dollar is doing its best work when seemingly dormant in the bank vault, for there its usefulness to business is multiplied four to six and two-thirds times." *Banker's Magazine,* 71 (August, 1905), 239. Typical discussions of the country-check problem are contained in *ibid.,* 67 (September, 1903), 293–97; 68 (January, 1904), 7–8; 72 (January, 1906), 7–8 and 91–93; 74 (January, 1907), 7; and 79 (July, 1909), 8–9; *Proceedings,* 1911, 37, 711–13; 1912, 38, 488; 1915, 41, 477–91; and *Jour. of the A.B.A.,* 5 (December, 1912), 359–60.

53. The Federal Reserve Banks began business on November 16, 1914. *Banker's Magazine,* 89 (December, 1914), 603.

54. In a kind of obituary note on its proposal for a great central bank in New York City, *Banker's Magazine,* 88 (May, 1914), 547–51, said, "Again, had the New York Clearing House been more ready to devise a system of clearing country checks much of the irritation which gradually developed against the banks of that city would have been avoided." Not all New York bankers were opposed to the use of the clearing-house system. Newton Dalling of the Nassau Bank described this feature of the Federal Reserve plan a "great boon to country banks." *Ibid.,* 87 (December, 1913), 636–37.

55. *Jour. of the A.B.A.,* 6 (January, 1914), 487.

56. A writer in the *Jour. of the A.B.A.,* 6 (June, 1914), 805, was impressed by this fact and ventured "the assertion that the financial importance of all three of these cities is largely due to the fact that they have built up a sound business and have been able to hold it on account of the fact that they have for a long time employed the best method for the collection of checks."

57. The Kansas City brief is printed in *Sen. Doc.* No. 485, 63 Cong., 2 Sess., "Location of Reserve Districts in the United States," 173–81 (6583).

58. Quoted by O. Howard Wolfe in an address entitled "The Clearing Function of the Reserve Bank in Theory and in Practice," *Jour. of the A.B.A.,* 7 (January, 1915), 448–49.

59. *Jour. of the A.B.A.,* 7 (January, 1915), 448–51.

60. In forming the Federal Reserve districts the location committee was required to weigh "convenience and the customary course of business." *Banker's Magazine,* 88 (February, 1914), 140. The Kansas City *Journal* carried almost daily reports on the activities and itinerary of the location committee. The *Journal* was critical of the Wilson administration in general and the Federal Reserve Act in particular, but once the law was enacted, it, like other critics, wanted a choice segment of the system. The *Journal* wanted the location committee to use the criteria most favorable to Kansas City, e.g., geographic convenience and "the established custom and trend of business as developed by the present system of bank reserves and checking accounts." Kansas City *Journal,* December 27, 1913.

61. The study of the Kansas City Federal Reserve District by Hurshel E. Underhill concentrates upon banking activities and operations. It was published by the Spaulding Moss Company about 1941.

62. The Reserve Bank Organization Committee consisted of Secretary of the Treasury William G. McAdoo, Secretary of Agriculture D. W. Houston,

and Comptroller of the Currency John Skelton Williams. The Kansas City brief was presented by the Associated Banks and Trust Companies of Greater Kansas City, but there is some reason to believe that Jerome Thralls played an active part in preparing it. The conclusion that the mechanism for handling country-bank checks, the railroad network, and the mail service weighed heavily in the location committee's decision is reenforced by the fact that originally the tenth district included much more than the Kansas City committee had requested. Among the tenth-district banks that were polled, 355 gave Kansas City as their first choice, 191—all but 10 from Nebraska—chose Omaha, and Denver received 132 votes. Of the thirty-two witnesses who testified at the hearings on Kansas City, many were from Kansas City or Kansas. The relevant data are to be found in *Sen. Doc.* No. 485, 63 Cong., 2 Sess., "Location of Reserve Districts in the United States," 173–81 and 377 (6583); and in *House Doc.* No. 1134, 63 Cong., 2 Sess., "First Choice Votes for Reserve Bank Cities," 3–15 (6755). Personal conversations with Mr. Calvin Manon, 1969, sometime railway mail clerk and presently a member of the staff of the Associated Press in Kansas City, Missouri. In addition to the statement that more railway post offices came into Kansas City than into any other city, he said that after the completion of the Union Depot in Kansas City at least two of the larger banks handled their incoming mail in offices in the depot, thus saving the time required for downtown deliveries.